A Critique of Pastoral Care

Stephen Pattison

A Critique of
Pastoral Care

★

Second Edition

SCM PRESS LTD

British Library Cataloguing in Publication Data

Pattison, Stephen
A critique of pastoral care.
1. Christian church. Pastoral work
I. Title
253

ISBN 0-334-02544-3

First published 1988
by SCM Press Ltd
26-30 Tottenham Road, London, N1

Second edition 1993

Photoset at The Spartan Press Ltd, Lymington
and printed in Great Britain by
Biddles Ltd, Guildford and King's Lynn

Contents

Preface to the Second Edition

It is a great pleasure for me to be able to write this Preface to the second edition of *A Critique of Pastoral Care*. The book seems to have found a useful place within the literature of pastoral care and I am pleased that its commercial life is to be prolonged.

The main text herein is largely the same as that which was originally published in 1988. However, there is a major addition in the form of an extended concluding Afterword. In this I undertake some re-assessment of wider developments in pastoral care theory and practice since 1987, comment critically upon the original chapters in the book, and provide some bibliographical updating. This by way of creating a partial critique of my original critique of pastoral care! I hope this will add substantially to the value of the book, as well as to its longevity. Readers may care to read my comments on particular chapters in the Afterword as they work their way through the text, rather than waiting to read them all together at the end.

In the first edition, I acknowledged the help of Peter Bellamy, David Ford, Janet Mayer, James Clarke, Sally Long and Paul Ballard. I would like to renew my thanks to them and add the names of Elaine Graham, Emmanuel Lartey and James Woodward to this list for their helpful comments in preparing the present edition. I should also like to thank my reviewers together with John Bowden and Linda Foster of SCM Press for their continuing interest in this volume.

The book is dedicated to the memory of my mother Audrey, to Theo, Rex, Fiona, and to Jill.

Birmingham   S.P.
April 1993

Acknowledgments

I am grateful to BBC Enterprises for permission to reproduce 'Dust and Ashes' from Lionel Blue, *Bright Blue*; to Chatto and Windus for permission to reproduce 'Big Top' from Norman MacCaig, *Collected Poems*; to Granada Publishing for permission to reproduce 'The Priest' from R. S. Thomas, *Selected Poems 1946–68*.

Introduction

Some years ago, a controversial TV programme brought to the attention of the public the fact that patients in a high security psychiatric hospital were being systematically abused by quite a large number of the nursing staff. Enough evidence was unearthed by this exposé to result in criminal proceedings and several nurses were convicted of offences against patients. While all this was going on a radio interviewer talked to the hospital chaplain. 'How do you see your role in the hospital in the light of these events?' he asked. The chaplain replied, 'I do not see my role, I just do it.'

This book is written with the deep conviction that such an attitude on the part of any pastoral carer is indefensible and irresponsible: even, as in the case cited, dangerous. If pastors have no perspective on their work they risk complacency, stagnation and possible complicity with that which is less than good or desirable. Ultimately, they risk harming those in their care. The broad underlying contention of this work is that acquiring and maintaining a critical perspective about what is, or might be done in pastoral practice is valuable, interesting and necessary. It prevents boredom, stimulates innovation, impedes unhelpful naivety, and gives a sense of direction and purpose to pastoral care.

Within this broad concern, there are three, more specific, subsidiary aims. The first of these is to provide basic outline discussions of topics which seem important for pastoral care but which have been largely, if not totally, ignored.[1] It seems almost incredible that theological students spend years studying the Bible and ethics, for example, yet there are no widely available detailed discussions of the relationship of these areas to the practical work of pastoral care.

A second aim is to point British readers towards some of the recent North American literature of pastoral care.[2] This is better developed than British writing, as much as anything else because there are many more pastoral theologians in the USA than there are in Britain. Unfortunately, it is relatively difficult to obtain in this country and is often expensive. A definite intention here is to present a critical introduction to some of the more important and interesting developments in theory, especially that emerging from the USA. In this sense, the present work is often unashamedly derivative; it points beyond itself to the work of other authors.

The third, and last, aim is to make an original and practical contribution to the situations which pastoral carers encounter. Rather than merely summarizing and evaluating the writings of other theorists, it seems more useful to try and draw out the actual implications that a set of theoretical insights and understandings have for actual pastoral practice.

This book can be read either as a whole or as a series of self-contained essays on particular topics. Allowing for the latter possibility has necessitated a certain amount of repetition. Typically, each chapter begins by discussing why this particular theme or topic has been neglected in pastoral care theory. Arguments for its importance and significance in pastoral care are then advanced. Finally, practical implications of theoretical insights and considerations are drawn out. Good and interesting theoretical considerations must show their value for practical pastoral care if they are to command the attention and respect of practitioners.

The first two chapters provide preliminary material and discussion on the nature of pastoral care and recent developments in its theory in the USA. This gives necessary background for the central four chapters which address themes arising from recent pastoral care literature in the USA and this country which are, or perhaps should be, important for contemporary pastoral practice. After an introductory interlude, the last two chapters, in dealing with the themes of failure and laughter, form a critique of the modern pastoral care movement on both sides of the Atlantic insofar as it has adopted ratio-technological methods and preoccupations. This critique suggests that both practitioners and theorists of pastoral care have been over-optimistic and over-serious about their desire to change the world and its people for the better. This has brought with it the dangers of distorting and misunderstanding the nature of the world and human beings. The keynote here is that people and the situations in which they find themselves are not always appropriately seen as problems. They, and the world in which they live, must ultimately be regarded as mysteries to be loved. The last chapter concludes with a brief discussion of ministry and pastoral care as primarily ways of seeing by analogy with contemplative prayer. This highlights the importance of gaining the correct perspective or critical stance in pastoral care as in religious life generally. Correct seeing, or theory, is a vital accompaniment to lively and enlivening ministry.

This volume is intended for all those who, at any level, would want to identify themselves as carers standing within the Christian tradition. It is primarily addressed to practising pastors and students in training on courses for ministry, but it should be useful to anyone who wishes to see more clearly or think more deeply about their caring work. In the discussion of definition of pastoral care which follows, it will be seen that I believe (largely on pragmatic grounds) that pastoral care must be closely associated with the people who form the authorized and recognized pastorate of the churches. The increasing and very welcome role of lay people in pastoral care suggests, however, that the noun 'pastor' may be too narrow a designation for the different kinds of people who now undertake pastoral care in practice. For this reason, as well as that of wanting to leaven the text by using different terms, the terms 'pastor' and the slightly cumbersome 'pastoral carer' will be used interchangeably. Where possible, the feminine forms of pronouns have been used in relation to pastors, pastoral carers, and those they care for. This is an earnest of the hope that one day pastoral care by and for women will be fully accepted as commonplace in the mainstream British churches. At that time, readers of theological books will have become entirely indifferent to the gender of pronouns because equality between the sexes has become more of a reality than it is today.

Chapter One

What is Pastoral Care Anyway?

It would be feasible, convenient and economical if a discussion of the nature and meaning of 'pastoral care' could be left out of this book. Many writers do, in fact, ignore the matter altogether. Most authors of the books in the SPCK 'New Library of Pastoral Care', for example, take it for granted that they do not need to define pastoral care. It is assumed that people already know what this is. Other writers might perhaps be expected to provide more in the way of definition and discussion. Alastair Campbell, for instance, in his well-known *Rediscovering Pastoral Care* clearly does discuss the issue, but surprisingly fails to give any clear definition of the area which he is re-discovering. Yet others provide summary definitions of what they take pastoral care to be but with relatively little discussion of why these definitions should be accepted by their readers. So Arnold, for example, presents a somewhat indigestible definition of pastoral care as

> the attempt to bring theology or the 'good news' (sic), to bear in a relationship where one is known as a member of the priesthood of all believers and seeks to care in a manner that is sensitive to the other person or persons and faithful to the theological commitments which have brought them together.[1]

Unwillingness to discuss or define the basic concept of pastoral care may be a reflection of several very different factors. First, pastoral pragmatism rears its head. Pastoral care is a matter of doing not thinking. You find out what pastoral care is by doing the job and definition is unnecessary. Secondly, it may be convenient both intellectually and practically to have a concept which can be used as a hold-all without too much attention to precision. This reflects a third and more positive factor; the multi-faceted nature of pastoral care as it is practised. There can be no doubt that many practical pastoral activities of a very diverse nature are to be accommodated under the general heading of pastoral care and any definition or discussion of it which excludes them on a narrow basis would be doing less than justice to reality. Lastly, it may be that the actual nature of pastoral care makes it impervious to analysis and definition. Analysis is primarily a process of taking things apart. There is something to be said for putting things together or synthesizing when it comes to understanding and defining the nature of an activity like pastoral care. This is Michael Taylor's approach. In *Learning to Care* he refuses to define or discuss pastoral care in narrow terms and tells six stories in which he believes pastoral care has been undertaken. By putting together the stories a picture of pastoral care is built up.[2]

It is tempting to follow Taylor, or even to take a less respectable commonsensical approach along the lines of 'I don't know what pastoral care is, but I recognize it when I see it!' There is a good deal of wisdom in this. Unfortunately, the matter cannot rest there, for it is important to be clear about the meaning of words and concepts. If a word or concept is so wide that it can contain everything and mean anything, then it is doubtful if it is of any real use. Indeed, it may help to convey considerable confusion. So at this point the reader is invited to follow a discussion which leads up to a definition of pastoral care which may or may not be helpful. Following through this discussion may in itself lead to more personal clarity about the problem of defining the nature of pastoral care. Even if it does not, there is a great deal of difference between the person who cannot define pastoral care for themselves having thought about it a great deal and the person who cannot do so because she has not thought about it at all. In this context the journey is at least as important as the destination.

One of the ways in which human beings know who they are and have personal identity is through the memory of past events. History is crucial to identity and so a glance at the history of pastoral care may help to construct some boundaries for the definition of this concept. This is also in accord with Oden's perception that modern pastoral carers, swamped with contemporary concerns, theories and techniques have developed a kind of amnesia about the Christian tradition which needs to be rectified. The past can indeed be a dead hand on the present and the future, or the source of nostalgic and unrealistic longings. On the other hand it can be a living and inspiring resource if critically and judiciously considered.

The *cura animarum* or care of souls, as pastoral care was designated in the past, seems to have been a feature of the life of the Christian community from the earliest times. Its content and nature have, however, been widely different historically according to factors such as denomination, context, era and place. Clebsch and Jaekle in their *Pastoral Care in Historical Perspective* which surveys this activity down the ages suggest that it has been characterized generally by the elements of healing, sustaining, reconciling and guiding.[3] Clebsch and Jaekle argue that while all these elements are present in the *cura animarum* throughout the history of the church, one predominates over the others at any particular time. In the early church, for example, sustaining Christians through the 'vicissitudes of life in this world' was emphasized.[4] Although this assertion seems somewhat arbitrary (surely discipline was also of the utmost importance at this time, a fact evidenced by some of the sources quoted by the authors in support of their claim), the broad elements identified by Clebsch and Jaekle seem valid and helpful. In more detailed and specific terms, pastoral care historically seems to have consisted, to a greater or lesser extent, of individual and corporate discipline (helping Christians overcome sin in themselves and in the Christian community); building up the church community; consolation (comforting and supporting Christians during times of personal or corporate sorrow); spiritual direction and guidance about the inner life; protecting the Christian community from external threats (trying, for example, to persuade temporal rulers not to persecute or destroy Christian groups); and healing (which might include the use of spiritual, sacramental and natural methods).

In concrete terms pastors (and it should be noted that the historical pastoral care tradition very much revolved around the activities of recognized church leaders) have at various times and to differing degrees undertaken some or all of the following activities in their pursuit of pastoral care. They have heard confessions; given advice and counsel, both spiritual and practical, verbally and in writing; offered consolation to the needy and given practical help; visited people in their homes and in prison or hospital; tried to cure people of their diseases using sacramental and medical means; become involved in educational activities; exercised a caring ministry both within the Christian community and outside it; undertaken social and political roles in the interests of their communities; conducted services or pastoral offices at crucial points in the lives of individuals, e.g. marriages and funerals. This rather dry and schematic account of the historical practice of pastoral care highlights the diversity of the activity. It seems that pastoral care has always been pluralistic, variegated and flexible according to need and circumstance, as well as having an identifiable core of healing, sustaining, reconciling and guiding. This variability should be borne in mind in any attempt to come to an understanding or definition of pastoral care today. The reader who is particularly interested in seeing the actual content of the pastoral care role in the past is strongly recommended to consult a good biography of one of the great historical pastors like Augustine.[5] At a slightly less exalted level, Russell's *The Clerical Profession* and Davie's *Pastoral Care and the Parish* give a vivid picture of the breadth of pastoral care amongst English Anglican clergy in recent centuries. The former is particularly valuable in tracing out the parish pastor's functions as, amongst other things, teacher, almoner, administrator of justice, local politician and public health official.[6]

Turning to the present day, the word 'pastoral' and the concept 'pastoral care' have even wider and more loosely construed meanings and connotations than they may have had in the past. The word 'pastoral' still retains something of the agricultural nuance which characterized its beginning when the care of flocks of animals began to be used in biblical times as a vivid analogy for the activity of leading and caring for God's chosen people. Once at a party when I volunteered that I was undertaking a course in pastoral studies the person who had asked me what I did appeared mystified until at last a look of comprehension came into his eyes and he blurted out, 'Ah, you're an agric.!' The metaphor of wise shepherds leading or guiding silly sheep has been challenged as dangerously one-sided, misleading and unhelpful in the egalitarian atmosphere of the twentieth century. This agricultural connotation still lives on, however, and is firmly enshrined in the cover design of the SPCK 'New Library of Pastoral Care'.

One of the main usages of the term 'pastoral care' is now that used in educational circles to denote the particular role of certain teachers in schools. In this instance, the personal welfare and adequate functioning of school students is the focus of pastoral care and there is no necessary reference to any religious dimension at all. Educational pastoral care has taken its own direction and become a highly specialized art in schools with its own practitioners and researchers. It is not appropriate to discuss it further here, but it is important to note that many of the books and conferences which have 'pastoral care' in their titles have nothing to do with the type of pastoral care under discussion here.[7]

Christians have no monopoly on the use of the term 'pastoral care'. Some would not want it anyway. In *Learning to Care*, Michael Taylor, for example, distinguishes between pastoral care and Christian pastoral care.[8] The former consists of any helping act done by any person, whereas the latter consists of acts undertaken by Christians. Many people apart from Taylor would want to affirm the enormous value of any kind of caring act, no matter who performs it. Some would see this as doing the will of God, even if God is not the recognized motivator or enabler, and it seems laudable in every way to see caring as something which happens outside the Christian community as well as within it. The trouble is that there seems to be no very good reason for describing such caring as pastoral. After all, many of those performing caring acts would not themselves want to attach the adjective 'pastoral' to it and it seems unnecessary to 'baptize' their caring actions against their will. The use of word in this way appears to come very close to depriving it of any distinctive meaning of content of its own at all.

At the other end of the spectrum from Taylor, there are those who would want to claim a very narrow functional definition for pastoral care. They would suggest that pastoral care is nothing other than the caring activity of recognized pastors of churches. Pastoral care is confined to a small distinctive group of people; but all the activity of those people, from stoking the church boiler to spiritual counselling, becomes pastoral activity. Here lies a lack of specificity of another kind.

There are others who would want to claim that care is pastoral not so much because it is the action of an ordained or recognized pastor, but because it is performed by people trained in particular methods. Those who have undergone training in pastoral studies or pastoral counselling might be deemed to be involved in pastoral work when they perform caring acts. The adjective pastoral is applicable in these cases because it denotes a particular training or discipline.

Yet other people would give little significance to the personal status or training of a carer as a means of determining whether an act was pastoral or not. For them, the content of an action, its context, or the motivation leading to it might be the key issue. Such people might argue that it is only when an action is directly concerned with a person's religious life and development that pastoral care is taking place. This would be the position of certain rather traditional pastoral theologians like Martin Thornton who would see spiritual direction as the content of the *cura animarum*.[9]

The context of care is an important variable for some who feel that pastoral care is essentially care undertaken in, for or on behalf of the church community. Frank Wright, however, is more concerned with direction and motivation. Rejecting the idea that care is only pastoral if it overtly brings God into conversations or encounters all the time (the use of theological language in an overt form does not necessarily make an encounter religious while its absence does not make it irreligious for God is either there all the time or not at all), Wright suggests that the important thing is that there is an awareness of another dimension,

> a transcendent reality, which is often lacking in a secular situation of pastoral care, and a conviction that the path to wholeness is not purely of human endeavour and through the interaction of human beings. It is sufficient, however, that that dimension is silently present, without any self-conscious references.[10]

The important, but implicit, religious content of Wright's pastoral care may be contrasted with the belief of the distinguished German theologian Eduard Thurneysen who defines pastoral care as

> A specific communication to the individual of the message proclaimed in general (i.e. to all) in the sermon to the congregation.[11]

Thurneysen is a Calvinist and sees pastoral care as part of the gospel-proclaiming task of the church. Its function is to bring the individual into a direct and explicit confrontation with the Word of God. There is no room here for Taylor's general helping acts conception of pastoral care.

The complexities of usage concerning the word 'pastoral' and the term 'pastoral care' are increased when the contemporary scope of pastoral care is considered. Many people would see pastoral care as essentially directed towards individuals. This does not do justice to more corporate and social aspects. Anglican dioceses, for example, often have pastoral committees whose role is not primarily to ensure the well-being of individuals, but to plan the deployment of manpower. This wider dimension is also implicit in the issuing of pastoral letters which are generally addressed by church leaders to whole congregations. Recently, Catholics and Anglicans have become aware of the very political nature of pastoral action in South Africa and South America, to take but two examples. Bishops like Desmond Tutu and Oscar Romero who appear to be indulging in overtly political action to resist established governments deny that they are politicians, claiming that they are pastors simply exercising appropriate pastoral care of their churches.

The width of usage and connotation associated with 'pastoral' and 'pastoral care' in both historical and contemporary settings is now at least to some extent apparent. It challenges the simplistic equation of pastoral care with individual counselling, a real danger in the North American pastoral care movement in the 1960s and early 1970s and something of a contemporary danger in this country. The trouble is that it also makes it look as if pastoral care has been, and is, such a variable activity that no precision is possible in its definition at all. It may be the case that it is very difficult to arrive at a definition which does justice to historical precedent, theological specificity and, perhaps most importantly, contemporary practice. Nonetheless, I want now to move towards a working definition which may do something to salvage the usefulness of 'pastoral care' without diminishing its proper diversity.

I shall proceed by way of Clebsch and Jaekle's definition in *Pastoral Care in Historical Perspective* which for many years was regarded as standard both in North America and in parts of the British pastoral care movement. They state that pastoral care consists of helping acts, done by representative Christian persons, directed towards the healing, sustaining, guiding, and reconciling of troubled persons whose troubles arise in the context of ultimate meanings and concerns.[12]

This definition clearly betrays its origins in mid-century North America, particularly in its use of phrases like 'ultimate meanings and concerns', a reflection of the enormous influence of existentialist ideas there at that time. Several criticisms can be made of it. First, in talking of 'representative Christian persons' it is apparent that Clebsch and Jaekle see pastoral care as primarily a clerical activity in which ordinary lay people have little part to play. This does not accord with developments which have taken place in the churches since the time they wrote which potentially allow lay people a much more significant sharing role in pastoral care. Secondly, the definition is problem-centred. Pastoral care is only concerned with troubled people. Again, this does not do justice to the needs of people who may not be troubled but do need to grow. The definition is implicitly individualistic in its focus in that it emphasizes helping persons rather than groups or communities. It has been seen that the scope of pastoral care goes beyond this in practice, although this is indeed an important part of pastoral care and it is certainly the main thrust of pastoral care conceived primarily as counselling. A fourth criticism is that the wider Christian community and its tradition are not seen as important either in terms of context or resource. Lastly, it is arguable that Christian pastoral carers should be responsive to needs and problems which do not necessarily 'arise in the context of ultimate meanings and concerns'. Although it is certainly true, as Clinebell points out, that the whole of human existence is lived out in the context of an awareness, however dim, of mortality, and so all troubles and problems have in some sense a dimension of 'ultimacy', this phrase is either so general as to be redundant or tends to concentrate the concerns of pastoral carers on so-called 'spiritual' and 'religious' problems. If the latter is the case the definition once again fails to do justice to the breadth of human need and pastoral concern. Having said all this, however, it must be acknowledged that this definition has been a very useful one, if only because it is at least a concrete statement which allows people to focus their own thoughts on a common core. Clebsch and Jaekle themselves are modest enough to allow that their definition has limitations and their own awareness of the changeable nature of pastoral care over the centuries would no doubt permit them to acknowledge that it should be revised as pastoral care evolves. While their definition was most useful and pertinent in counselling-centred pastoral care done in the context of North American existentialist theology it cannot be unequivocally accepted in the Britain of the 1980s. A wider and more general definition which takes more factors into account is needed.

Here, then, is one possible definition of pastoral care which may help to give the term some clarity and finitude without being unduly restrictive: *pastoral care is that activity, undertaken especially by representative Christian persons, directed towards the elimination and relief of sin and sorrow and the presentation of all people perfect in Christ to God.* More must be said about the precise constituents of this definition in a moment. Here it should be emphasized that I have drawn on pastoral practice, the historical tradition of pastoral care and a passage from the Bible to make this formulation. A reading of the historical tradition of pastoral care makes it quite clear that, despite its very varying forms, a constant underlying common denominator has been the struggle against sin and sorrow in whatever way it has arisen in personal or corporate life.[13] The biblical passage, Colossians 1.28 supplements the rather negative image of struggling with destructive aspects of life by putting the whole enterprise of pastoral care in a positive light. The aim of pastoral care is not only to concern itself with sin and suffering, but also to bring people to a positive goal through growth and fulfilment. This is consonant with Paul's aim for his ministry of which he writes in the verse cited:

> Him (Christ) we proclaim, warning every man and teaching every man in all wisdom, that we may present every man mature in Christ.[14]

Turning to particular elements of the definition, the following features should be noted. First, pastoral care is described as an activity. This assertion has its dangers. I have already noted the tendency towards pastoral pragmatism amongst pastors which can degenerate into simple mindless activism. Writers like Campbell and Wright have eloquently and effectively tried to change the notion that pastoral care is a matter of good works performed with ever more sophisticated techniques. The former suggests that pastoral care requires carers to become a particular kind of person rather than simply a highly trained professional (an ever-present danger with the plethora of new techniques and theories which continue to emerge).[15] Wright resists the notion of the pastor as activist/technician by counterposing it with the idea that the pastor is an artist or visionary. Pastors are fundamentally people with a distinctive vision and perception.[16] (You could say that Campbell believes it ain't what you do, it's the person who does it, while Wright maintains it ain't what you do, it's the way that you see it!) Depth, direction and being are important in pastoral care. It should not always be a matter of overt and conspicuous busyness. One pastoral skill that is sadly lacking amongst many people is the ability to stand still long enough for people to be able to know the pastor. Likewise, there is much wisdom in the saying, 'Sometimes, the best thing is to do nothing.' Action of an immediate and direct sort without reflection can be precipitate and harmful.[17] On the other hand, if action is understood to include reflection and assessment, as it does in the Marxist notion of praxis, it can be seen as indispensable. While acknowledging the corrective note sounded by Campbell and Wright it seems important to emphasize the very practical or 'operation-centred' nature of pastoral care. Being a certain kind of person, or seeing in a particular way are themselves actions, and if there is a tendency to activism in pastoral care there is an equal, if not greater, tendency towards inaction and passivity which must be resisted. Pastoral care is part of changing the world as well as simply being in it.

Some readers may be surprised that the significance of 'representative Christian persons' is emphasized in my definition in the light of the growing and proper contribution of lay people to this activity. They should note the strategically placed 'especially'. If pastoral care becomes too loosely applied to all kinds of care undertaken by all manner of person it is evacuated of distinctive meaning. It is most useful to see pastoral care as carried out in or on behalf of the Christian community. Care outside that context, or undertaken on some other body's behalf, should just be called 'care' (God-given though it may well, and rightly, be held to be).

Within the Christian community, it is undoubtedly, and happily true that much, if not most, pastoral care is exercised by lay people. It is right that this should be acknowledged in any definition. Nonetheless, most churches do have a distinctive ordained pastoral ministry, for better or worse, and it would seem incontrovertible that this ministry in some way sums up, encapsulates, serves as an example for, and is paradigmatic of, pastoral care carried out by all the members of the church. If it is not like this, it needs to be radically changed. Clericalism, the domination of ordained over lay persons in the church, should be deplored and resisted. This should not mean that lay people find it necessary to reject the central and exemplary role of ordained pastors. The word 'pastoral' must continue to be closely associated with the role of clergy, but it need not be confined to them in a narrow way.

The definition does not limit pastoral care to caring acts for individuals, one of the elements of Clebsch and Jaekle's definition which was pointed up and relativized by a consideration of the width of pastoral practice both historically and contemporarily. Much sin, sorrow, and capacity for growth finds its roots outside the individual person. Poverty, inequality and injustice can be the agents and tools of evil and can stunt people just as effectively as personal misery or loss. Throughout history, pastors have sometimes taken it upon themselves to involve themselves in social and political questions in a very direct and active way as being the most important way of exercising pastoral care (I shall discuss this further later on). Any useful definition of pastoral care must, therefore, resist the temptation to become chained to individualism. Pastoral care needs to be flexible, variegated and able to respond at different levels of existence, according to human need. The historical tradition suggests that this is permissible and necessary and so this possibility is included in the definition.

One feature of the experience of pastoral care today which is very important is the fact that while pastoral care may be carried on primarily in, or on behalf of particular Christian communities, it cannot be directed solely towards Christians. Full-time pastors in established denominations will be very well aware of the way in which they are required to give pastoral care to many who never normally aproach churches, but may need help in a time of need or require one of the so-called 'pastoral offices' (baptism, marriage, funeral) for themselves or those close to them. Pastors in sector ministries like hospital chaplaincy may spend most of their time working with non-Christians. These are eloquent and actual examples in practice that the ministry of the church which includes pastoral care is not just for the church but for the world. Practice and experience confirm the example of Jesus who set out to serve the needy of the world. It is right, therefore, that any definition of pastoral care should contain a universal element. Whatever it means in practice in a pluralistic society such as ours is becoming, pastoral care should be directed towards presenting *all* people perfect in Christ to God and not just a faithful remnant.

Finally, I want briefly to point out the explicitly theological and transcendent content of this definition. Pastoral action, if it is to be effective, must pay close attention to people, the human situation and the world in which we live. To this end, pastoral care must obtain understandings from many different 'secular' sources. This brings the danger that pastoral care loses any real distinctive Christian or religious identity and becomes a species of social work or counselling. I have already dismissed the idea that religious language or overt reference to theology or gospel is necessary for an encounter to be religiously significant or pastoral. It is important, however, that pastoral carers should maintain a Christian vision, a spiritual life and a sense of being rooted, grounded in and orientated towards God, whatever the means they use to undertake their caring. The end which is sought, the motivation for seeking it, and the means used to attain it may not be externally significant in care, but their underlying significance cannot be ignored, for they will significantly colour all encounters.

Pastoral care can be given even greater character, structure and definition if its forms and overall aim are considered. The overall aim of pastoral care, Campbell asserts, is the aim of ministry as a whole, i.e., to increase love between people and between people and God. He writes,

> Pastoral care is, in essence, surprisingly simple. It has one fundamental aim: to help people to know love, both as something to be received and as something to give.[18]

This assertion has great value. It is direct, uncluttered and easily comprehensible (a welcome change, perhaps, from the complexities of the foregoing discussion). It also links pastoral care with ministry as a whole and this is important, for it is sometimes a temptation to treat pastoral care as a wholly separate entity. Teaching, preaching, organizing and worshipping must be held in tension with pastoral care in ministry as a whole.[19] Since all aspects of ministry have the same aim, and are essentially practical, it is not surprising that they often appear to overlap and have substantial implications for each other. Worship, for example, is primarily oriented towards giving glory to God but it does many of the things which pastoral care would also do. It builds up people as individuals and a community, it helps to form Christian identity, it shares many of the same themes and concerns like guilt, grace and new beginnings as well as bearing upon situations of human need such as death and bereavement.[20] The boundaries between the various aspects of ministry are never absolute. Nonetheless, it is important not to reduce one ministerial activity to another so that there is no distinction between them. Pastoral care is not the same as worship. It may have the same ultimate aim as the latter, and often be closely associated with it, but it has its own distinctive ethos methods and forms which maintain a degree of practical and theoretical separateness which is valid and useful.

A helpful way of conceiving the unity and diversity of the various different aspects of ministry is to be found by analogy with crystals. All the crystals of a particular substance, salt, for example, share the same basic structure and angles, whatever their individual size and shape. Each crystal shares a basic similarity with all others of the same substance, yet each has its own separate distinctive identity and shape as well. This, then, leads on to the distinctive forms which characterize pastoral care, as opposed to other ministerial activities sharing the common aim of increasing love between people and between people and God.

The characteristic forms of pastoral care are largely encapsulated by Clebsch and Jaekle in the definition set out earlier. These are healing, sustaining, reconciling and guiding. An additional form which embodies the positive, preventive and growth emphasis which is also present in pastoral care has been added by Clinebell. This is that of nurturing.[21] As I suggested before, in different circumstances one or more of these forms of activity may be very prominent while another may be almost wholly absent. Nurturing, for example, was largely ignored in the pastoral care exercised in North America under the aegis of problem-centred pastoral counselling. It is appropriate that pastoral care should have a somewhat chameleon-like character so that it can be related to particular human needs at different times and in different places. It is important, however, that all the valid forms of pastoral care enumerated here should be borne in mind, for together they provide a basis for critical dialogue which stops unwitting distortion and one-sidedness which may threaten the practical responsiveness of pastoral care.

I once saw a cartoon of a man standing outside the door of a psychiatrist's office. He was looking bemused, having clearly just been paying a visit to that luminary. The caption beneath read, 'It's not that I'm *not* confused any more, but I *am* confused on a higher level!' One may feel much the same way about the nature of pastoral care. The discussion above has illustrated the width of this activity, its complexity and its close relation to other ministerial activities. Can it really be separated from lots.of other things and talked of as an independent, meaningful field in its own right? Perhaps it is right that it should remain a vague *portmanteau* concept whose boundaries cannot be sensibly charted. It certainly seems vital that no definition should be employed which is rigid, narrow and exclusive. The saying, 'People are right in what they affirm and wrong in what they deny' might be usefully re-membered here. Surely, too, there is much wisdom in the attitude that it is more important to recognize pastoral care when one sees it in action than to have set ideas about what it is which are then brutally and insensitively imposed on the reality of pastoral practice. Yet to recognize something, literally to re-know it, is to have some notion of what it is that is known before encountering it. Everyone who uses the concept pastoral care has some presupposition about it in their minds based on a combination of theories and experiences picked up in all sorts of ways. Because of this, perhaps largely unconscious but operative fact, it is necessary to open up the possibility of at least designating a broad field which can provide some context for the meaningful use of this term. If pastoral care has no very firm outer boundaries, it should have some kind of coherent, rationally discernible centre which provides some theoretical and practical direction for its practitioners. Such a centre has been suggested here in the belief that confusion is not a virtue, though it may be a necessity, and land-marks, though they may be disputed, do at least allow some kind of orientation.

Chapter Two

Stepping Westwards: Recent Developments in North American Pastoral Theory

The most important feature of pastoral care in the USA since the last war has been the dominance of the counselling and pastoral psychology movements. As the British writer R. A. Lambourne noted in his paper 'With love to the USA' at the beginning of the 1970s, counselling and humanistic psychology appeared to have ousted all other ways of understanding or helping human beings.[1] One of the roots of this dominance was the Clinical Pastoral Education movement which was inaugurated by Anton Boisen in the 1920s and which emphasizes the importance of examining closely the individual pastoral conversation. Boisen's use of the supervised *verbatim* record of the pastoral conversation has now become a main aspect of ministerial training in America. Seminarians in most mainstream denominations now take Clinical Pastoral Education semesters as a matter of course. A large and sophisticated organization, the American Association for Clinical Pastoral Education arranges and monitors the supervision, training and accreditation of students and supervisors.

It was shortly after Boisen that the psychotherapeutic theories of Freud and his followers began to gain widespread acceptance in North America and this was a second very influential shaping force for pastoral care. In the words of Thomas Oden,

after Boisen, pastoral care soon acquired a consuming interest in psychoanalysis, psychopathology, clinical methods of treatment and the whole string of therapeutic approaches that were to follow Freud.[2]

Many humanistic psychological theories and methods emanating from people like Carl Rogers, Eric Berne and Erich Fromm have been considered, adopted and adapted by those involved in pastoral care in the USA. Oden himself is a good example of someone who has experimented with many different approaches. He admits to having started in Rogers' client-centred therapy and then moving on to existential psychotherapy. In the late 1960s he was exploring intensive group process ranging from T-groups and growth groups to psychodrama and Gestalt awareness training. The 1970s were taken up with Transactional Analysis and crisis intervention theory. Now Oden is more interested in re-discovering the classical Christian tradition of pastoral care.[3] I shall return to Oden, but the point to emphasize here is the omni-pervasive nature of humanistic psychology and counselling in pastoral care prevailing until very recently in North America.

Why did psychotherapeutic theories and techniques come to hold such sway in North American pastoral care? There is no clear answer to this but the following may have acted as contributory or buttressing factors. First, the new psychological understandings and therapies seemed to offer concrete ways of helping suffering individuals. People are now so accustomed to the notion that talking to someone in a therapeutic or counselling situation may be helpful and alleviate distress that they fail to realize the relative novelty of this kind of therapy. Any kind of technique which seems to have a concretely beneficial effect on individuals being broken by 'sorrow's mighty rod' is obviously attractive to concerned people like pastors.

A second attraction for pastors, particularly in the main stream liberal protestant tradition in North America, may have been the fact that training in psychotherapeutic or counselling methods not only seemed to make them practically more useful, but also enhanced the significance and importance of their professional role. In a highly professionalized society where competence and expertise are held at a premium, the prospect of developing a high degree of competence in 'talking cures' must seem desirable to many pastors.

In many ways, North America is more religious than Britain; proportionately more people attend churches and more are likely to go and consult ministers when they are in need or trouble.[4] This presumably provided a third predisposing reason for the popularity of counselling and psychotherapy amongst pastoral carers.

Fourthly, North American society is predominantly individualistic in its concerns rather than corporate. There seems to be an implicit ideal that everyone should be responsible for themselves in a free market and there is relatively little enthusiasm for socialism or the supremacy of corporate needs or plans. Many pastors share this fundamental presupposition as to the value and supreme importance of the individual and the methods and insights of counselling and psychotherapy are also congruent with it. It may be one of the attractions of counselling for pastors that by undertaking it with individuals they can help to change things for the better without having to become involved in more complex, and apparently less appropriate, activities such as political action for justice.

Finally, the dominance of counselling in pastoral care in the USA in the middle part of the century was reinforced by the interests and concerns of contemporary theology and philosophy. The humanistic and existentialist concerns of theologians like Tillich and Bultmann which emphasized the centrality of human experience, the experience of the transcendent in the present, and the importance of persons and personal experience amongst other things had an enormous influence in post-war America. Books like Tillich's *The Courage To Be* (1962) very much addressed the interface between psychology and theology and helped to provide a powerful undergirding rationale for the growth of religious counselling and pastoral psychology.[5]

The account of Oden's pilgrimage through various types of counselling and psychotherapy brings out the fact that the US pastoral care and counselling movement has been extremely dynamic. It continues to change and adopt new insights, a fact also well illustrated by Howard Clinebell's work. Clinebell's books *Basic Types of Pastoral Counseling* (1966) and *Basic Types of Pastoral Care and Counselling* (1984) reveal a remarkable desire and ability to synthesize and make use of new insights and theories.[6] The former work draws on the findings and methods of role-relationship marriage counselling, family group therapy and transactional analysis, types of supportive counselling, crisis counselling, referral counselling, educative counselling, group counselling, religious-existential counselling, confrontational counselling and depth counselling. Each of these methods is itself often a complex synthesis of diverse insights and methods. In the latter, Clinebell expands the former and reveals that he has gained yet more useful counselling material. Growth counselling, for example, plays a more prominent part.

It is difficult and, for the purposes of the present book, unnecessary to describe and characterize the shape of contemporary pastoral care in North America precisely. The following features are, however, worth noting. First, there is the continuing dominance of counselling methods and ideas both in the training and practice of pastors. A feature closely associated with this is the professionalized ethos of North American pastoral care. Professionalism and its implications are discussed in much greater depth in Alastair Campbell's book *Paid to Care?* (1985) which was originally written for a North American market. Some of the features which characterize professionalism here include specialized and assessed training; membership of, and accreditation by, a corporate professional body, e.g. the American Association of Pastoral Counsellors; the possibility of charging fees for services rendered and of having only limited contact with 'clients' by seeing them in an office setting for an agreed length of time, e.g. one hour. It may well seem alien to the British reader to conceive of pastors spending a good deal of their time in office-based, specialized practice charging fees for expert counselling; of course, not all or even most American pastors do this. Nonetheless, many of the innovations and influential writings in North America have been heavily influenced and coloured by thinking emanating from the direction of professionalized pastoral counselling, a point criticized by William Arnold:

> I am quite conscious of the number of times pastors, including me, have found writing in pastoral care to be focused on the concerns of specialists. Too little knowledge is shown of the more frequent locus of pastoral care-the community, where there is far less opportunity for structure or control.[7]

A third feature, apart from the dominance of pastoral counselling and its concomitant professionalization, is the sheer dynamism of pastoral care and counselling in North America. Americans seem willing to continue to learn and develop and to experiment with new techniques. If a standard British attitude is response to any suggested change is, Why?, in America it seems much more likely to be, Why not? Not all new ideas or methods are of lasting value. Sometimes it does look very much as if North Americans are prone to jumping on band wagons from which later they have to make a hasty and perhaps undignified exit. It cannot be denied, however, that at least they do have the courage to keep moving and take chances. This must be regarded as in some ways a real virtue.

Finally, it is important to emphasize the inter-denominational, and even inter-religious, nature of the North American pastoral counselling and pastoral psychology movements. The British Marriage Guidance Council uses as one of its standard teaching texts a book called *The Skilled Helper* which is written by a North American Jesuit, Gerard Egan. Readers may be familiar with the Catholic writer Eugene Kennedy who has written, amongst other books, *On Becoming a Counselor*.[8] Several rabbis now contribute to the literature of pastoral counselling in the USA and one of them, Robert Katz, has recently produced *Pastoral Care and the Jewish Tradition*.[9] This is an attempt to relate pastoral counselling to the rabbinic tradition, a move made necessary by the fact that rabbis in liberal Judaism are now under considerable pressure to imitate Christian pastors. So although the original impetus to establish a *rapprochement* with 'secular' counselling and psychotherapeutic insights and methods came from liberal protestants it has become accepted in many areas of American religious life ranging from evangelical protestants to liberal Jews.

By this point, the British reader may be beginning to wonder what all this has to do with our own side of the Atlantic. While it is perhaps interesting from the point of view of general interest to know a little about North American pastoral care, if only to wonder at its very different and almost exotic nature, what has it got to do with our own less specialized, more general and parochially-based pastoral care? There is a tendency in this country to think highly of amateurism and versatility which runs very deep in the traditional professions such as the civil service and the ordained ministry. In theory, organizations like churches are becoming more enthusiastic about the further training of pastors and the development of specialized skills such as parish management. But in practice there is still a very real suspicion that activities which claim a certain expertise and demand specialized training are worthy more of contempt than respect. It may rightly be pointed out that pastoral care based on confidential conversations between parishioners and their pastors has been successfully conducted for many centuries without the benefit of so-called 'counselling skills'. Furthermore, it is sometimes, again correctly, said that pastoral care and the pastoral role must be far wider than simply counselling people.

Sophisticated British critics like R. A. Lambourne point out the dangers of therapeutically-inspired professionalized care by suggesting that even if professions do not intend to be conspiracies against the laity (George Bernard Shaw's contention in *The Doctor's Dilemma*), they can easily become so. As soon as a group claims for itself an exclusive expertise it can rapidly start to assert the ignorance and incompetence of those who are not in its view properly, that is to say, professionally, trained and qualified. Thus doctors discourage patients from making decisions about their own treatment and often deplore diagnoses and remedies gained from non-medical sources like chiropractors or homeopaths. In objecting to a British professional national pastoral organization, mooted in the early 1970s, Lambourne argued that it would not promote pastoral care which was 'lay, voluntary and diffuse in the community' and which was 'motivated as much by a struggle for corporate excellence as a struggle against defects'.[10]

It is certainly a strength of the British pastoral care tradition that, on the whole, it has resisted narrow specialization and professionalism for reasons like these. The negative side of this, however, is that there is much unthinking ignorance about ways in which caring could be made more effective and the skills of pastors improved. Frank Wright points up the suspicion that many people in the churches still have of psychology and that this is based more on prejudice than on positive rejection born out of close acquaintance and study.[11] Such attitudes cannot be applauded. While it is right that there should be more room in the churches for the ministry of all kinds of amateurs (including those who are paid and prize their generalist outlook and abilities highly), it must be remembered that there are 'blithering amateurs' as well as talented ones, and that even those who are naturally gifted in, say, counselling can improve their effectiveness and minimize their capacity to harm others.

In spite of native resistance, or perhaps apathy and reluctance to try anything new and challenging, counselling is beginning to make a significant impact on pastoral care here as in the USA. A national pastoral organization, the Association for Pastoral Care and Counselling which is affiliated to the wider secular organization, the British Association for Counselling, has come into being and it now offers training, supervision and accreditation for those pastors who want it. The Westminster Pastoral Foundation performs a similar function and clearly betrays the training of its founders who trained in the USA. Perhaps the most well-known organization promoting the importance of counselling and psychotherapeutic, as well as theological, insights in pastoral care is the Clinincal Theology Association which was founded by the late Frank Lake. People in towns and cities all over the country have benefitted from courses organized locally by this Association. At the same time many Anglican and indeed Catholic dioceses, together with other churches, have appointed counselling advisers and these officials frequently organize courses for clergy and lay people on a local basis. Most theological colleges now include an element of basic counselling training in their courses for those seeking ordination and many ordinands would like much more of this in preparation for pastoral ministry. Pastoral counselling has also caught the imagination of lay people who will often attend courses at their own expense and in their own time in order to increase their confidence and practical ability in pastoral work. Clinical Pastoral Education now flourishes in some parts of the country, for example in Edinburgh and London, because there are now American-trained supervisors available in this sphere. On the theoretical level, many of the most interesting and stimulating books being published in pastoral care build on the insights of counselling. Michael Jacobs' *Still Small Voice* could be mentioned but other books in the SPCK's 'New Library of Pastoral Care' are also written by skilled pastoral counsellors and supervisors. John Foskett's *Meaning in Madness*, for example, gives an excellent insight into the method of using *verbatim* reports in Clinical Pastoral Education. Peter

Selby's book, *Liberating God* relates counselling to wider social and political factors and context.

The advent of counselling as a method in pastoral care may even have helped to produce a new species of minister in the 1960s and 1970s in Britain, the therapeutic clergyman, identified and described by the sociologist Bernice Martin. She writes,

> one role drawn from the modern professions, that of the pastoral therapist, does have a ready appeal. . . . So clergy learn less Greek, Latin, Hebrew, and classical theology but more social science. They become a species of semi-professional therapist with a roving brief, generic case workers for the parish with a mildly spiritual aura. [12]

Martin claims that many clergy abandoned the religious in favour of either secular politics or 'a mildly therapeutic pastoral role: "only the humane"; no dog collars; no mystery, just good citizenship and informal mateyness.' [13]

Whether or not pastoral counselling can be blamed (or lauded) for bringing about the phenomenon of 'therapeutic clergymen', there can be no doubt that over the last twenty years it has become more and more influential in pastoral care in this country and continues to grow and flourish. It is true that there are all too many pastors still wilfully and woefully ignorant and unskilled in counselling and that much British pastoral care remains amateurish, traditional and unselfconscious in the pejorative senses of those words. Nonetheless, the gospel of counselling is gradually leavening pastoral practice even at the level of general and subconscious assumptions. It therefore seems appropriate for us to hope to learn something from the American writers on pastoral care who have been working with pastoral counselling in a much more coherent manner over a much greater period of time. This is especially the case now that the pastoral care movement in North America is moving beyond a somewhat euphoric and uncritical acceptance of counselling as *the* way of understanding and conducting pastoral ministry. A new and more critical, sceptical spirit is now evident in the USA, which may allow a greater area of learning and dialogue between British and American theorists and practitioners. To put it briefly, American writers are beginning to lift their eyes beyond the individual counselling situation to address more general issues which are of enduring and universal interest and importance.

Since the middle of the 1970s a sea-change has been taking place among American pastoral care writers. The whole nature and direction of pastoral care has come into question and criticism has particularly focussed on the hegemony of secular counselling theories and methods. Perhaps the most vociferous critic, certainly the most incisive, is Thomas Oden, one of the people who had done most to promote pastoral counselling in North America and the author of many distinguished and thoughtful books critically relating various types of therapy to the theological tradition.[14] In *Pastoral Care in the Classic Tradition*, Oden, with the zeal of a convert renouncing his former evil ways, attacks many of the central values implicit in contemporary psychotherapies which have been assumed into pastoral care. These include autonomous individualism (the idea that the welfare of the individual is paramount and the focus of care must be upon the individual not, say, the community), naturalistic reductionism (the idea that there is nothing beyond what is concrete and can be studied or grasped empirically or scientifically) and narcissistic hedonism (the idea that the individual should always seek the best thing for herself). Insofar as these values have been assimilated into pastoral care – and there can be no doubt that they have been both in America and here – they should be rejected, together with the assumption that only new ideas or methods are valuable. Oden points up the neglect of classical Christian authors in the modern pastoral care tradition in favour of contemporary, often non-believing, psychotherapeutic authors. In a fascinating survey of twentieth-century pastoral care writers like Howard Clinebell, Seward Hiltner, Wayne Oates and Paul Tournier, Oden finds no references to authors like Augustine, Gregory the Great, George Herbert, Luther, Calvin or Jeremy Taylor, while these same books are replete with allusions to people like Freud, Jung, Carl Rogers, Erich Fromm and Eric Berne. It is almost as if the churches' pastoral tradition has been completely forgotten as being of no value. In the light of this, Oden believes, the ideology of modernism should be abandoned and that an attempt should be made 'to recover classical ecumenical orthodoxy amid postmodern cultural consciousness'.[15] He talks of his own conversion to the riches of the Christian tradition which he describes as 'a joyful decision on my part to turn again toward the classical Christian pastoral tradition, especially as expressed by the ecumenical consensus of Christianity's first millenium of experience in caring for souls'.[16] The remainder of *Care of Souls in the Classic Tradition* is an attempt to elicit the wisdom of one particular classical writer, Pope Gregory the Great. This work is complemented by a much larger textbook, *Pastoral Theology*. which adopts the same perspective but deals more with specific issues.[17]

Apart from the dismissal of the uncritical acceptance of modernism and modern secular pastoral therapists brought out by Oden, there are other new directions and trends in contemporary American pastoral care literature. One way of bringing these out is to compare Clinebell's *Basic Types of Pastoral Counseling* written in 1966 with his recent *Basic Types of Pastoral Care and Counselling* published in 1984. (Incidentally, both these books are widely and easily obtainable in this country and are useful and readable.) The respective titles of the two books, the latter containing the word 'care' as well as 'counselling' indicates that pastoral counselling is now being placed by American thinkers in a much broader perspective. Counselling is no longer the only paradigm for pastoral care as it perhaps seemed in 1966 when the two words seemed to be synonymous. Clinebell now believes that pastoral care should be 'the nurturing context of pastoral counselling'.[18] The sub-title of the earlier book is 'New Resources for Dealing with the Troubled' while that of the more recent one is 'Resources for the Ministry of Healing and Growth'. Implicit in these once again is a major shift towards a different and broader perspective. There is a move away from simply dealing with problems and crises towards continuing nurture and a focus on growth. Clinebell describes the book as presenting 'a more holistic and explicitly liberation-growth paradigm'.[19]

The use of words like 'healing' and 'ministry' in the sub-title of *Basic Types of Pastoral Care and Counselling* brings out another major change in emphasis. These words are overtly religious and have substantial theological connotations and this points up the far more consciously religious, spiritual and church-centred turn which is becoming evident in Clinebell's work as well as others like Arnold, Browning, Hulme and Oden. Clinebell claims that his revised book 'stresses spiritual and ethical growth as central and unifying goals of all care and counselling that is truly pastoral. . . .' Apart from having this more overtly religious content and interest with its insistence that theology must be taken into account and be used as both source and critique in pastoral care rather than being ignored or regarded as an embarrassment, a further feature of the new book is that it takes into account parish and general ministries and it is not solely based on, or directed towards, specialized counselling and counsellors. The corporate and ecclesiastical bases for pastoral care are recognized and welcomed. Clinebell does not merely broaden his concerns beyond the individual or small group counselling situation. In his holistic liberation-growth model of pastoral care and counselling, he points out that people must be seen in the context of social systems, and even biological systems![20] He emphasizes the need for social and political awareness. Feminist insights, for example, must be incorporated and used in pastoral care as must those of liberation theologies. While the latter do not appear to have influenced the book to any great extent, the fact remains that at least this broader perspective is believed to be of value and significance.[21]

To sum up: Clinebell's recent work, which I am taking as reasonably representative of some of the important new directions evident in contemporary pastoral care literature in North America, exhibits the following features: (1) A move away from counselling as the only paradigm for pastoral care. (2) A move away from focussing only on crises and problems to seeing pastoral care as also a positive, nurturing and ongoing activity. (3) A new emphasis on the importance of the Christian theological tradition with its accompanying concerns for spirituality and ethics as a resource and critical element in pastoral care. (4) A new emphasis on the Christian community as the context of pastoral care and lay people as participants in pastoral care away from the former preoccupation with specialized counselling undertaken by clergy divorced from their ecclesiastical context. (5) A new emphasis on the wider social and political context and implications of pastoral care. Clinebell shares these traits with many other contemporary writers in North America to a greater or lesser extent, although it must be acknowledged that not all of them would want to assent to his priorities in quite the same way as he does. Oden's *Pastoral Theology*, for example, is enthusiastic in trying to base pastoral care in the Christian tradition but, disappointingly, appears to give little place to lay people in pastoral care. Much of the most interesting material illustrating these new emphases is to be found in the series of volumes 'Theology and Pastoral Care' to which I have already drawn attention.[22]

Before going on to look at some of the substantial issues raised by this literature, however, some critical points must be made about the new developments coming from the USA. First, it is important that while people in Britain are prepared to learn from writers in North America and to overcome some of our insularity, we should not be too uncritically accepting of all their ideas. There are real differences of context and emphasis, and these must be recognized. What is required is enlightened conversation or dialogue, not total conversion. Secondly, we should be wary of the North American tendency in pastoral care of rapidly and enthusiastically embracing 'new' ideas and perceptions (even if, as in the case of Oden, they are claimed to be old or classic ideas).

Writing on pastoral care does seem to have something of the character of a roller coaster. It is tempting to groan when one finds in Oden's work this sort of statement, 'So this is where I am coming from – but where am I headed?'[23] There is a tendency in American writing towards following fashion and trendiness. Pastoral care is not an area in which this should be emulated.

Related to the dynamism and changeability of the American pastoral care scene is a degree of superficiality. American academics (and most of the books to which I shall refer are written by full-time academics) are under considerable pressure to produce books regularly and rapidly. The casualty of this in some cases is depth and wisdom. An example of this is found in Clinebell's *Basic Types of Pastoral Care and Counselling* where Chapter 5 deals with spiritual direction and counselling in thirty-four pages. To me, at least, it seems that Clinebell has little experience of that about which he writes and the attempt to write about it in such a short space is ill-advised, if well-intentioned. Spiritual guidance, like counselling of other sorts, is very skilled work requiring much wisdom and discernment born out of long personal experience. It cannot be tackled, written about or learned about in the superficial and cursory way Clinebell attempts.

One of the real strengths of the British tradition of writing in pastoral care is that while it has been all too sporadic and infrequent, it does often emanate directly from pastoral practice or experience. The SPCK 'New Library of Pastoral Care' embodies this 'feet on the ground' approach which, at its best, combines critical awareness, pastoral experience and practical and practicable theory. It is often hard to believe, when reading authors like Browning and Capps that they have really tried to work their theories out in practice, not least because the theories themselves are often difficult to comprehend and understand.

My final criticism concerns the more religious and theological emphasis noted above in North American pastoral care literature. There can be no doubt that the theological tradition has been extensively ignored or forgotten about by those involved in pastoral care on both sides of the Atlantic. Attempts to take it with new seriousness are to be applauded. It does seem, however, that this venture may be partially the product of forces which may be less welcome. In North America there appears to be a two-fold, predominantly conservative, movement at work. This involves a turning away from modernity to the classical roots of the past and it is closely linked with a quest for distinctive Christian identity which is to be sharply distinguished from the identity and values of the civic American religion which has been dominant hitherto. Clearly, there is nothing wrong with seeking a greater sense of identity in itself, nor with seeking roots in the past. It is unfortunate, though, if it means that little attention is paid to society outside the church which becomes very much a secondary concern. It is also a pity if it means that pastoral care ceases to learn from, and dialogue with, secular insights and disciplines. The achievements of the American pastoral care movement in developing counselling should not now be denigrated in favour of idealizing historical theological sources (and it should be noted that selection of traditional sources is in itself a somewhat arbitrary process which is largely determined by contemporary concerns) any more than they should have been unquestioned. Similarly, it should be recognized that the Christian community finds its distinctive identity in relation to the secular world and not apart from it.[24] For this reason, it would be very sad if British pastoral carers who work within a tradition of concern for wider society in many cases were to imitate, whether consciously or unconsciously, all the aspects implicit in some of the new directions being taken by the North Americans.

Chapter Three

Ethics and Pastoral Care

The Christian God is paradoxical in character. He is thought of as being loving, accepting and compassionate, full of mercy and loving kindness to all. But he is also perceived as being just and moral, a judge who demands righteousness and obedience to his commands. Christianity has sometimes been seen primarily as an ethical religion, or even simply as a collection of ethical precepts. For most of its history, Christian pastoral care has maintained a tension between these two aspects of the divine character; love and justice have co-existed together in pastoral practice, with some bias perhaps towards the latter. Pastors have not been afraid to admonish and advise those in their care to keep them on the straight and narrow way. This has led to pastors being regarded as upholders of high moral precepts who act as moral 'policemen' both within and outside the church, a view which persists in the popular consciousness to the present day.

It might surprise those who continue to see pastors as primarily an embodiment of the judgment of God to learn that in the present century there has been a flight from this role, particularly in the liberal wing of the church. Modern pastors often prefer to see themselves as representing the love and compassion of God. They are confirmed in this not only by aspects of the Christian tradition such as the dictum of St Augustine, 'To understand all is to forgive all', but also by the precepts of counselling which suggest that acceptance and unconditional positive regard are the keys to helping people to gain their full statute and potential. Gone are the days when telling people what to do or giving authoritative advice was seen as effective care. The emphasis now lies on developing a warm relationship based on valuing those cared for, understanding them and refusing to judge them. No doubt there are many good things about this bias towards compassion and acceptance in pastoral care. The trouble is that liberal pastors who assume this bias often become oblivious to the ethical or justice dimension in Christianity. An essential element of religion is hived off and forgotten about.

In this chapter some aspects of the contemporary relationship between ethics and pastoral care will be examined. The last part of the chapter will deal with the place of ethics in actual pastoral encounters. It is preceded by an account of the American theologian Don Browning's critique of the place of ethics in pastoral care and his proposals for practical moral thinking as a background against which pastoral care can be exercised. I shall begin by saying a little more about the reasons for the divorce between ethics and pastoral care within liberal Christianity and then outlining a typology of the ways in which ethical aspects impinge on pastoral care.

One of the reasons for minimizing the importance of the ethical dimension in pastoral care has, as has already been implied, been the judgmental connotation associated with ethics. There are several other reasons as well. One has been the desire to acquire techniques for helping people. Pastoral care is a practical activity and human needs are urgent; far more important to actually help people than to indulge in extensive reflection on philosophical and theoretical abstractions, for so ethical considerations can appear. The decline of pastoral power and authority in society is a further factor. People no longer want to be told what to think and do by those who are no better and no wiser than they are themselves. Even if pastors are interested in the ethical aspects of care, there are problems within the realm of ethics itself, for it seems to be in considerable disarray. It is a prey to individualism (everyone must make their own decisions and the decision of each is as valid as that of any other), personalism (everyone must choose her own code of ethics), privatization (there are no, or very few, publicly agreed moral precepts which everyone should obey). Both within and outside the church, there is a vast range of more or less valid opinions and perspectives on each moral issue. Religious ethics have lost their unquestioned supremacy due to the influence of secularization and it seems that the only virtue accepted by most members of society is that of tolerance for the moral codes of those who differ from oneself.[1]

In the light of factors like these, it is small wonder that ethics has occupied a very minor part in contemporary pastoral practice. It is so much easier to get on with the job of caring for people than to try and unravel the knots which ethical considerations bring to the fore. Easy, but dangerous. For the fact is that where pastoral care ignores ethics it is in peril of promoting values or dealing in practices which, on reflection, it might find rather undesirable, dubious or harmful. All human activities have ethical aspects and consequences. These may be implicit and unconscious or conscious and explicit. In the latter case they can be examined and changed; in the former, there is always the possibility that the wrong aims, methods and tools may be unwittingly promoted to the detriment of those who care, as well as those who are cared for. Enlightened common sense is a good guide to ethically responsible behaviour for much of the time. Occasionally, however, it can be very misleading and inadequate. It certainly should not be regarded as wholly adequate by pastors standing in the religio-ethical system of Christianity whose God is moral as well as compassionate.

At this point it is useful to distinguish four different ethical aspects of pastoral care. The first of these concerns the *ultimate aims* and *ends* of pastoral care. All actions and endeavours embody and promote particular norms and values. Pastoral care is no exception to this. It can therefore be asked, What are the norms and values which pastoral care should promote? What are its ultimate aims? What values and behaviour patterns should it be encouraging? What vision of being human should it adopt? What sort of person is it trying to shape? This, then, is what might be designated the *normative* or *prescriptive* aspect of pastoral care and ethics and it concerns the ideals after which pastoral care strives.

The second aspect is that of *description*. This focusses on pastoral care as it is actually practised and seeks to describe the values and ideals which *are* in fact promoted by it rather than those which should be promoted by it. The presumption lying behind this is that if human activities ebody values and ideals, it should be possible to discover and analyse what those values and ideals are. An example of descriptive analysis is given by Thomas Oden who suggests that pastoral care based on the insights and methods of counselling tends to promote what he considers to be harmful modernistic values such as individualism, narcissism and hedonism.[2] The prescriptive and descriptive aspects of ethics in pastoral care are complementary. The former gives it a sense of purpose and direction in outlining ideals to be aimed for, while the latter makes clear what ideals and goals are being fostered in practice. Both areas have been neglected in pastoral care.

A third aspect is that of *ethical issues* which form part of the content of pastoral care in practice. Sometimes people go to a pastor to seek counsel on a moral problem. A doctor might go to her pastor to talk through the morality of taking part in abortions, for example. Often issues arise in pastoral encounters which have covert or implicit ethical aspects. Marital problems, for instance, almost invariably bring up the whole question of what view of marriage is to be taken, what are the rights and obligations of the partners involved, and so on. In this sort of situation the pastor has the task of relating the Christian ethical tradition to the specific circumstances of the person in her care. The process of doing this is sometimes called 'ethical confrontation' and a great deal more will be said about the practicalities and difficulties of doing this later.

One very important aspect of the relationship between ethics and pastoral care can only receive a very brief mention here. This is the area of *professional ethics*. All caring raises questions of an ethical nature for carers themselves. Confidentiality is an example of this. Like doctors or social workers, pastors are sometimes privy to sensitive information about those in their care. How should they use that knowledge? Are there circumstances in which it should be made known to others, perhaps family, friends, other ministers? There can be no doubt that the way in which pastors conduct their caring for others deserves careful attention, but it requires a book in itself. Readers who are particularly concerned about this area are referred to the works in the note if they wish to pursue the matter further.[3]

Constructing Norms for Pastoral Care

No one has done more to highlight both the importance and neglect of ethical norms in pastoral care than Don Browning,

Professor of Religion and Psychological Studies at the University of Chicago. This section of the chapter is based almost entirely on his work, for two reasons. First, he is almost alone in considering the place of values in pastoral care. Secondly, while Browning's writings are rich and suggestive, they are also somewhat dense and obscure in places. It seems useful, therefore, to give a clear and critical account of them.

In his first book on the subject of ethics and pastoral care, *The Moral Context of Pastoral Care* (1976) Browning begins his critique of the neglect of norms and values within the care of a religious community which might be expected to have a deep concern for them.[4] Browning deplores the way in which pastoral care has opted out of determining goals and norms for society in favour of short-term therapeutic activity. Surely, he suggests, one of the things which makes people unhappy or distressed is the absence of appropriate meanings and values in their lives:

> Without a fund of normative religiocultural meanings and symbols, the general confusion about the nature of good in living will itself be enough to cause untold personal difficulties, muddled lives, overt illnesses, and emotional conflicts.[5]

By the same token,

> To minimize value confusion, to clarify the objects and values worthy of people's loyalty, is to contribute to their emotional and mental well-being.[6]

In the light of this, Browning calls for the revival of the traditional role of the church as a community where 'practical moral reasoning' takes place. The place of pastoral care in this community lies not so much in responding therapeutically to the needs of individuals with problems but in 'facilitating a mode of enquiry that will help the members of the church to develop a framework of meanings relevant to all aspects of their life'.[7] With more than a little hyperbole to emphasize the point he is making, Browning concludes

> How to enter into sensitive moral enquiry with troubled and confused individuals without becoming moralistic is . . . the major technical and methodological task for training in pastoral care in the future.[8]

It is important to point out that Browning does not envisage all pastoral care encounters as being primarily ethics seminars or occasions for giving moral advice. He believes that in specific situations it is right for ethical and value considerations to be 'bracketed' so that emotional needs can be dealt with. The immediate and urgent pastoral encounter should, however, be situated within an ongoing process of discerning and exploring meanings, goals and values.

In very basic terms, the fundamental criticism that Browning advances against the modern pastoral care movement is that it has sold out on the business of morals and values. To caricature, it is almost as if the only thing which the needy *cannot* get from the Christian community, which has always stood for the importance of the good and right ways of living, is help with this specific area. The person seeking care can have her emotional and dynamic concerns dealt with in pastoral care, but receives a stone not bread when she expects, or asks for, her value and meaning needs to be taken into account.

Browning is surely right to point up the absurdity of this situation. The emphasis on psychological understanding and counselling methods has made pastoral care lop-sided at times, a fact which even secular counsellors and psychotherapists have recognized.[9] People simply do not live by emotional and psychological support and understanding alone. Given the historical concern of the church for morality and the goals and purpose of human life it is a nonsense if pastoral care is conducted in total isolation from this concern. It might be a dangerous nonsense if this means that values implicit in secular caring methods are allowed to seep unconsciously into religious pastoral care. It is certainly a pathetic nonsense if pastors, who are actually trained in ethics, put aside their particular expertise in this area when they become involved in caring for people in practice and are unable, or unwilling, to offer one of the few things that they distinctively have to give.

Browning is, therefore, absolutely right to draw attention to the neglect of ethics in pastoral care. Some criticisms must, however, be made of his case. In the first place, it is somewhat overdrawn and exaggerated at times. This is perfectly understandable; Browning wants people to take note of what he is saying and needs to correct an overwhelming bias away from ethics and towards the emotional and dynamic in pastoral care in America. Secondly, but related to the previous point, Browning is in danger of being reductionistic about the nature of pastoral care. If others have been in danger of turning pastoral care into nothing more than psychodynamically informed therapy, Browning is in danger of implying that it is nothing more than ethical discourse, or training in morals and values. It is a common failing amongst writers on pastoral care to assert that their particular interest should be central. This does not do justice to the multi-faceted nature of pastoral care, nor, sometimes to the nature of the church community. In Browning's case, he is prone to forget that, while goals and values certainly underlie and are part of the totality of pastoral care, some aspects of this activity (healing, sustaining, guiding, reconciling and nurturing) cannot give primacy to moral discourse at all times. A similar point can be made in relation to Browning's view of the church as a community of moral discourse and practical moral reasoning. Of course this is an accurate and desirable description of part of the church's role, but it is not the totality of it. The church is not just, or even primarily a seminar group of moral philosophers; it is a community of lovers and worshippers as well. Religion is more than ethics and morality, although these elements are a vital part of the outworkings of religion. Finally, a theological and ethical criticism might be made of Browning's position. It has often been asserted that at the heart of the Christian gospel, and so of Christian ethics, lies the command to love. Christianity may be characterized as the religion of love. As a perfectly logical corollary, many pastors would therefore suggest that the task of pastoral care is to mediate love to those cared for so that love between people, and between people and God, can be increased.[10] Although love certainly has radical ethical implications and does not reject moral reasoning, arguably within pastoral care it is primarily mediated through the emotional and dynamic, rather than rational discourse. The experience of love comes first and rational/ethical discourse follows. Perhaps, in his proper concern to redress a very uneven balance, Browning has been tempted to forget the primacy of love and with it, the damage which giving primacy to ethics has done to people in the past. When Christians have allowed ethics to come first, love has often been forgotten and pastoral care has seemed cold, detached, theoretical, cerebral and unresponsive to human need. Mediating

love and grace must precede, and be given primacy over, moral
discourse in pastoral care. If pastoral care ignores the latter,
however, it will be distorted, weakened and less able to respond
adequately and comprehensively to the needs of those who seek
care.

In *The Moral Context of Pastoral Care* Browning raises the
problem of goals, values and morals in pastoral care. In his later
book, *Religious Ethics and Pastoral Care* (1983), he begins to
outline a method for the practical moral reasoning in the church,
which he believes to be such an important back-drop for pastoral
care.[11] The aim of practical moral reasoning is to develop properly
thought-through goals and values to which pastoral care should
conform. The people who undertake this activity Browning
designates as 'critical practical theologians of care'.

The process of practical moral reasoning which moves towards a
normative practical theology of care begins with the identification
of a problem or particular pastoral situation; marital breakdown,
or the pastoral care of young people, for example. The idea is that
the pastor or congregation should move away from an unexam-
ined, *ad hoc*, or pragmatic response to a particular situation or
problem towards having an overall concept of the norms which
should be aimed at and ideally desired. To do this, they would
move through three further stages once a situation or problem is
identified. First, they would attend to the situation and the various
possible interpretations relevant to it very carefully (Browning
describes this as a hermeneutical process). Secondly, they would
undertake critical analysis and comparison using the five levels of
practical moral reasoning which will be described shortly. Finally,
they would be in a position to make practical decisions with regard
to their treatment of the situation or problem and to evolve an
appropriate strategy of action which would embody the norms and
understandings which had come to light.[12]

These steps or stages form part of 'a revised correlational
approach'. This is derived from the work of the theologian Paul
Tillich who sought to correlate questions from contemporary
human existence with answers derived from revelation. Tillich's
work has been modified by later theologians like David Tracy,
hence the term 'revised'. The characteristics of this approach as
expounded by Browning are first, that it attempts to correlate
interpretations of the central Christian tradition with questions *and*

answers implicit in various interpretations of ordinary contemporary human experience. The emphasized words are important modifications of Tillich's original concept; 'interpretation' acknowledges that there is no one direct way of obtaining access either to human experience or the Christian tradition, only a number of different and possibly contradictory interpretations; the possibility of discovering answers to questions posed by the Christian tradition in ordinary human experience where God is also at work presupposes a greater mutuality between these two elements than in Tillich's method. Secondly, the method has the nature of a critical conversation in which the different elements question, confirm and deny each other in a dynamic manner. Thirdly, it takes seriously and involves in conversation the Christian tradition, human powers of reasoning, experience, scripture and the social sciences. The inclusion of experience and the social sciences as full partners in the dialogue or conversation is particularly significant; traditional theological methods have often given a very subordinate place to contemporary experience as a significant element in discerning the truth. Only recently has it been recognized that the social sciences are an important way of discerning the nature of human being. A final obvious, but important feature, is that there is, of course, the potential for conflict between these various elements. The interpretations offered by each will often differ significantly, hence the method is a critical method which will not quickly or easily arrive at convenient or glib synthesis.[13]

At all stages in the method, but particularly at that of critical analysis and comparison, the five levels of practical moral reasoning would be relevant in order to move towards a normative practical theology of the problem, action, or situation under consideration. The first level is the *metaphorical level*. Browning suggests that underlying all human experience and interpretations are basic metaphors which determine and shape basic perceptions, beliefs, actions and characters. The Christian tradition, for example, contains three basic metaphors, or symbols, of God; God is creator (therefore creation is good), governor (therefore there is a moral order in the universe) and redeemer (therefore redemption and renewal are possible). The existence of these fundamental understandings of the world does not in itself determine moral action, right and wrong, but it does colour human behaviour. The person who believes that redemption or renewal is in fact possible, may behave and perceive in very different ways from the person who believes there is no hope or no possibility of change. Examination of the metaphorical level of existence poses the question, 'What kind of world or universe constitutes the ultimate context of our action?'

At the *obligational level* the question posed is, 'What are we obligated to do?' At this second level people are invited to consider what the central and general principles of morality are which should be regarded as obligatory. Browning himself believes that the central ethical principle of Christianity is that of impartiality, i.e., the need to give others equal consideration with one's own interests. In the first instance this principle, derived from the Golden Rule ('Do unto others as you would they do unto you') and the second Commandment ('You shall love your neighbour as yourself') is an invitation to *think* about the needs and interests of others. Other theories or principles of obligation exist elsewhere in the contemporary world. These include, for example, utilitarianism (the greatest happiness of the greatest number should be sought) and ethical egoism (what is best for oneself should be sought).

The third level is the *tendency-need level*. Here the practical theologian of care has to consider the question, 'Which of all our tendencies and needs are we morally justified in satisfying?' To be able to apply the general principles identified at the obligational level to particular human beings, non-moral information must be gathered as to the nature of contemporary needs, tendencies and ends. This can be gleaned from personal intuition and experience, religious and cultural traditions and from the human and social sciences which give insight into human nature. An attempt must be made to discern which of all the available needs, desires and tendencies should be responded to or encouraged, and which are not legitimate.

Having as far as possible tried to discern the nature and destiny of humanity, the next level turns outward to look more closely at the context in which pastoral action takes place and the ways in which it may modify the understandings gained at the third level. The *contextual-predictive* level considers the question, 'What is the immediate context of our action and the various factors which condition it?' Interpretation of the actual situation confronting the practical theologian of care demands assessing psychological, sociological and cultural factors. When this has been done and critical comparison has taken place with the findings of the tendency-need level it is possible to advance to the fifth and final level, that of *rules-roles*. Here the relevant question seems refreshingly simple: 'What specific roles, rules and processes of communication should we follow in order to accomplish our moral ends?' This is really the point at which it becomes possible to consider in what way it is appropriate to implement the moral ends which have been discerned by critical comparison of the material gained at the previous three stages.[14]

Browning suggests that the stages he outlines should be worked through in the order given. Although they are closely related and mutually dependent, they form a hierarchy. He further believes that it should involve theologians from all the theological specializations at each level. (Traditionally, systematic theologians would be most interested in the first level only, ethicists in the second, and practical or pastoral theologians in levels three to five.) The method is prescriptive and normative in its final outcome but it is also a useful analytical and descriptive tool. The stages with their questions can be used to clarify what is presently believed and practised as well as suggesting what should prevail. Its analytical potential is not confined to pastoral care. The same questions can be put to secular methods of caring or to social sciences, thus exposing their assumptions and limitations. What, for example, are the underlying metaphors and theories of obligation implicit in contemporary counselling practices? In the same way, these questions can be used diagnostically in relation to particular individuals or cases. It is possible to ask about a person's basic assumptions about the world, about their working theory of morality and so forth, thus exposing their relative adequacy.[15] Clearly, the procedure which Browning outlines is time-consuming and might be expected to require a great deal of knowledge of, for example, the social sciences. It comes as a relief, therefore, to learn that Browning does not envisage practical moral reasoning as being a process to be undertaken by individuals, nor on a regular basis. It only becomes relevant when a particular area of care or life becomes problematic or muddled and, when this happens, it is a corporate venture involving many different people with different kinds of expertise and knowledge.

Browning's method is certainly abstract and sounds very complicated. It becomes less intimidating, perhaps, if it is pointed out that all that is really being suggested is a systematized step-by-step account of something that people do anyway in a rather haphazard way. Everyone has basic metaphors and basic moral principles which they regard as obligatory. In confronting every situation we all have a view of what it is to be human and what ends should be satisfied or rejected. Often our view of human beings and of the context of action is informed by insights gained perhaps very indirectly from the social sciences and this modifies our sense of what is appropriate action. Finally, in confronting any situation or problem, we have to adopt particular rules and roles. The difference between what we do anyway and Browning's method of practical moral reasoning is that his method is systematic and makes us self-conscious of our assumptions and perceptions. This makes it less likely that we will deceive ourselves or take short cuts which may lead to norms being arrived at which may not be critically- or well-informed.

Apart from systematizing the way in which Christian pastors and others might arrive at ethical norms for pastoral care, the revised correlational method as a whole, as well as practical moral reasoning in particular, has several further attractive and commendable features. It not only establishes a value context and goals for pastoral care which can give it an appropriate direction, but it also improves understanding of what is actually happening in individual pastoral situations at specific moments with regard to the promotion or denial of values. The method is characterized by being rational, publically accessible and critical. This means that anyone, Christian or not, can attain a better understanding of why particular practices or values might be preferred in pastoral care. It allows pastors to justify their work more adequately to the general public as well as the Christian community. The method allows a useful and full integration of the insights and methods of the social sciences, while ensuring that their voice does not overwhelm the distinctively theological in seeking norms for pastoral care.[16] Finally, the revised correlational model is applicable far beyond the bounds of pastoral care. It is really a practical theological method which could be used by Christians of very varied concerns to sort out the norms and priorities which they might pursue in relation to a specific issue or problem.

Inevitably there are limitations to the revised correlational model, too. First, and most obviously, the method is complex and time-consuming if rigorously prosecuted. How many pastors or congregations are really going to have the time or specific knowledge to pursue the method properly? Is it right that they should? It could be argued that the kind of exercise which Browning advocates is really most suitable for people with sophisticated intellectual skills who have access to enormous amounts of information. Perhaps, then, it is of more use to academics like Browning himself than to people in parishes. It is difficult to conceive of professional theologians specializing in, say, biblical studies wanting to get involved in revised correlational method. Their knowledge is very specialized and it might well be a real waste of their time to become involved in a very general enterprise, however worthy that enterprise might be in itself. A similar problem arises in relation to the social sciences. How many theologians, much less pastors, are really competent to evaluate and engage in a critical dialogue with social sciences? All too often their vision of the findings of the social sciences will be partial or distorted. And which social sciences should be attended to, and to what extent? There is an explosion of knowledge in sociology, psychology, anthropology and other disciplines. They also have their own foundational metaphors and assumptions which need a rigorous critique from the theological perspective if they are not to be uncritically assimilated into the norms informing pastoral care. Perhaps one has to conclude that Browning has done a great service by showing what it would mean to conduct an exhaustive and scrupulous quest for a normative theology of care, but that what he has emerged with is hopelessly unwieldy for ordinary pastors involved very busily in local pastoral care. If pastors had to resort regularly to the revised correlational method then they would have little time to actually exercise much practical care and analysis would be in danger of displacing action. Perhaps the most appropriate place for the use of the revised correlational method in its pure form lies with central church bodies or with academic institutions which may be able to work with local communities providing resources which can lead to appropriate norms being formulated for pastoral care. Whether or not this is the case, it should be remembered that the rejection of the revised correlational method or other methods aimed at producing practical theologies or norms for care will not lead to a lack of norms. It will simply mean that norms are unrecognized, implicit, inadequate or plain undesirable. With this dismal thought, it is time to turn to the way in which ethics, norms and values should be allowed to impinge on actual pastoral encounters.

Ethics in Pastoral Encounters

It is one thing to evolve norms and goals for pastoral care in general. It is another to integrate the ethical dimension in practical pastoral care. A real problem arises when the pastor has to represent to the person who seeks care a concern for the right and the good as well as love, acceptance and compassion.

> Without love, acceptance, forgiveness, there is no healing, no regeneration, no restoration of a broken life or a poisoned relationship. But equally, without a strong moral witness which is willing to affirm goodness and condemn evil, without the courage to risk oneself and one's relationship for a principle a people perish.[17]

There can be no doubt that there is a real tension here, albeit that it is expressed in a rather extreme and polarized way. Tensions are difficult to live with, and it is therefore not surprising that pastors try to get away from this one. Some do so by ignoring the problem altogether and by responding to each pastoral encounter as it seems best at the time. Sometimes they may be compassionate, sometimes they are judgmental; in either case, they are pragmatic and unreflective. Others opt for giving a clear priority to their role as moral guides and teachers. They believe that the primary task of the pastor is to make clear what the standards are to which people should adhere and find a place in their care for straightforward rebuke and admonishment, together with the giving of direct advice or instruction. A third group solves the tension in the opposite way, emphasizing the supreme importance of love and acceptance and tending to de-emphasize the importance of moral and ethical factors raised in pastoral encounters. These pastors are often of a liberal disposition, strongly influenced by the recent insights and methods of secular counselling which maintain the paramount importance of acceptance and empathy in care if it is to be effective and compassionate. It is the position of the last group which is addressed here. Is it possible for pastors who believe in the value of acceptance and empathy to integrate into their thinking and practice a concern for ethics and values which does justice to their position as representatives of a community of moral discourse and concern?

The reluctance of some liberal pastors to incorporate any overt emphasis on ethics and values in their pastoral care seems very understandable when some of the evidence gained from modern counselling and psychological theories and practices is considered. Freud, for example, postulated the existence of an element of the personality called the superego which represents the commanding voice of the parent. Any emphasis on morality may reinforce the superego in the person and so maintain repressive forces within the personality which prevent personal growth. A similar negative effect is postulated in regard to the neurotically guilty. Sufferers from neurotic guilt have committed no offence in fact but perceive themselves to be permanently in the wrong. Such people may actually obtain temporary relief from being rebuked by an authority figure such as a pastor. Having been punished or 'spanked' they are better able to cope with life for a while but their deeper malaise is left untouched.[18]

There can be little doubt that in some circumstances the introduction of moral standards, considerations or judgments can have a very inhibiting effect on helping relationships. If a person is made to feel guilty or inadequate, or if they feel that their beliefs and standards are unacceptable, it may be very difficult for them to be open with the person who is trying to help them. Defences remain high and personal change or growth is therefore prevented. A further observation from the counselling sphere is that moral advice and evaluation seldom helps people to change the way in which they behave. People will usually only act upon advice or principles which accord with their own deeper desires and instincts. In an age of radical individual autonomy, giving advice or demanding adherence to particular moral standards is ineffective, as well as being alienating, in the caring encounter.

Lurking behind these objections to the overt inclusion of ethics and values in pastoral practice lies the spectre of judgmentalism. Judgmentalism implies some or all of the following characteristics: the condemnation of sinful behaviour; working with fixed or prior notions and so being inflexible and lacking in understanding; the possession of an authoritarian or disciplinarian character which demands conformity from others; manipulating or protecting other people so that they lose their individual freedom and autonomy; coercion, exhortation and prohibition; the possibility of sadistic control and gratification which may be enjoyed by self-righteous people; a negative and uncreative reaction to situations.[19] This unattractive constellation of characteristics is thrown into relief by those associated with acceptance, the key factor needed if helping relationships are to be successful. Acceptance implies a relatively passive attitude which allows people to articulate their real feelings; a willingness to build up the empirical particularity of the situation under consideration rather than judging it beforehand in a general way; finally, acceptance is avowedly and vehemently non-authoritarian.[20]

Faced with the unacceptable and harmful effects of judgmentalism and moralism, many pastors feel strongly that they should err on the side of empathy, acceptance and compassion in helping encounters. But this option brings its own difficulties. First, it ignores the fact that values or ethics surround and permeate pastoral care itself. Pastoral care is exercised in a social and moral context. It promotes some values and aims and it discourages others. Pastors bring their personal values to their helping relationships and, although they may not make their personal convictions explicit, there is reason to believe that those for whom they care quickly discern their basic outlines and tailor their behaviour and responses accordingly.[21] The idea that helping, much less pastoral care, can be wholly value-free is a fallacy. Indeed, some people seek help from pastors precisely because they wish to be cared for within the context of specific values. Sometimes, of course, they come to a pastor with an explicit moral problem with which they need help. More often moral dimensions may be brought up in the context of a broader situation or problem; Don Browning only slightly exaggerates when he claims, 'All problems of care are finally, in some way, moral problems. . . .'[22]

It cannot be denied that each person has a moral or ethical dimension to her existence, just as much as she has an emotional dimension. It is strange if this whole dimension is dogmatically ignored, especially in the pastoral care of the Christian church which is a community of moral discourse. Care which does this might be deemed to be rather partial and one-sided. It could also be accused of being disrespectful, for it does not show much respect for a person if a pastor refuses to be honest about ethics as well as emotions. The principle of genuineness, (meaning openness and honesty) which together with unconditional positive regard and empathy forms part of the essential 'therapeutic triad' for effective counselling, demands the possibility of dealing with the ethical dimension if that becomes relevant in a helping relationship.

All the points made above add up to one conclusion; it is not a case of *whether* a value and ethical dimension should be a part of the pastoral relationship, for that cannot be avoided. Rather, it is a matter of trying to sort out in *what way* it can be part of the relationship so that it avoids the negative features of judgmentalism or moralism and has some compatability with acceptance and compassion. It is at this point that the work of Ralph Underwood on empathy and confrontation comes into its own.[23]

As we have seen, it may sometimes look as though a pastor must make a choice in pastoral care between offering acceptance or empathy and offering challenge and raising value issues overtly – a type of confrontation. Underwood believes that this is a false polarization. In fact, empathy and confrontation are *both* important aspects of respect for the person seeking help. God acts with respect towards humanity. This means that sometimes he has primarily shown love and acceptance towards us, sometimes his challenge and justice. Both of these things communicate respect and regard. Ultimately, neither diminishes the person and both affirm her:

> Respect is a moral connection that discloses how empathy and certain ways of being confrontive require each other. Respectful considerate confrontation goes hand in hand with empathy. . . . Respectful confrontation communicates in essence, 'Having gained some understanding of you, I now trust you to deal openly with some things you have not considered.' That is, for all their differences, there is no fundamental contradiction when ministers who are empathic are also confrontational, so long as there is respect.[24]

Confrontation is absolutely essential in pastoral care. It allows the enlargement of people's self-understanding, prevents self-idolization, affirms sociality and communality, helps people to be more objective in their analysis of themselves and their situations, turns them away from total self-reliance, expands the horizons of the pastoral encounter spiritually and morally, and can help people to realize that judgment is a means of grace when it is sensitively and appropriately administered. It is good for the pastor in that it allows her to be herself and not to smother her own views and positions.[25] The trouble with empathic listening which remains non-directive or non-confrontational, is that eventually it can leave the person seeking care trapped within the boundaries of her own horizons. People need the challenge, guidance, opinions and perspectives of others if they are to grow and change. To permanently deprive them of these things in the name of acceptance is neglect. That is not to say, however, that the way in which people are confronted is not enormously important.

The first, and most important precept to be remembered when contemplating bringing an element of ethical confrontation into a pastoral encounter is that this should take place within a context of acceptance. The person who is being cared for must have an experience of being cared for and understood if they are not to feel rejected or judged by the introduction of a moral element into care. This makes good sense theologically, for the Christian perception of grace suggests that the experience of grace precedes that of judgment; it is because we perceive ourselves to be forgiven and accepted by God that we are able to face up to our sinful condition and to begin to amend our lives. It also makes practical sense because, as has been noted, the introduction of law or judgment can cause a person to actually raise their defences or flee from a relationship where they feel hopelessly inadequate and condemned. Imagine, for example, going to a pastor to discuss marital difficulties and being immediately greeted with a digest of biblical teaching on the virtues of family life. The implied rebuke in this may well prevent someone from being able to be open about the real situation which faces them, particularly if they are already feeling very guilty. So the first thing must be to establish, as far as possible, a warm, trusting, and understanding relationship in which the person being cared for has the experience of being listened to and understood. This opens the way to ethical confrontation at a later point.

Pastors have a right to confront and raise the ethical dimension only when they have earned this by showing to those in their care that they are willing to be patient and to try and understand or empathize with that particular person's situation. They may have to 'bracket' the moral dimension in order to do this. It is not an easy thing to suspend judgment and put aside general principles, perhaps very passionately held, in order to pay attention to the specifics of a situation. Sometimes it is tempting for those who preach sermons to transfer at least some of their desire to expound very general principles into the context of their individual pastoral care. Resisting doing so is, however, of paramount importance. Only by disciplining oneself to listen very carefully to the particular story of the person seeking care can some of the worst aspects of judgmentalism be avoided. These include responding too rapidly and inappropriately ('I think you should do this because this is what people would normally do in this sort of situation'); stereotyping ('This is a case of simple adultery and so it is quite clear that you should do this'); superficiality; imposing dogmatic judgments. A clear corollary of this precept is that sensitive pastoral care which is alive to the empirical reality of a person's situation will often take a great deal of time. If a pastor is not willing to spend time in this way, it may be better not to get involved in the first place, or to refer a person to someone else. Far better that this should happen than that a person should feel misunderstood ('Pastors do not understand what it is like for me'), superficially judged, or rejected, because moral judgments have been introduced at too early a point in the pastoral relationship.

So far, the impression may have been given that the introduction of the ethical dimension into the pastoral encounter is a matter of listening and understanding but then confronting people with a series of moral commandments or propositions which must then be accepted or rejected in a straightforward way. This is a distortion of both the nature of moral discourse and the empathic style of the pastoral encounter. Moral discourse does not consist in re-iterating traditional precepts but in exploring and discussing various important questions. It is well known that many different moral standpoints can now be adopted with equal seriousness and sincerity. Ethical confrontation in pastoral care is therefore an invitation to consideration, exploration and discovery rather than to conformity. This means that when ethical points are raised in the pastoral encounter it is often best that they should be raised tentatively and in the form of questions. This is functional, in that the person being cared for does not feel rebuked or condemned. It is also respectful of the autonomy of the individual, itself an important pre-supposition of both ethics and care. Each individual is to be regarded as rational and responsible for their own moral code and behaviour. It is they who must consider and give free assent to certain important questions and principles. The pastor can only facilitate this process, she cannot short-circuit it by providing pre-formulated solutions, however desirable she may think those solutions are.

The introduction of a moral dimension in care is an invitation to growth and discovery and should not be experienced as wholly negative moral denunciation. It is creative and appeals to people's reason, not their fear of the pastor or of God. Only that which people become convinced of themselves can truly be called moral. The negative, authoritarian and repressive connotations of judgmentalism should therefore be resisted in thinking of ethics in relation to pastoral care. People should be invited to undertake their own moral enquiry and, as far as possible, to make their own judgments. This reflects the way in which Jesus Christ appears to have dealt with ethical questions; instead of telling people directly what to do, Jesus frequently told a parable or a story which left people to make up their own minds. There seems to have been no attempt to morally coerce people into the Kingdom of God. If people judge themselves, together with their attitudes and behaviour, they are much more likely to accept this judgment and, perhaps, to be able to change. The pastor provides the opportunity for this judgment, she does not do the judging herself.

It is very important to recognize that ethical confrontation in pastoral care is not a one-way process. Entering into a moral enquiry which is a genuine conversation involves all participants. The pastor who eschews the role of authoritative moral teacher will find that she, too, is drawn into the process and may be challenged or confronted in her attitudes and beliefs. Mutuality is becoming a key note in contemporary pastoral care and it is a welcome feature of ethical confrontation in that it reduces the dangers of authoritarianism and judgmentalism. No pretence can be made that one party knows better than the other or can solve the other's problems or dilemmas. Instead, each can offer her own skills and insights for scrutiny, criticism and consideration. One very practical benefit of this for the pastor is that she does not have to take total responsibility for the principles, beliefs or behaviour which may emerge from the pastoral encounter. The responsibility for their own principles and actions remains firmly with each respective participant.

When the pastor tries to become conscious of and develop the moral or ethical dimension in pastoral relationships several temptations emerge. Some of these have already been considered: the temptation to confront before empathizing, to generalize, to make snap judgments, to move too quickly towards the ethical dimension, to tell people what is right and wrong rather than letting them take responsibility for finding their own answers. Two further temptations must be mentioned. First, there is the temptation to build on people's guilt and shame. Some people, as has already been mentioned, actually want to be found guilty and condemned by an authority figure like a pastor. It gives them a strange kind of relief or even pleasure. It is vital that pastors do not collude with the kind of guilt which exists where no offence has taken place. True morality flows from an appeal to what is best in the person, to rationality and to the inspiration of a gracious God. It does not come from cowering obedience to an overweening superego or from neurotic guilt.[26] By the same token, entering into the ethical dimension in pastoral care must not be an excuse on the part of the pastor to vent aggressive feelings against the person cared for, or to make the pastor feel that she is doing her job. The ethical dimension is explored because the needs of the care-seeker demand that it should be, and the raising of moral questions should not be a way of 'beating' those who may already feel guilty and inadequate.

Finally, as preparation for the possibility of the mutual encounter of ethical confrontation it is essential that pastors become aware of their own ethical beliefs and principles. This allows a free and honest exchange within the care situation. More significantly, it will help the pastor to be able to be open and direct when this is required by another's needs. Sometimes this kind of self-awareness and knowledge may suggest to a pastor that they are not the right person to help someone. A person who believes strongly that abortion is wrong in all circumstances for example, may think that it is unlikely that they can really give good and objective help to someone who is wondering whether or not to have an abortion. The knowledge that this is how she thinks herself means that the pastor can share her position openly with a person seeking help. The latter then has some choice as to whether to carry on with this pastor or to go elsewhere. Where ethical presuppositions and values are explicit, at least in the pastor's own mind, the potential for self-deceit, suggestion or manipulation is minimized.

The term 'ethical confrontation' used in conjunction with pastoral care sounds cold, forbidding and unpleasant with its connotations of being 'told off'. It is to be hoped that this discussion may have modified that first impression, and that it has shown what a vital part the ethical dimension can be in pastoral care, complementing rather than destroying empathy and acceptance. Justice and compassion, law and grace can be reconciled in pastoral care, even as they are in the nature of God himself. Exploring the ethical dimension in pastoral care is, therefore, an integral part of discovering what it is to be human and of realizing human potential.[27]

Chapter Four

Discipline and Pastoral Care

'Caring and sadism are separated by a hair's breadth only.' I was brought up short by this comment made by my supervisor when I was a student in a psychiatric hospital. We had been talking about a certain kind of nurse sometimes to be found in hospitals who seems both parental and kind but also sometimes rigid and cruel, ruling patients with a rod of iron. Since that time, I have often been struck by the close relationship between care and control in many parts of life. The parent wants her child to grow up conforming to certain values and standards of behaviour. She shapes the child's behaviour by a mixture of positive encouragement and a measure of restrictive control or punishment. A probation officer genuinely wants to help her client to find a decent and appropriate way of life in the community and may spend a great deal of time and energy talking with the client and trying to create opportunities for her. But she also has a responsibility to the courts and to society at large which may lead to her using the threat of punitive measures to obtain some conformity. Social workers in the community may wish to side with the deprived families in their care but sometimes have to exercise a controlling role by taking a child into care, ostensibly for the good of all concerned. This may lead to their being perceived more as policemen than helpers by their clientele.

Care and control are often inseparable in the helping relationship where one individual or group has some power over another. Sometimes it can even seem that care is just a word with positive overtones used to disguise what is actually nothing more than control. We are all familiar with the stereotyped and probably imaginary Victorian father who beats his child severely for the child's own good. The torturers of the Inquisition believed themselves to be benevolent, seeking only the ultimate salvation of their victims. A more contemporary and more relevant example of care being perceived as control can be illustrated from my own experience:

> Miss X was in her eighties. She was blind and nearly deaf, and lived on her own. Some days before I met her in hospital she had been found behind the door of her kitchen by the police who had been summoned by anxious neighbours who had not seen Miss X for some days. When I saw her, she expressed her extreme disappointment that she had not been left alone to die. A cultured woman, she said that now all her friends and relations were dead and she could do none of the things she enjoyed doing like reading, there was nothing left for her. 'I do so want to die,' she said, 'I'm so looking forward to meeting God – aren't you?' She asked me if I would be able to get her a gun so she could shoot herself and pleaded, 'Please promise that you won't let them give me that kiss of life.'

For Miss X the benevolent intervention of social workers, the police and medical staff was an unnecessary and unwelcome intervention in the process of dying and it simply prolonged her misery and frustration. In this case, the caring institution of the hospital put the preservation of life at any cost above the wishes of the person living that life and so became an institution of control and conformity. This ambivalence is potentially present in many helping acts and institutions, including pastoral ones, and is one of the factors which leads to a consideration of discipline here, for discipline is precisely a blend of care and control undertaken for the supposed benefit and good of individuals, groups or even whole societies.

Discipline is also one of the keys to a very widespread activity amongst pastors, pastoral visiting. Two days after my ordination in the Church of England I was given details of my duties. A large proportion of my time, afternoons and evenings when there were no meetings, was to be given to visiting people of the parish in their homes. Generations of Anglican pastors have been initiated in this way and it was not unexpected on my part. But I was puzzled then, and became even more puzzled as to the purpose of all this visiting for which no particular rationale was provided in terms of the overall strategy in the parish. It was only when I became aware of the historical background to visiting and learned of its disciplinary functions that I began to understand fully what the origins and purpose of visiting were. I shall return to the historical and disciplinary background to pastoral visiting soon. In the meanwhile, it should be said that although I did not think of my pastoral visits in homes or in hospitals as having a disciplinary function clearly some of those visited did! I recall the look of horror on the face of one person as she opened the door to find a man in a clerical collar there, and many occasions on which people have in a completely unprompted way started to lay out their faith and personal beliefs, apparently for clerical inspection and approval. For many people, even now, an encounter with a pastor is like meeting a policeman. It is an experience of judgment: 'I don't go to church, but I do believe in God. I try to live a good life and I would help anybody. Anyway people who go to church are hypocrites. . . .' Such people are all too well aware of the disciplinary (in the negative sense), controlling aspect of pastoral care which continues to reverberate in the common consciousness even in a very secular society.

Discipline has rather negative associations for most people living in Western societies today. It seems to imply punishment, negative sanctions and control. A person is disciplined or punished when they offend against the rules and norms of the group or society to which they belong. The application of discipline in this negative sense often involves some kind of penalty or loss of freedom and rights, these latter being highly prized in our society. Most people would want to avoid discipline of this sort at all costs. It is important to put it alongside a comprehensive and positive view of discipline which is much more to do with growth, formation, acquisition and training.

In academic circles, a scholarly discipline is not primarily something which is inflicted on people as a way of punishing them, but a means whereby a person's capacities are appropriately expanded and enhanced. In Christian spirituality a person undertakes a disciplined prayer life to draw closer to God. Both academic work and prayer may require hard work, but they are positive disciplines closely related to discipleship rather than to punishment. Saint Benedict referred to his monastery as a school for the spiritual life and in his *Rule* set out many disciplines to be undertaken by monks. The *Rule* is designed to be merciful rather than punitive and its sole reason for existence is that people should have a way of becoming more perfect and reflecting the image of Christ. Nonetheless, it does contain punitive elements. The lesson which might be drawn from all this is that discipline has positive and negative aspects. Anyone undertaking the life of Christian discipleship should be involved in the process of discipline for the sake of formation. This may involve negative sanctions as well as positive encouragements. However, Christian discipline is predominantly positive, undertaken for positive reasons and not just a system of punishment, control, or conformity for its own sake. Both positive and negative aspects of discipline are relevant to pastoral care in its historical and contemporary forms.

The Historical Background

The church is a community of deviants! Or, to put it in more traditional language, the church is a community of sinners. All the members of the church, including its ministers, are supposed to strive after the perfection of Christ and at the same time they all fall short of this. The Christian life is one of constantly battling against sin in oneself and the world at large and attempting to be conformed to the image of Christ. This task has been with Christians from the earliest times and it is the main aim of pastoral care which, it will be recalled, 'is directed towards the elimination and relief of sin and sorrow and the presentation of all people perfect in Christ to God.'[1] In this context, discipline is enormously important for it is a major aspect of helping people grow towards perfection as well as being, in its negative sense, a way of trying to ensure that sin and evil are eliminated or alleviated within the Christian community.

Discipline has helped to establish the norms of the church and ensured conformity to them by means of both encouragements and routine exercises and, on occasion, by the use of negative sanction and punishment. Once again, it may be that the negative connotations of discipline are most apparent historically. Anyone who has read any church history will recall the numerous occasions on which people were excommunicated by the Christian community as well as the punitive discipline exercised by the

Inquisition or the Puritans of the seventeenth century. It should not be forgotten, then, that discipline in the positive sense of shaping people through teaching and spiritual exercises was taking place simultaneously, and is ultimately of far more significance for pastoral care.

A modern pastoral theologian, Seward Hiltner, sees discipline as absolutely central to the history of pastoral care:

> John T. McNeill's great book *A History of the Cure of Souls* is primarily a history of what came to be known as Christian discipline – what the pastor or the church did, in order to keep itself pure and to correct the sinner, to those who offended against the Christian community.[2]

Hiltner points out that discipline was an integral part of the church as far back as the time of Paul who gives one of the first recorded examples of someone being punished by the church for his sins.[3] As the church grew, Hiltner suggests, discipline for the sake of the purity of the community became ever more important and in those less individualistic days the good of the offender was regarded as secondary to the good of the whole body, although ultimately the interests of individual and community were believed to coincide. Hiltner tends to dwell on the negative aspect of discipline, omitting the positive aspects like the gradual growth of, for example, personal confession. Nonetheless, he is surely right to point to the centrality of discipline in the *cura animarum* before the Reformation and to its decline since. Discipline, especially corporate discipline, has all but disappeared in the mainstream Western churches to the extent that it may now seem wholly alien to pastoral care.

Discipline did not disappear entirely at the Reformation. It forms a central element in both its positive and negative aspects in George Herbert's treatise on parochial pastoral care *The Country Parson* (1632). Herbert is best known as a poet, but he was also a clergyman of the established Church of England and spent the last few years of his short life (1593–1633) in a small country parish in Wiltshire. Interestingly, *The Country Parson* was written while he was still a don at Cambridge and so it is a somewhat idealized description of parochial pastoral care.

Herbert seems to have conceived of the parish as a 'School of Religion'.[4] The keynote of pastoral ministry is thus to educate people in the Christian life and help them to grow:

The task of the priest, in Herbert's terms, is to find each parishioner where he is and move him from that place toward fuller involvement in the Christian life.[5]

Herbert himself describes the pastor's job thus: 'A pastor is the Deputy of Christ for the reducing of Man to the obedience of God.'[6] This sounds like discipline with a vengeance, although the word 'reducing' simply means 'bringing back'. Discipline is central, however. It is educative and didactic and the pastor must be teacher, preacher and example. It can also be admonitory and concerned with the preservation of order and with sanctions. In order to be effective in his work, the parson must visit a good deal. Herbert has a chapter entitled 'The Parson in Circuit' which describes the way in which the faithful parson will visit throughout his parish on weekday afternoons, monitoring and observing the lives of his parishioners. The reason for visiting was not to be pleasant, or pass the time of day, but to see whether the candidates for paradise were up to the mark and whether they could be assisted further towards perfection by the pastor. Herbert has no qualms about admonishing the wayward although this is to be done with sensitivity to the individual concerned:

> Those that the Parson finds idle, or ill-employed, he chides not at first, for that were neither civil, nor profitable; but always in the close, before he departs from them: yet in this he distinguisheth; for if he be a plain countryman, he reproves him plainly; for they are not sensible of fineness: if they be of higher quality, they commonly are quick, and sensible, and very tender of reproof: and therefore he lays his discourse so, that he comes to the point very leisurely, and oftentimes, as *Nathan* did, in the person of another, making them reprove themselves. However, one way or other, he ever reproves them, that he may keep himself pure, and not be entangled in others' sins. Neither in this doth he forbear, though there be company by: for as when the offense is particular, and against me, I am to follow our Savior's (sic) rule, and to take my brother aside and reprove him; . . . Besides these occasional discourses, the Parson questions what order is kept in the house, as about prayers morning and evening on their knees, reading of Scripture, catechizing, singing of Psalms at their work, and on holy days;

who can read, who not; sometimes he hears the children read himself . . .[7]

This short extract illustrates many points, not least the degree of intrusiveness which pastors expected to be able to exercise in the lives of their parishioners. The whole parish was to be open to the surveillance of the pastor and a certain amount of this expectation of automatic access remains amongst Anglican clergy to this day. The aspect of surveillance and control is to be found throughout *The Country Parson*. Wherever he is, he is to watch, to judge and to assess:

> the Country Parson, where ever he is, keeps God's watch: that is, there is nothing spoken, or done in the company where he is, but comes under his Test and censure.[8]

Ultimately, Herbert's pastor is also bound to punish evil-doers and support the magistracy against sinners and the idle, the latter seen as the great scourge of late Elizabethan and Jacobean society. A Chapter is devoted to 'The Parson Punishing'!

Herbert's country parson seems to be a mixture of schoolmaster, saint and policeman. There can be no doubt that this person is to be loving, humane and benevolent in his concern to conform people to the laws of Christ as well as the laws of the land (of which Herbert in common with other clergy of the established church was a staunch supporter). For Herbert and his kind, discipline was absolutely necessary and completely unproblematic. It was an integral part of pastoral care. The reasons for this are not hard to find. First, Jacobean society, in common with all Western societies up to that point, was hierarchical. The peasantry expected to obey their social betters and the clergy were amongst these. Secondly, pastors had a very high social status and were main stays of the social order. They expected people to take notice of what they said and to allow them to interfere in their lives. Thirdly, all the people living in a particular parish were Christians and most were (or should have been) members of the Church of England. This meant that the pastor automatically had responsibility for the spiritual well-being of all the parishioners. In this situation admonitions and rebukes might be expected and tolerated.

The sort of pastoral care undertaken by George Herbert together with its very overt disciplinary aspects is almost unimaginable today in mainstream liberal churches, though it does survive in some very traditional settings, in the attitudes of some very traditional ministers, and also in very committed and enthusiastic sectarian groups. Almost all the things which made that kind of pastoral care possible for Herbert have changed. There is greater equality in society so people will not automatically regard the opinion of a minister as better than anyone else's. Pastors have fallen from their exalted and superior position and are now regarded with contempt or amusement rather than with respect by many members of the community in which they serve. It is highly unlikely that any pastor will find herself in a parish which consists solely of members of the Church of England or any other single denomination; the community of faith and the community in general cannot be regarded as coterminous. Parish clergy often have huge numbers of people living within their boundaries and are wholly unable to keep a watchful eye on the homes of all inhabitants. There has been a growth in the value given to individuals rather than communities, so even committed Christians might not take kindly to gratuitous admonition from their pastor. Individual autonomy is enhanced by mobility and the pastor who tries admonition and rebuke on a regular basis may well find that her flock has wandered to pastures new, no longer compelled by law or predominant social custom to be in any church. Finally, there is a strong sense that people's homes are private places and that no one has the right to enter them unless freely ivited, much less to quiz them on matters of faith while they are there. The all-seeing eye of the autocratic benevolent paternalist pastor must now stop at the front door. Spiritual policemen can get no search warrants!

Discipline as George Herbert conceived it is outmoded. It would, however, be foolish and presumptuous to suppose that something which has been such an important element of pastoral care in the past can simply be forgotten about or lightly discarded, particularly amongst those who now choose to belong to churches of their own accord. A re-interpretation is needed to make this aspect of pastoral care relevant to secularized, Western, predominantly urban Christians. New interest is now being taken in this area, particularly in North America.

Discipline Today

In his book *The Moral Context of Pastoral Care* Don Browning identifies two primary functions for pastoral care historically:

> (1) the incorporation of members and their discipline in the group goals and practices of the church, and (2) the assistance of persons in handling certain crises and conflicts having to do with existential, developmental, interpersonal and social strains.[9]

Latterly in Western liberal churches the second function seems to have almost totally supplanted the former so that

> churches are giving up earlier efforts to socialize their members into a distinctive style of life. These churches are renouncing disciplines that might induce and maintain significant alterations in the behavior and attitudes of their members. Pastoral care is now more readily seen as something done by ministers to help people in a situation of emotional conflict and crisis.[10]

The consequence of this kind of movement is, amongst other things, that the churches lose any kind of distinctive identity over against the societies in which they are situated. People come to church 'not for ethical direction and a change of life-style but for social affirmation and for emotional and spiritual comfort.'[11]

There are now signs of a reversal of this trend in pastoral care. Writers like Browning and more recently Oden and Duffy have become very interested in discipline, especially in its positive, formative and educational sense. The reasons for this revival of interest in discipline are complex but fascinating and I shall use them as 'pegs' upon which to hang the material derived from individual writers. Together, they form a strong case for discipline occupying a much more central place in pastoral care in this country as much as in North America, though it has to be said that our circumstances are not exactly the same. England and Scotland, for example, still have established churches with a formal link to the political state.

Eight factors underlie the contemporary revival of interest in discipline in pastoral care:

1. *The nature of the church and changing understandings of ecclesiology*   It is not possible to summarize accurately in a small space all the developments taking place in Western churches but some general points can be made. There is a trend towards churches becoming smaller numerically. There is an emphasis on Christians meeting together in small groups (this country has seen the rise of the house church movement and even mainstream churches now set great store by people meeting in small groups rather than just in main services in the church building on Sundays). In many countries, churches seem to be becoming more critical of the societies in which they live. It used to be the case that churches, particularly majority or established churches, allied themselves closely with the dominant values and rulers of the societies in which they were situated. This is now much more controversial; witness the growing opposition to totalitarian governments by the Catholic Church or the criticisms made of the British government recently by bishops of the Church of England. In America, too, there seems to be a general disillusion with the sort of civic religion which has hitherto been dominant amongst mainstream churches.

Practical developments of this sort are reflected in the thinking of theologians studying the nature of the church. Moltmann and Pannenberg, for example, visualize an end to the old established churches and look towards a voluntary, highly committed, but not necessarily numerous, fellowship.[12] There is growing feeling that traditional institutional churches which are geographically coterminous with a particular state, authoritarian, hierarchical, clerically dominated and omni-inclusive in terms of membership, should give way to a servant church which is committed, small, a faithful remnant, to some degree exclusive, and which claims no monopoly of the truth.[13] Even so staunch a defender of the established Church in England as the Archbishop of York is sympathetic to this view and sees the importance of a highly committed core of Christian parishes who are nonetheless open to the less or un-committed people around them.[14]

This highlights the importance of discipleship and so of discipline and it underlies and amplifies many of the other factors leading to interest in this area.

2. *Christian identity*   A great deal of recent American theological writing has concentrated on the importance of developing a distinctive Christian identity. Surely Christianity must consist of

more than simply being a good citizen or a nice person, there must be something distinctive about the members of the Christian community and the values which its members adopt.[15] In pastoral care, Don Browning has been the most outspoken advocate of the need to form a 'community of moral discourse' with its own distinctive culture of meanings and values. This needs to take place for the benefit of individuals and church communities, but also for the benefit of society at large. If Christians have nothing distinctive to offer then the salt has lost its saltness and they cannot act as an effective leavening force in society. Discipline is of crucial importance for forming such a community of distinctive moral discourse:

> Discipline is first of all a matter of deeply implanting within the character of a people the basic norms, patterns, values and sensibilities that govern the culture of the group. Discipline as the task of forming and maintaining the emotional sensibilities, values, and behavioral norms of a people called Christians was very much the central task of pastoral care – in the early church, during the Dark Ages, and in the medieval church.[16]

3. *Rediscovery of tradition*   For individuals or communities, identity is closely linked to what has happened in the past. Something has already been said about the place of discipline within the history of pastoral care, and also about the rediscovery of historical emphases and wisdom by modern American writers on pastoral care. Suffice it here to point to Oden's assertion that the rediscovery of the historical tradition of pastoral care would, amongst other things, demand a rehabilitation of discipline, particularly self-discipline or *askesis*. This would, in Oden's view, act as a counterbalance to the exaggerated self expression which presently prevails.[17]

4. *The corporate dimension of Christian life and community*   A common criticism now made of the history of the church in the West since the Reformation is that it has been primarily concerned with individual piety and individual salvation rather than with the formation of a community with a strong sense of corporate identity and direction. This imbalance is now being redressed. Alongside the growth of small groups of Christians which meet together and learn to worship, work and pray together, there is enormous interest being shown in experiments in Christian community.

Even the formal worship of churches like the Church of England now demands the active participation of all the people in the church and attempts to reinforce a strong corporate or family atmosphere and identity.[18] The rediscovery of the body of Christ made up of Christians relating closely to each other rather than each simply relating personally to God is another predisposing factor towards an interest in discipline. The discovery of group norms, values and practices is vital to bind the Christian community and this lies at the heart of positive discipline.

The most vivid example of a corporate emphasis with substantial disciplinary overtones in recent pastoral care literature is to be found in E. Mansell Pattison's pastoral care of systems.[19] Pattison suggests that rather than paying exhaustive attention to needy individuals, the pastor of a parish should be 'shepherd of systems'. The idea lying behind this comes originally from science. The point is that social groups can be seen as dynamic systems which are either good for the individuals involved in them because they meet their needs or bad. These systems exist anyway and we all belong to them. The task of the pastor is to identify the various systems operating within his church and to ensure that they grow and evolve in health-giving ways. This kind of thinking is a refreshing change from single minded concentration on individuals and their needs. It also offers a way for individual pastors to exercise effective pastoral care over a large group of people involving everyone in creating a caring environment.

5. *Rediscovery of the distinctive mission of the church*   As the church gradually realizes its separateness from the secular world by which it is surrounded it is also becoming more aware of the need for mission to that world. The servant church has a job to do. Pastoral care is not divorced from the main task of the church; indeed, it is there to help people be equipped and fitted for it. If the Church has a distinctive shape and direction, pastoral care must take part in shaping or disciplining Christians rather than only providing a relief service to those individuals in need or distress.

This kind of thinking is most apparent in the writing of Regis Duffy who has attempted to formulate a Roman Catholic theology of pastoral care.[20] Duffy argues that pastoral care must be situated within the mission of the Christian community. The redemptive needs of individuals should be met within the context of evoking a commitment to the gospel, this evocation being, of course,

discipleship. For Duffy vocation and salvation cannot be separated, so pastoral care enables people to do something in relation to
the gospel mission of the church, it does not just make them feel
better:

> Commitment to gospel tasks and responsibilities is a key factor
> in effective pastoral care. We are healed for the sake of others.
> The praxis of the community and its individual members must
> be evaluated in terms of this gospel perspective.[21]

Duffy further suggests that 'pastoral care is the continuing effort
to assist Christian communities and their members to deepen their
baptismal commitment and penitential recommitment so that they
may do the work of the gospel in our time.'[22] It has to forge
credible communities of Christians that can proclaim the gospel
and to call forth the manifestations of the Spirit that are needed for
this. Duffy believes that effective pastoral care always leads to
ongoing conversion and renewal and enables Christians to clarify
their intentions. Healing sacraments similarly enable the healed
person to do the work of Christ. The quality of effective pastoral
care is ultimately tested against whether the Christian community
and its members have gained a wider vision and deepened their
commitment. If they have not, pastoral care has in some way
failed. The sense of purpose, direction and mission in pastoral care
together with the importance of deeper discipleship is very
attractive. It puts discipline in a prominent place but within the
context of positive discipleship which is where it properly belongs.

6. *Nurture, growth and prevention* These are characteristics of
much of modern pastoral care literature which reflect a movement
away from concentrating on crisis intervention when things go
wrong for people after they have happened and towards positive
and continuous growth, nurture and prevention. The way of
discipleship does not always lie in the valley of the shadow of
death. It is important that people should be being formed and
educated on all levels of their existence. Once again, the concept of
discipleship implies the importance of positive discipline here.

7. *Emphasis on norms and values* Browning's interest in making the Christian community a place with distinctive norms and
values which are different from those of society round about has
already been mentioned. It is not just in the church that there is a
renewed interest in this area. Western society generally is

witnessing a reaction to the permissive attitudes of the sixties when it seemed that each person was being urged to find their own morality and behave as they liked as long as it did not harm others. Some Christians at that time advocated a principle of love as the ultimate measure of any act and more specific moral guidance or conformity to the rules of the past was questioned. This kind of thinking is now held to be anarchic and irresponsible by many, and there are calls within and outside the church for a return to traditional values. This background forms a fertile seedbed for the call to discipline and not only positive discipline is advocated. Some are referring to imposed discipline of a military sort ('Bring back conscription for the young.'). In some evangelical circles, particularly in the USA, the merits of corporal punishment based on biblical principles ('Spare the rod and spoil the child') are now being advocated with great seriousness.

8. *Spiritual life and guidance*   There has been an explosion of interest in the life of the Spirit and in prayer over the last two decades. This has reached all parts of the church and with it has come a new appreciation of the value of systematic effort and disciplined practice ranging from regular times of prayer to occasional fasting. Many ordinary Christians are beginning to see the necessity of supplementing grace and spontaneity with human effort and system so that discipline as a positive way of deepening discipleship and commitment is again brought to the fore. One evangelical writer entitles a book on the subject of spiritual discipline *Celebration of Discipline* and emphasizes the fact that the keynote in discipline is joy not drudgery.[23]

This is a good point on which to end this review of some of the factors which lie behind the interest which is now being shown in discipline, particularly in pastoral care. To understand why this topic is of such interest is one thing and has some value. But it is much more important to begin to think about the sort of discipline which should be being encouraged and practised in pastoral care. This more immediate question will now be explored.

Discipline in Practice

Pastoral care has all but ignored the discipline dimension of the tradition of the *cura animarum* which emphasizes growth, positive action, education and aspects of specifically religious spirituality in favour of quasi-psychological means used largely to meet the needs of distressed individuals. It is good that the tide is now turning. The trouble is that the insights of the tradition need considerable modification if they are to be relevant now. The sort of discipline in pastoral care practised by George Herbert was paternalistic, authoritarian, intrusive, admonitory and sometimes punitive. For reasons already discussed, this cannot commend itself wholly to Christians living in an ecclesiastical and social situation which is completely different in many ways. Where pastoral care is exercised in a context of large populations, secularization, religious pluralism, personal privacy, individual autonomy and at least notional social equality, where pastors no longer have recognized authority and sanctions at their disposal, what guidelines can be offered?

To be compatible with life in modern Western society where people voluntarily commit themselves to the Christian faith discipline needs to have some or all of the following features. First, and most importantly, discipline must not be separated from discipleship. It must find its place within the positive, and ultimately joyful, journey of Christians towards God and each other. This is a point which is well put by the Catholic pastoral theologian Henri Nouwen:

> Discipline and discipleship can never be separated. Without discipline discipleship is little more than hero worship or fadism; without discipleship discipline easily becomes a form of emulation or self-assertion. Discipline and discipleship belong together. They strengthen and deepen each other.[24]

Discipline, and the habits and virtues it encourages, is not an end in itself. If it becomes a form of self-justifying, joyless work, then somewhere its purpose has been lost sight of. In *Celebration of Discipline* Foster warns against the very real danger that the attempt to order human activity and orientate it systematically towards God can be a way of denying divine grace. This must not be allowed to happen.

Related to this point is the importance of keeping the positive developmental view of discipline to the fore and resisting the temptation to make it primarily punitive. Sometimes discipline is costly to undertake and individuals or communities may from time to time wish to undertake apparently punitive exercises, for example fasting. This is acceptable only if it is part of the road to sanctification. There is a good deal of false guilt around in Western churches, that is, feelings of guilt which are not actually related to wrong actions which have been committed. People who are guilty in this way may seek punitive discipline in order to feel they have been 'spanked' and so feel a little better about themselves. Such people need to become aware of the joy, grace and love that comes from God and which is essentially liberating and healing rather than being caught up in guilt-feeding rule keeping. Rules and disciplines should be primarily adopted as a response to grace and because of the desire to grow in all aspects of one's life.

It is still helpful to see discipline along educational lines. Benedict and Herbert regarded the monastery and parish respectively as schools of sanctity where people were, in a very positive way, learning to deepen their Christian commitment. Although education has now changed considerably so that it is no longer simply a matter of rote learning the wisdom of the past, the function of the school is still fundamentally the same. It is a place where people's capacities are expanded and drawn out. There is still a place for rote learning (e.g. the alphabet) in schools and the same is true of Christians in churches where much more could be learned of the essentials of religion by studying the Bible and the works of the great saints. But education is now seen as far more exploratory as well. It is not just a matter of assimilating answers from the past but also a case of learning to ask the right questions for oneself and seek one's own answers. The school is sometimes perceived by its pupils as a place of punishment and control entered unwillingly and left as soon as possible. The Christian 'school' must not have that feel to it if it is to be a place of joyous sanctification.

The necessity of putting discipline within a positive educational framework has been laboured because there is a real danger that the contemporary revival of interest in discipline could lead to some very negative and harmful distortions. As I said at the outset of this chapter, care and control are very closely linked; it is easy for discipline which starts out as a free response to grace and as a desire for growth to turn into a cage rather than a springboard. The contemporary crisis in state sector schools in this country at the moment presents a salutary reminder of the way in which a very positive institution can find itself becoming more and more bogged down in control rather than care or education.

Christian discipline must always be willingly and voluntarily entered upon. This has always been the case when people have sought spiritual direction. They are not compelled to do so but do so of their own accord. Discipline visited upon people without their glad consent is likely to be of little use anyway (even if people will tolerate its imposition for whatever reason) and it goes against the spirit of free response to God. To be of real value, discipline must ultimately be accepted as self-discipline. There are two closely related points to this one. First, discipline must be tailored to the needs and gifts of particular individuals. This has always been the case in spiritual direction. The idea is not to produce standardized robots or clones but, in Duffy's terms, to bring forth the many gifts of the Spirit required for the church to be able to undertake its mission. Secondly, the desire for discipline must spring from the presentation of a vision rather than from coercion. The followers of Jesus should be inspired not driven.

By the same token, although discipline is important for its normative value-shaping functions, for the way it fosters particular practices and virtues and helps develop particular habits and personal rules, there must always be room for spontaneity as well. Where dour normativeness and legalism threaten, it should be remembered that the early Christian fathers in the desert and the founders of monasticism where discipline found its earliest exponents were very keen that there should always be scope for spontaneity. The point of the rules and disciplines was not to kill life and zest but rather to provide structure and training which would provide a vehicle for spiritual progress, not a substitute for joy and spiritual experience.

Another important thing which can be learned from the monastic tradition about discipline is that it should be humane. In his *Rule* Benedict requires the abbot of the monastery to set mercy above judgment. There is certainly scope for admonition and punishment but it is there primarily as a vehicle for human beings and should not be an unbearable yoke.[25] When people enter the religious life as monks or nuns they take upon themselves obedience to the rule of the order they are joining. Many people today would find the prospect of taking a vow of obedience daunting and apparently very repressive. This difficulty is overcome if the word 'faithfulness', is substituted for 'obedience'. Christopher Holdsworth, a Quaker, in advocating the value of rules like that of Benedict to ordinary lay people, suggests that obedience can still make a great deal of sense if it is interpreted as faithfulness to a person's true self and values as expressed in a discipline voluntarily undertaken with a view to growing as far as possible into the fullness of the stature of Christ and into friendship with God.[26]

A good way of summarizing the points I am trying to make about the place of discipline in Christian life is by comparing it with worship. Both discipline and worship are essential aspects of the Christian life. Both are voluntary activities freely undertaken if they are genuine. Each involves, and has an impact on, both individuals severally and the community as a whole. Worship and discipline both affirm and reinforce corporate identity and consciousness and help to develop particular values and behaviour amongst Christians. Both come into being as a response to the grace of God, but human activity and effort are also essential. Neither worship nor discipline is solely concerned with ethics and changing patterns of behaviour but each has ethical implications. Each is part of the sanctification of individuals and the community and each points beyond itself to the Kingdom of God. Discipline and worship are essentially practical things and they involve adherence to rules and some agreed order. Nonetheless, if they are effective they also allow room for human failure, for joy, spontaneity and the work of the Spirit. A view of the pastoral relationship itself has been implied by all the things said so far but it is now time to make this explicit. If the key note of Herbert's pastoral care and disciplinary activity was benevolent paternalism, that of contemporary pastoral care and discipline must be mutuality.

There is no room for bullying, coercion or demanding that people undertake certain practices or adopt certain views just because the pastor says so and she is the pastor. Finding an appropriate discipline for an individual or a community involves a process of mutual seeking and discussion, not ministerial *fiat*. It is not a question of a parental authority figure disciplining the naughty children in the congregation (though it is still common to find clergy attempting to do this in pulpits and elsewhere, often appealing to false guilt). Instead, all the members of a community should recognize their mutual need to find ways of growing together as a community and as the body of Christ, both severally and corporately. The pastor is just one of the people seeking a way towards God and needs the discipline of others. For the most part, this discipline will take the form of encouragement rather than admonition or rebuke; Herbert was right in thinking that, given time and understanding, most people will judge themselves rather than having to be explicitly judged by others. In fact, many people judge themselves much more severely than anyone else would, hence the need for encouragement and reassurance rather than condemnation. The church is a community of deviants and sinners. All have fallen short of God's love and there is little scope or point in one Christian condemning another while there is a great deal of value in Christians encouraging each other to be true to what is most precious in themselves and in their community.[27] The kind of mutual disciplinary relationship between adult Christians sharing the same journey is perhaps best characterized as friendship.[28] This notion may seem very distant from the pastoral ministry exercised by Herbert's socially superior, authoritarian and all-seeing country parson, but perhaps Herbert would sympathize with it if he were living in present social circumstances. It is, after all, a description which Jesus himself uses of his relationship to his disciples:

> I shall not call you servants any more, because a servant does not know his master's business; I call you friends because I have made known to you everything I have learnt from my Father. (John 15.15 Jerusalem Bible)

Visiting Re-visited

This chapter began with my own experience of visiting parishioners in their homes. I said that I was given no real rationale for this activity, but that I believed that one of the keys to it was its historic disciplinary function as exemplified in writers like George Herbert.[29]

Herbert had the clear purpose in his parochial 'school' of sanctifying the people of the parish. One of the main tools he used for this was regular home visiting in which he cared, taught, catechized, encouraged, admonished and rebuked. Herbert's aims and methods were entirely admirable for the times in which he lived, modelled very closely on the image of the shepherd. The shepherd is, by implication, stronger, wiser and more far-seeing than his flock. He uses a mixture of encouragement and punishment to ensure the compliance of his sheep so they eventually arrive at their destination: individual and corporate sanctification. Times have changed. Some things, however, remain the same. One of these is the belief on the part of pastors that they should regularly visit 'their' people (and the possessive pronoun here is very significant for implicit in it is the all-responsible parental authoritative shepherd rather than the fallible, limited human being involved in relationships based on shared responsibility and mutuality). The trouble is that it is no longer clear what the purpose of routine visiting is. Discipline from on high is no longer required or welcomed amongst ostensibly equal adults. Where people do ask to be told what to do by a pastor or seem to want to be rebuked, it may be that childishness or masochism is being encouraged and growth is stifled. Pastors feel they ought to visit, but often neither they nor the people they visit are very clear about the purpose or value of what they are doing.

There may be great discrepancies between the significance a pastor attaches to visiting and the perceptions of the people visited. Often professional workers see and understand things in a completely different way from their clientele. A doctor telling of an encounter with a patient may say, 'I explained everything to her and she seemed grateful for my help', while the patient says, 'He told me nothing and I didn't find the visit a lot of use!'[30] Examples based on experience of such discrepancies can be given:

1. Pastor: 'Visiting is part of my work.'
Parishioner: 'Drinking tea with people in the afternoons isn't work, it's leisure. Anyway there are lonely people who need visiting more than I do. I don't mind being friendly to the minister if he wants to come and see me but I'm blowed if I'm going to be seen as his work. It's like being an object!'

2. Pastor (to person who has only been to the church once and who comes from another part of the town): 'I must come and visit you.'

Visitor: 'Help! Why does this person who is a total stranger to me want to come to my house? He seems to think that it is natural to visit people who don't know you, may not like you and haven't invited you. It's like the Mormons – you can't even call your home your own!'

3. Pastor: 'Visiting people is consistent with the teaching of the Bible. Jesus came to visit us so I visit people to incarnate God's love and concern for them. Like Jesus, I go to where they are.'
Parishioner: 'I feel I am being judged by this man. Why is he here? I don't know why he is so interested in me. It is a bit nosey to want to come into the house when you hardly know someone.'

4. Pastor: 'I hate visiting and feel very uncomfortable about going into the homes of people I don't know very well. But it's part of my duties.'
Parishioner: 'I do wish he wouldn't come. I don't think he feels comfortable with us and it is very embarrassing. I think he only does it because it's his duty and that doesn't say much for us as people does it?'

5. Pastor: 'I haven't got much time to visit, but I think it is a good thing to get lay people involved with so we've set up a visiting team.'
Parishioner (perhaps elderly): 'The minister never visits. I know there are visitors from the church who come round but it's not the same. After all, it is his job, he is ordained to be the representative of the church and ministers always used to visit.'

I cannot go into all the theological and practical points which these examples raise. I would like to underline some key issues however. First, there is often no agreed understanding about why a particular visit is taking place, or indeed what pastors *think* they are doing when they visit. Second, even when a pastor does have a clear purpose, e.g. simply to get to know people better, this often does not communicate itself to those whom he is visiting. Third, it would be good if all pastors were to ask themselves why they are undertaking visits, both specifically and generally. Is it a matter of duty or desire, and who primarily is supposed to benefit from the visit? Fourth, attention needs to be given to the judgmental and symbolic aspects of pastoral visiting, still very much present despite the decline of its overtly disciplinary function. It is common for patients in hospital to turn over and pretend to be asleep when a minister approaches and for patients in the day room to start apologizing for swearing. Whether pastors like it or not, they are often perceived to be figures of judgment because of their symbolic role. This has been the case ever since St Paul in his visits to the earliest Christian communities came as both a figure of encouragement and rebuke. This aspect of ministerial '*parousia*' (a word which is used to describe Jesus coming to judge the world at the end of time) raises important questions about how the ascribed judgmental aspect of the ministerial role can be used creatively and for the benefit of those who are visited. It also raises the issue of who may appropriately visit and in what circumstances. The pastor who has the symbolic authority to represent the Christian community may be feared or disliked more than a lay visitor in some circumstances because of the judgmental connotation associated with her visiting.

It is the same symbolic authority and role, however, which enables clergy to visit homes, hospitals and prisons which might be closed to lay members of the church. A residual right of visitation for ministers is still retained in our society and this, too, is left over from the days when discipline was dominant in visiting and the pastor had a role of surveillance over the whole of his parish. This raises the fifth point, How far should pastors in secularized, pluralistic, and privatized societies like our own presume to have a duty, right, or responsibility to visit people, especially non-members of their own churches, if they are not invited to do so? This is the issue of unwanted intrusion which, again, has not been adequately thought out. Clearly, some people find the visits of pastors invasive, mystifying and oppressive. This is a particular problem when people are not able to get up and walk away, for example, when they are ill in hospital. There should be no automatic assumption that pastoral visiting is a good thing, particularly if it is based on the residual remnants of supposed 'rights' inherited from the disciplinarian, authoritarian, paternalistic pastoral care systems of the past. One can no longer applaud King's advice to Tractarian ordinands at Oxford: 'Keep on going to them, Dissenters and all, until they say they won't have you.'[31] Lastly, all these points must be taken together with the reinterpretation of discipline and the model of the pastoral relationship as a kind of friendship described above. Somehow, modern pastoral visiting must take account of the need for mutual care and positive discipline oriented towards growth and sanctification. Once again, this raises questions of who should visit whom, with what purpose and under what circumstances. To be practical for a moment, it seems to me that mutuality and friendship imply that the pastor might be *visited* just as much as anyone else in a congregation and that the rejection of the autocratic, all-responsible shepherd role might put a question mark against visiting people without their active consent or invitation.

Books and articles commending the value of pastoral visiting (but still failing for the most part to provide very much in the way of a rationale for it) continue to be produced.[32] The most stimulating discussion of the subject is to be found in William Oglesby's *Biblical Themes for Pastoral Care*.[33] Oglesby believes strongly in routine visiting and regrets the fact that it is often neglected for lack of time or because pastors do not know why they are doing it. It is valuable because it allows the pastor to see people in their own space, a privilege denied to most professionals who therefore have a more limited knowledge of the people they are dealing with. If there are problems in a family, the pastor can get to know of them and help with them before they get desperate. It also allows people to learn of what resources there are available before they absolutely need them. Oglesby thinks it is equally important to visit whether there is no known need present, where there is a manifest need or where a need is simply suspected. The crucial thing is that in each visiting encounter there should be elements both of initiative and freedom. This model is drawn from the Bible. God acts, takes initiatives; human beings can then respond, or not, for God respects their freedom of choice. This model of allowing both initiative and freedom in pastoral visiting is summarized by a verse from Revelation:

> Behold, I stand at the door and knock; if anyone hears my voice and opens the door, I will come in to him and eat with him and he with me (Rev. 3.20).

The point is that, like Jesus, pastors should be willing to take initiatives in approaching people to offer them pastoral care but that they should not force themselves on people. This way of thinking seems much more consistent with modern respect for individuals and a non-coercive view of pastoral care. No right of entry or expectation that people must accept the care tendered is required. The pastor may even be firmly rejected. If this happens she should not give up knocking on the door nor should she force her way in. Oglesby parodies the verse from Revelation: 'Behold I stand at the door with a fireaxe; if anyone will not open the door, I will chop it down and come in, anyhow!' The pastor must be patient. She should ask in advance if it is all right to visit, and when she visits it should be clear why she is there. In jargon terms, a mutually understood if unwritten contract should be formed. When undertaking such a visit which she has herself initiated, the pastor should allow the conversation to go the way the person or family visited want, rather than imposing her own concerns. Once again, this affirms their freedom. Equally, respect for freedom demands that the pastor should be sensitive to the right time to terminate a visit or conversation. At all times the pastor must avoid being coercive:

> In any pastoral conversation, the minister has a responsibility to prevent silences becoming coercive. This is primarily true when the minister has taken the initiative in the call. [34]

Oglesby recognizes that it is very difficult to respect another person's freedom and withdraw when they want you to. Nonetheless, even Jesus withdrew when asked to do so, or when not welcome. [35] Initiative is absolutely necessary in pastoral care, for it overcomes isolation and aloneness and brings reconciliation and communion. There is always a need for carers to make a first move and to be prepared to move towards people who cannot move towards them. Pastoral relationships in the modern world cannot be genuine and mutual, however, if people's freedom and ability to say no is not respected.

Oglesby's sensitive, theologically and psychologically well-informed discussion does much to begin to move thinking about visiting away from the merely pragmatic. [36] It takes into account the existence of adult Christians making a free response and is consonant with the views of discipline and mutuality which should now begin to be taken into account in thinking about pastoral visiting. This activity is as old as Christianity itself

('Blessed be the Lord, the God of Israel for He hath *visited* His people and set them free.') and there is no reason why it should continue to be a vital part of pastoral care. The historical, and largely tacit, assumptions upon which it rests do, however, need to be reviewed and new ways of conceiving it and practising it need to be developed. In the Bible visiting is always undertaken for a purpose and it is an integral part of God's mission to the world. It is indeed sad, then, when visiting, having been a tool of a particular type of pastoral discipline, is regarded as purposeless, or a waste of time. It is even worse when pastors persist in visiting without those being visited having the least idea why or desiring it.

Conclusion

The revival of interest in discipline amongst pastoral theologians is a very welcome corrective for pastoral care. There are, however, some anxieties about the possible dangers of this revival. First, there is the danger of a new legalism and its associated evils of ministerial authoritarianism, appeals to guilt, and the death of spontaneity. Secondly, discipline is most feasible and creative in small groups. When churches have already declined so they are small groups there is not much problem, but there is a question whether the emphasis on discipline might cause established churches like the Church of England to seek actively to become smaller and to want only a highly committed membership. If this is the case, the church will be relinquishing its claims to be the church of the whole people, whether or not they attend church, and this will be a fundamental change in orientation. The third anxiety is related. Where a group of highly committed people who are involved in a distinctive common discipline springs up it is easy for less committed people to feel excluded. In building up the body of Christ by nurturing discipline within it, it is important to consider whether an unhealthy and unnecessary exclusivity is also being fostered. The last point concerns care and control. I have suggested at a number of points that care and control are in many ways inseparable, two sides of the same coin. Pastors who seek to make discipline an important aspect of their care will need to beware of letting it become a way of manipulating or controlling groups or individuals. This will demand constant re-assessment and vigilance on the part of the whole Christian community.

George Herbert's poem 'Discipline' places discipline of a very negative punitive kind within the love and providence of God and the journey towards him. While his treatise on pastoral care now seems dated, his poems are fresh and of lasting relevance:

Discipline

Throw away thy rod,
Throw away thy wrath:
 Oh my God,
Take the gentle path.

For my heart's desire
Unto thine is bent:
 I aspire
To a full consent.

Not a word or look
I affect to own,
 But by book,
And thy book alone.

Though I fail, I weep;
Though I halt in pace,
 Yet I creep
To the throne of grace.

Then let wrath remove;
Love will do the deed:
 For with love
Stony hearts will bleed.

Love is swift of foot;
Love's a man of war,
 And can shoot,
And can hit from far.

Who can 'scape his bow?
That which wrought on thee,
 Brought thee low,
Needs must work on me.

Throw away thy rod;
Though man frailties hath,
　　Thou art God:
Throw away thy wrath.

Chapter Five

Politics and Pastoral Care[1]

Some readers may already have decided that there is no connection between pastoral care and politics. They may agree strongly with Frank Wright's assertion that it is the individual person who should be the central and over-riding concern of pastoral care, not any kind of amorphous social collectivity:

> Under the compulsion of the Kingdom, the pastor will never settle for the impersonal, but always seek the welfare of the person. There, at least, is pastoral distinctiveness.[2]

It is, of course, unthinkable that pastoral care should ever lose sight of concern for individuals. Nonetheless, a moment's reflection will make it obvious that many of the things which affect the well-being and growth of individuals for good or ill originate in the wider social and political order. The advent of mass unemployment with its attendant carnage of personal deprivation, misery and mental disorder is a poignant and topical example of the way in which the welfare of particular persons is in so many ways vitally affected by collective social forces. The individual may be regarded as in some ways the specific locus for suffering caused by wider social ills.

The contention of this chapter is that effective pastoral care, if it is truly to alleviate sin and sorrow and to nurture human growth, must widen its concern and vision beyond the suffering individual. Psychologically-informed, individually-focussed pastoral care has become unnecessarily narrow and straitened, sometimes with consequences bordering on the disastrous.

Relating pastoral care to the social and political dimension of life has, on the whole, not been a major concern of American writers. There was a burst of interest in this area in the 1960s when President Kennedy's liberal social welfare programme was at its height, but since then interest has been limited. There are honourable exceptions to this. Dieter Hessell's *Social Ministry* puts socio-political concern and action at the centre of ministry and Howard Clinebell's *Basic Types of Pastoral Care and Counselling* follows up a long-standing interest of Clinebell's in this area in proposing a 'holistic liberation-growth model of pastoral care and counselling'. This allows the inclusion of the socio-political dimension in pastoral care, but it is somewhat vague and lacking in clear direction or analysis.[3] Reasons for the relative lack of interest in the USA might include the greater specialization of pastoral care round the counselling model and a general social context which is less politicized and more individualistic.

In this country, by contrast, there has been a great deal of interest over the past few years, a fact borne witness to by numerous papers and at least one important book.[4] It is not easy to account fully for this development, nor for the interest previously expressed here by people like R. A. Lambourne and James Mathers in the 1970s, but some factors can be postulated.[5] First, our political context has been radicalized over the past few years. Secondly, there has always been a close link here between church and state and so broad political concern. (Recent interventions in public life by Anglican bishops and other church leaders remind of the living nature of this link.) Thirdly, pastoral care, and training for it, have always been more generic and broadly-based here than in America. British pastoral care has never been solely, or even mainly, a matter of counselling troubled individuals. Lastly, there is the considerable influence of political theologies, especially Latin American theology of liberation. Even high up in the Anglican hierarchy, the view has been expressed that such theology is necessary in Britain today.[6]

The socio-political dimension is a central concern of British writing on pastoral care today.[7] Its significance should not be overestimated, however. Many people, perhaps particularly working pastors, would still see it as unrelated to the sort of pastoral work they do. The continuing, almost exclusive, emphasis on caring for individuals still holds sway. Why is it, then, that British pastoral care trapped within individualistic and psychological understandings and practices?

The Psychological and Individualistic Encirclement of Pastoral Care

There are at least seven very powerful factors which, to a greater or lesser extent, have predisposed pastoral carers in this country to see their activity in primarily individualistic and psychological terms.

1. *The theory and practice of psychodynamic psychology, psychotherapy and counselling*   The discovery of 'talking cures' by Freud and his followers has had an enormous effect on pastoral care both in this country and America. Pastoral counselling continues to grow and flourish. The disadvantage of it is that it focusses the attention of pastors more and more on the one-to-one relationship with all its fascinations. At best, it also takes groups into account, but on the whole does little to encourage pastors to look carefully at social and political context or the need for social change as a solution to individual problems.[8]

2. *The influence of individualism in religion and theology*   The concentration on individuals and individualized ways of helping them fostered by pastoral counselling is reinforced by the high priority given to individuals in Western Christianity and many of its theologians. Dorothee Sölle describes some of the effects of this:

> We Protestants reduced our symbols and confined them to ourselves, to our personalities. We used religious concepts and images for one purpose only: they had to serve the supreme value of middle class culture – individualism . . . Religion becomes a tool of the ruling classes, and only continues to function in order to comfort the sad, enrich personal life, and give the individual the feeling of significance. Sin then becomes personal transgressions . . . The cross then becomes my unique suffering, and the resurrection my individual immortality.[9]

Many twentieth-century theologians have taken the individual person as the most important category in their thinking about human beings. Paul Tillich's work is one example of primarily individualist and existentialist theology which still has a wide influence.[10] This emphasis is greeted with disgust by some of the political theologians of Latin America. Comblin talks of Western theology as being 'saturated to the point of nausea with existentialist and personalist themes'![11] There are now signs that this tendency is being countered. J. G. Davies for example writes

> To be set free from sin is not to be understood in terms of individual, personal and private sin . . . freedom if it is to be anything other than private self-adulation, has to be embodied in corporate life.[12]

David Jenkins also warns against the dangers of thinking that each individual is separable from society and that personal growth is possible without taking into account the communal, social dimension:

> The process of the growth of the image out of the potentialities of the image towards the fullness of him who is imaged (Jesus) is not an individual process. Indeed, I am increasingly of the view that 'the individual' is a myth and a dangerously dehumanizing myth. We are not individuals, we are persons . . . The process of the development of the potentialities of the image of God which is the process of being and becoming is the process of the development of community. We cannot be human until all are human.[13]

Despite this kind of protest against individualism and exclusive attention to the person in isolation, the prevailing ideology remains largely intact in our religion and theology and is congruent with the individualism dominant in society as a whole.

3. *Individualism in Western Society* For various reasons, enormous importance is attached to individuals as opposed to wider social groups or classes in our society. The freedom of the individual, for example, is taken to be one of the greatest goods for people living in the West. All sorts of areas of life are shot through with this emphasis. In medicine, for instance, it is becoming increasingly well-known that many of the diseases and disorders from which people suffer have social causes. Smoking is an example of a disease-creating habit which may lead to lung cancer. Despite this knowledge, relatively little was done until recently to prevent tobacco firms from vigorously promoting their products, while at the same time a great deal of time and money was given to

treating the individual sufferers from lung cancer. The point is that, in many ways, there is a reluctance to look beyond the individual. Because this is a dominant feature of our society, movements, practices and ideas which are in tune with it are more likely to be supported and successful than those which swim against the stream. In terms of pastoral care this means that pastors are more likely to be encouraged (perhaps unconsciously a lot of the time) to exercise care focused on individuals than to find support for social and political action.

It is indeed very hard for pastors to break out of a ministry centred on individuals or small groups when Christians, like other members of our society, are predominantly aware of, and concerned about, individual people and not large collectivities.[14]

4. *Secularization*   Secularization is the term used to describe the decline of the formal influence of religious institutions in society accompanied by the privatization of religious faith so that it simply becomes a matter of personal choice.[15] A corollary of this process is that the churches, and in turn their pastors, have become less prominent and influential in the world at large. Whereas once they were powerful in their localities and had at least a notional responsibility for everyone in the country, churches and pastors may find themselves redundant or unwanted. Now that churches and their representatives have so little influence on the secular social order as a whole, it is possible that they are being more and more tempted to minister to individuals and to abandon the larger social structures to their own devices. Pastoral care which concentrates on individuals, especially if it is informed by the insights of psychology and pastoral counselling, may be a way some pastors find meaning and a role in a world which does not seem to want them. Pastoral counselling can give structure, goals and job satisfaction which it is difficult to find in the complicated secularized social and political structures of society at large. What could be more satisfying than feeling that you have really helped an individual person with a difficulty, especially if they actually say thank you for it afterwards!

5. *The discrediting of political solutions to human problems*
Sociologist Paul Halmos suggests that we are living in a post-political society where social and political reform as an answer to human problems has been rejected.[16] This has occurred because social issues are very complex. The task of trying to understand

them is enormous. Political life is perceived as being filled with double-think and half-truths. It seems wasteful of human sympathy to attempt political action and more productive to express compassion in individual human problems. Politics is stereotyped, political involvement is taken to require that people should become hard and impersonal, and the needs of the many lonely individuals in society are ignored. All these features have contributed to the growth of the flourishing counselling movement which allows people to feel that they can directly contribute something personal and of worth to their fellow human beings by expressing practical compassion in this way. It seems very likely that disillusion with political solutions has hit pastors as much as anyone else in society over the last two decades, if not more so. It has almost certainly contributed something to the interest expressed in individual counselling by pastoral carers and has provided a strong impetus for more training and expertise in this area.

6. *The adoption of professional role models by pastors*   The adoption of professional role models by pastors towards the end of the last century has also probably exercised an influence on the individualistic focus of pastoral care. Anthony Russell has traced the rise of the clerical profession and shows clearly the way in which clergy gradually came to specialize in more narrowly religious and spiritual matters, forsaking more general aspects of their work which were taken over by people like teachers and doctors. Simultaneously, clergy began to adopt many of the trappings of professions including, for example, special clothing and training. Crucially, an emphasis on the importance of the individual client-professional relationship was taken up. The prominence of the one-to-one professional relationship, coupled with an understanding that religion is essentially a personal and private matter, probably forms an important predisposing factor towards pastoral care which is psychologically, spiritually and individually orientated.[17]

7. *The influence of the pastoral care tradition*   This is an obvious but significant point. The historic pastoral care tradition clearly testifies to the importance of individuals as the 'objects' of its activity. There can be no doubt that pastors have always prized people as individuals and have entered into intimate relationships with them. One has only to think of the habit of personal

confession to a priest in the Catholic tradition to illustrate this point. People sought advice and consolation from pastors long before modern counselling and psychotherapeutic understandings and methods came into being. These methods simply build on a tendency which was already there and the existence of this tendency has, no doubt, provided fertile ground for those who wish to concentrate on individuals and their needs rather than those of the wider community in pastoral care.

Arguments for the Inclusion of Socio-political Action and Awareness in Pastoral Care

It is beyond dispute that pastoral care has always given a high priority to the care of individuals. There are many factors both within the church and society today which reinforce an individual, psychologically informed approach. The question is, 'Is there room in pastoral care for attention to be paid to what I have called the socio-political dimension?' Some people would probably answer, 'No. Pastoral care has its own limited function. If it starts getting involved in politics and paying attention to social context, it will lose its essence and no longer do what it is good at, i.e. caring for individuals.' These people might argue that it is good for the church or its leaders to be involved in politics and shaping society, but that this is a very different activity from pastoral care. 'Horses for courses,' they might say, 'leave pastoral care to get on with looking after individual people.' This is not an adequate response. Clearly, if pastoral care lightly ignores individuals ('I cannot take your mother's funeral because I am going on a demonstration in London that day') it forsakes part of its essential function. But seeing the nature of pastoral care as being solely concerned about individuals is a misrepresentation. Pastoral care has social and political implications and consequences. Sometimes the only truly pastoral action is political action. There are factors which might suggest that the social and political dimension is, on occasion, integral to the nature of pastoral care.

1. *Holistic thinking* The words 'holism' and 'holistic' have become very fashionable these days. The term simply means seeing things together or as a whole rather than looking at bits and creating artificial divisions and separations. In the case of alternative medicine, it is argued that conventional medicine just treats

bits of people – their bad legs, for instance – while a holistic view connects the bad leg to the life, situation and being of the complete person within their social context. In the case of pastoral care, holistic thinking suggests that individuals must not be isolated from their social context in either conceptualization or action. Failure to have a total or holistic view results in harmful and unreal dichotomies and separations.

Holistic thinking can be found in Howard Clinebell's 'holistic liberation – growth model' of pastoral care. Clinebell argues that

> Pastoral care and counselling must be holistic, seeking to enable healing and growth in all dimensions of human wholeness.[18]

He suggests that it is not adequate to see human beings as atomized psychological entities. People should be seen instead as open systems with six equally important dimensions: mind, body, intimate relationships, relationships with nature and the biosphere, relationships with significant institutions and relationships with God.[19] For Clinebell wholeness is a relational thing which involves the community and society, not just individuals regarded as separate isolated entities. It is the job of pastoral care to foster liberating wholeness which enables everyone to develop their full potential and so, by implication, a social and political dimension becomes inevitable. Unfortunately, despite his holistic systems-orientated vision, Clinebell does little to spell out how pastoral care should take into account, say, the biosphere or social institutions in concrete terms. It remains a somewhat vague, if daunting and attractive, hope.

A more gritty and complete approach which also displays underlying holistic tendencies is found in Peter Selby's *Liberating God*.[20] Selby starts by pointing out the way in which the public and private spheres have become very detached from each other in contemporary society. Pastoral care cannot accept this for two main reasons. First, God is to be found in, and is concerned about, both areas (if he is not, he is not a universal God). To be concerned only about the private and not the public in pastoral care is therefore a fundamental theological error. Secondly, human beings are at all points in their lives inextricably bound up with, and formed by, social and political groupings. A corollary of this is that the causes of suffering or growth often lie outside the individual. As a result, pastoral care which only focusses narrowly on the individual must be regarded as limited and partial. The practical outworking of this kind of partial vision is firmly rejected by Selby:

> To presume to care for other human beings without taking into account the social and political causes of whatever it is they may be experiencing is to confirm them in their distress while pretending to offer healing.[21]

The same kind of assertion is also made, more trenchantly, by the American writer Robert Bonthius:

> You cannot take good care of persons without doing something about the environment which makes them what they are . . . My thesis is that pastoral care for structures is fully as important as ministry to persons. Indeed, that unless a clergyman is giving 'equal time' to changing structures, he is just as surely neglecting his pastoral duties as when he fails those who can use pastoral counselling.[22]

2. *The inevitability of socio-political involvement*   Many pastors pride themselves on being a-political or neutral and regard this as a great strength for it enables them to minister to all types of people. It sometimes comes as a shock when the point is put to them that, whether they like it or not, their pastoral work is inevitably caught up in wider social currents and values. Liberation theologians have graphically shown how the Roman Catholic Church in Latin America has supported values and political systems which militate against the interests of poor people, despite the fact that the church claims to be neutral and not interested in politics. The fact is that whatever is done, in any area of church life, tends to propagate some values and practices at the expense of others. Even claiming to be neutral and doing nothing, in particular politically, is a political stance for it maintains the *status quo*, leaving things as they are. All pastoral care takes place in a specific social and political context and its ideas and practices either question or affirm the values and structure of that order. The ostensible neutrality of pastoral care has been questioned by a number of writers of whom Bonthius is once again the most outspoken:

> It is not a matter of choice for clergy whether they will or will not assume the sociological role of pastoral activity. To the extent

that a clergyman chooses not to be an agent at this (social change) end of the mental health continuum he sides with the status quo, and therefore supports existing systems in their demonic effects on some individuals. The true choice is what kind of agent he will be in his pastoral activity: whether he will act with insight and effectiveness on the environment, or whether he will act in ignorance and prejudice or simply by default, to oppose necessary social change.[23]

3. *Ethical and theological context* The criticisms made by writers like Don Browning that pastoral care has become separated from ethics and values have been noted before.[24] Browning argues that pastoral care should be situated within the values that the church seeks to promote and these include, of course, the vitally important socio-political values of justice and peace. Justice and peace must become a significant backdrop for pastoral care and searching questions should be asked about the extent to which pastoral care promotes or minimizes these and other values. Selby accuses pastoral care of having for too long simply engaged in trying to adjust individuals to the social circumstances which prevail rather than helping them to become involved in a long-term and painful struggle for justice and peace. He suggests that 'too narrow and too private a perspective makes human living lose both its grandeur and its tragedy'.[25] Pastoral care should not so much make people content with their lot, however unjust or dismal; it should induce a divine discontent with the world as it is instead. This concern is also reflected by R. A. Lambourne who memorably deplores 'the separation of the theory and art of loving from the theory and art of justice' in pastoral care as in the contemporary social order.[26]

4. *The actual experience of pastoral care* Some people argue that the actual experience of giving and receiving pastoral care gives those involved in it some of the vision, means and determination to change the social order. Peter Selby suggests that those who experience pastoral care are empowered and inspired with a liberating and subversive vision which enables them to see that things can be different and that faith and vulnerability are possible and worth fighting for in this world.[27] The same sort of concern is also found in Lambourne who argues that the whole point of pastoral care is to form communities which can then serve the

needs of the world and, where necessary, change it. Pastoral care should be concerned with 'the radical progressive formation of the behaviour and conscience of the church fellowship as it exercises its corporate responsibility in being a holy servant people'.[28] Where effective pastoral care is taking place, people gain self-respect and learn to take responsibility for themselves and for their world. Social and political awareness and involvement will follow automatically. In this way, pastoral care could be regarded as directly subversive of the social and political order in which it is situated insofar as that order is oppressive and de-humanizing.

5. *The Bible* The Bible has been a fertile source for insights into the socio-political dimension of pastoral care. These are most easily seen in a little-known, but very fascinating article by a British psychiatrist and pastoral theologian, James Mathers.[29] Going back to the Old Testament Mathers points out that in the first instance the pastoral role was associated with the rulers of Israel. It is these rulers who are referred to as the 'shepherds of Israel' in, for example, Ezekiel's rebukes (Ezek. 34). The pastoral role was focussed on corporate and public problems while the priestly function in Israel was an entirely different one, centring on the preservation and teaching of the religious tradition. Starting from this basic distinction, Mathers asserts

> There is very slender historical warrant for the present-day notion that the professional healers of disease, whose special concerns seem still to be individual and private rather than public and corporate, have anything to contribute to the pastoral role.

Mathers goes on to suggest that

> There are good grounds for giving priority to the leading rather than the caring function wherever there is doubt – so to speak the priestly or prophetic function should take precedence over the obviously pastoral – because in the long run this is more likely to preserve the flock.[30]

Moses is cited by Mathers as a good and effective pastor because, although he paid little attention to individuals and was far from gentle and kindly, he did actually preserve his people and get them to the destination God had prepared for them. Mathers believes it is a mistake, in the light of this kind of insight, for pastors to dwell exclusively on individually-focussed models of care drawn from other contemporary professional disciplines like medicine.

A second theme which is found in the Old Testament and has been developed recently is that of prophecy. This is understood as the protest against social injustice and the call to a reform of social structures. William Hulme calls for ministry which is both priestly, i.e. to do with the care of individuals, and prophetic, i.e. to do with acting on the structures which influence the lives of individuals.[31] It is often assumed that pastors should be prophetic but, arguably, this term is diluted for it seems to denote any form of questioning, however gentle, of the socio-political *status quo* rather than the impassioned demands for radical social change such as that called for by the Old Testament prophets. Browning suggests that the term 'rabbinic' is more appropriate for the kind of questioning which most pastors undertake. Writing of hospital chaplains he states,

> On the whole the chaplain should resist seeing his or her moral concern in analogy to the prophet. Because of the high degree of autonomy which most secondary institutions have from the direct power of the church, the model of the ancient scribe and rabbi will serve the chaplain better. The moral concern and counselling of the chaplain should take the form of a midrash (a 'search' or 'enquiry') which can elicit the collaborative efforts of the other professional.[32]

Turning to the New Testament, two themes have been of particular significance. One is the theme of healing whose social and political implications in the ministry of Jesus have been drawn out by R. A. Lambourne.[33] Lambourne suggests that Jesus' healings were not only significant for individuals but for whole communities in confronting them with the grace and judgment of God. The second and more obvious theme is that of the kingdom of God, a central motif in Jesus' teaching. Jesus proclaimed a socio-political structure not simply individual salvation. Bonthius writes,

> In Christian terms it is a 'structure', an ideal community, that we are taught to pray for and asked to work for. Ministry to structures is not simply subordinate to ministry to persons. It is not even, strictly speaking, 'for the sake of persons'. Ministry to

persons is ultimately for the purpose of enabling them to serve a structure: the Kingdom of God. [34]

The significance of the socio-politically related themes in the Bible could be developed much further but no more space can be devoted to them here.

6. *The pastoral care tradition*   The pastoral care tradition itself shows considerable evidence of socio-political awareness, concern and activity. Two elements are particularly prominent in the tradition as a whole; the overcoming of sin amongst the faithful, and church discipline. [35] Both have strong corporate overtones. They have more to do with the building up of the whole body of Christ and enabling it for its missionary function in the service of the kingdom of God than with the simple relief of individual suffering or matters of personal and existential concern. Within the historical practice of pastoral care there has often been an important element of political involvement for the sake of maintaining the body of the church and bringing those outside the realm of salvation within it. The extreme examples of Augustine and Calvin illustrate this point. As bishop of Hippo in North Africa in the fourth century, Augustine evolved a doctrine of coercion to draw the schismatic Donatist sect back into the Catholic Church. He had no hesitation in using the military power of the Roman empire to further this aim and saw this as absolutely necessary if he was to exercise his duties as pastor properly. [36] In rather different circumstances, the Reformation theologian Calvin created a theocracy in sixteenth-century Geneva in which public discipline was a primary pastoral goal. He also devoted a good deal of his energy to writing pastoral letters to contemporary rulers in 'an attempt to reach the conscience of the man, while suggesting the policy of the ruler'. [37] In both these examples, overtly political activity formed an integral part of pastoral care. Further examples of ways in which pastors have exercised a direct social and political influence in carrying out the cure of soul can be found among the Anglican clergy of the eighteenth and nineteenth centuries. Apart from their liturgical and preaching roles, parish clergy acted as officers of law and order, almoners, teachers, officers of health and as magistrates and often active politicians, usually of a Tory persuasion. [38]

The pastoral care tradition illustrates that a social and political dimension to pastoral care is not as alien as it might be expected to be. At some times and in some places it has been central and essential either for building up or preserving the people of God. To have failed to have taken note and action in this dimension and merely to concentrate on the needs of individuals would have been both inconceivable and irresponsible. Sometimes, of course, socio-political action was disastrous or unfortunate. Arguably Augustine's cry, 'Compel them to come in!' backed up by military force falls into this category. The significant point here, though, is that the modern view that pastoral care should only be directed towards individuals is not required from the perspective of history. In at least some circumstances, history suggests, the social and political aspect should be allowed a more prominent part both in understanding and action.

The point of assembling all the points above is to make a cumulative case for re-thinking the assumptions lying behind the contemporary fixation on pastoral care being an activity which should only take individuals seriously. Individualized pastoral care can sometimes be arbitrary. At other times it can even be harmful. This is particularly likely to be the case when practitioners of pastoral care see themselves as having nothing to do with the wider social and political dimension and as being neutral. A practical contemporary example of the potential tragedy which can occur when pastoral care sees its task only through individualistic and psychological 'spectacles' and eschews socio-political understanding and action now follows.

The Exclusion of the Socio-political Dimension: Pastoral Care in Psychiatric Hospitals

There are around a hundred and fifty psychiatric hospitals in this country, mostly dotted round the edges of the main urban areas, many of them largely built in the last century. During the 1970s, some 10% of these hospitals came to public attention, mostly in a sensational way, when conditions of neglect and cruelty were exposed, particularly on wards for chronically ill and elderly people. A number of public enquiries were established and duly reported.[39] Here I shall just summarize some of the things which one enquiry found.

At one hospital the following allegations were found proven.

Patients were sworn at and hit around the head as well as being threatened by one nurse. One patient was slapped for not urinating. Electro-convulsive therapy (ECT) was given to an unwilling voluntary patient (i.e. a person not compulsorily detained under the Mental Health Act) who had to be bodily manhandled to be made to comply. Another patient was kept locked in a bare, smelly side room for a month. Psychogeriatric patients on some wards received baths only very infrequently. Patients' property, and presents brought in for them, were denied them. They were deprived of their spectacles and had little opportunity to engage in any kind of stimulating activity. Patients did not receive the pocket money to which they were entitled. On one ward, patients were deprived of liquid if they were incontinent. Sometimes patients were made to 'perform' in front of groups of students by a ward charge nurse. Clothing supplies were inadequate (a very serious problem if dealing with repeatedly incontinent patients). One charge nurse deprived a patient of food for several weeks. Some patients were verbally abused and called 'dumbos' openly by nurses. One patient was kept in his pyjamas and dressing gown for nine months. Some patients almost never saw their doctors. A patient was given ECT without first being examined by a doctor. It became apparent subsequently that she was not physically fit to have the treatment.

This horrifying picture of life in one particularly bad hospital is made worse if one considers that these were only the allegations which were actually legally proved. It seems likely that all sorts of other undesirable things were going on which were not reported or were unproven. You do not have to actually hit someone to make their life a misery. When mostly junior staff were horrified by witnessing this kind of treatment in what was supposed to be a hospital not a concentration camp, their complaints were dismissed or they were ostracized by their colleagues. Some even received personal threats.

At this point two things should be emphasized. First, while conditions in this hospital were particularly bad they should not be seen as extraordinary or unconnected with the condition of many other psychiatric hospitals which escaped enquiries. Conditions which actually provoked enquiries may be seen as the tip of an iceberg of poor treatment which pervades most old psychiatric hospitals, at least in parts. Secondly, and most importantly, it is

important to see individual acts of cruelty and neglect against a
very broad background. Popular press reports of poor conditions
in institutions tend to focus on individuals committing particular
acts. Particular acts and situations should in fact be seen as acute
instances of a general underlying *malaise*, so blaming individuals is
of limited use.

A wide variety of factors lies behind the sort of scandalous
conditions outlined above. The psychiatric hospitals are old and
limited architecturally in what they can do. Although they were set
up ostensibly to cure people, it is clear that for much of their
existence they have acted as controlling or warehousing institutions, places where mentally ill people could be out of sight
and out of mind. Psychiatric hospitals have nearly always been
required to meet enormous needs with very inadequate resources.
Hospitals built to house, say, four hundred patients comfortably
have often had to accommodate over a thousand. Institutions used
mainly to control the misunderstood and unwanted attract little
public interest and few resources. Throughout their history,
psychiatric hospitals have lacked the financial and human resources that they would need to do an effective job of rehabilitating
people into society. Other sectors of the health and social services
where the clientele is younger and more interesting (and will also
get better more rapidly) tend to attract a disproportionate amount
of the available resources, so psychiatric hospitals, along with
services for the mentally ill generally, have been Cinderellas.
Within the hospitals leadership is often not very effective,
psychiatry tending to attract less able doctors than other branches
of medicine. There are frequently conflicts between the different
staff groups in the hospital e.g. between nurses, administrators
and doctors who may have very different views of what they want
to do for patients. Often acute, younger patients receive more time
and resources from medical and nursing staff than the growing
number of elderly or chronic patients who are consigned to live on
what are sometimes known as 'back wards'. Institutional life can
nurture great rigidity and authoritarian attitudes. Patients easily
become institutionalized while overworked staff can quickly
become inflexible, using their considerable power over patients to
try and obtain a quiet life for themselves (readers may recall Nurse
Rached in *One Flew Over the Cuckoo's Nest* who manages to
oppress her patients in the name of giving them therapy).

Psychiatric hospitals have become even more demoralized places over the last two decades because they are now under perpetual threat of closure in favour of patients going into the community and attending smaller psychiatric units in local general hospitals. Where psychiatric hospitals remain open, their clientele will be mostly chronic and elderly. This does not commend itself to able young people choosing a career in medicine or nursing. At the bottom of the psychiatric hospital's problems lies its clientele. The people who end up in these hospitals are disproportionately from the lower classes of society. They are regarded as second class or stigmatized citizens because of their illness (until a few years ago some patients did not even have the vote). For the most part neither patients nor their relatives have any political or economic influence. It is not surprising, therefore, that these hospitals have the greatest difficulty in attracting positive public interest, human and financial resources and staff of the right calibre.

The case of psychiatric hospitals described above should, one might think, evoke considerable interest and concern from Christian pastors. Undoubtedly they are places of much sin and sorrow, a great deal of it caused not by mental illness itself, nor by wicked individuals, so much as by social and political factors which have their roots outside the hospital. The question is then, 'How do Christian pastors react to situations such as that exposed at the hospital described?' Each hospital has a number of part-time chaplains and some have full-time chaplains. How do they respond to the issues of justice, equality, power and human rights raised by the unacceptable conditions prevalent in some psychiatric hospitals?

The answer seems to be that on the whole chaplains respond by ignoring these issues. This judgment is based on talking with a large number of chaplains, on the things that they have written about their work and on the reports of the committees of enquiry which took place in the 1970s. Despite the fact that there was evident suffering of a very basic kind taking place, a background of considerable demoralization and not a little personal wickedness, there is almost no evidence that those involved in pastoral care took any notice of these things at all. Only one report records a chaplain giving evidence to a committee of enquiry. No reports show any evidence of chaplains initiating complaints or exposing diabolical conditions in their hospitals. Saddest of all, there is no record that pastors gave any support to those who risked their meagre incomes, their jobs, and their personal comfort to bring unsatisfactory conditions to the public notice.

The failure of chaplains to recognize and act against the palpable structural evils which diminished all those living and working in psychiatric hospitals needs explanation. These chaplains were not evil, callous or uncaring. Their vision of pastoral care was, however, too limited, largely as a result of becoming ensnared in individualism. Few chaplains seem to have much understanding of the social and political structure of the institution in which they are working. They believe that they should be neutral and are often keen on the one-to-one individual relationship. Many chaplains I have encountered speak warmly of being part of the therapeutic team, and some have undertaken therapeutic training themselves so they can take a fuller part in the team. For the most part, it does not seem to strike them that membership of the staff team might separate them from the patients and give them a 'professional' view of the world which might make them deaf to the stories of those who are powerless in the hospital. Nor does it seem to occur to them that therapy might give direction to the sometimes unstructured life of chaplains, but at the same time reinforce norms, roles, and values which should perhaps be fundamentally changed.

All these criticisms can be summed up by pointing to John Foskett's book, *Meaning in Madness*, a guide to the pastoral care of mentally ill people. The book focusses on individuals and small groups and counselling with them. Issues of power, justice, inequality and human rights are entirely omitted. It is the kind of mind set embodied in this book which enables chaplains to continue to concentrate only on individuals and methods for trying to alleviate their suffering and sorrow in personal encounters while leaving social structures completely out of the picture. A lack of awareness of the social and political dimension in the theory of pastoral care in this instance reflects a lack of action in practice. By this means pastors become *post hoc* alleviators of small and individual evils, while legitimating by their silence the greater social and institutional evils which ensure the long-term suffering of oppressed and unwanted minority groups.

Towards a Socio-politically Aware and Committed Pastoral Care

When pastors only pay attention to individuals and are oblivious to the socio-political dimension and implications of their pastoral care, the results can be disastrous. This has been demonstrated by referring to pastoral care in psychiatric hospitals. In a curious and devastating way, honouring and paying attention to particular individuals or small groups can contribute to many other individuals continuing to suffer. It is therefore urgent for pastoral carers to become more aware of their social and political context, not because it is fashionable, but because the war against sin and sorrow and the promotion of human potential extends far beyond the individual. Pastoral care must broaden its scope of understanding. Sometimes, perhaps often in some situations, there may be a necessity for the immediate needs and interests of individuals or small groups to be subordinated to the wider and longer-term interests of larger communities. This chapter concludes with a short discussion of the practical outworkings of this assertion. It is all very well to make general statements, but it is also important to suggest some starting points for putting them into effect.

The first and most important thing for pastoral carers to do is to become clear about their own socio-political context. This involves a process of analysis. Any pastoral action takes place within a context of social and political factors. The mentally ill person, for example, is at the apex of a very complex system of factors which extends far beyond that person's actual illness. Even the illness itself may have social and political factors involved in it. Social researchers have demonstrated that the type, duration and treatment of mental illness is related to social class position and economic recession. The daunting task before the pastoral carer is to try as far as possible to unearth the relevant social and political factors bearing on a specific pastoral care situation. This is undoubtedly a very complex and demanding activity which requires looking at sociology, social policy, and even economics, to be done properly.

Many pastoral situations look completely different when they have been exposed to this kind of analysis which allows pastors to become more aware of the influence of social class, status and power. Pastors are then in a position to look at very important issues such as: Who has power in a particular context? How is that power used and to what ends? What are the values being served and who benefits and in what way from the way things are? These are essentially ethical questions. Once a context has been analysed in this way, it is possible to ask how pastoral care fits into it: How does the practice of this kind of pastoral care fit into the situation? Does it maintain the dominant values inherent here? Does it serve the interests of the powerful or the powerless? Should it be working to change the situation by other than individual therapeutically informed means? Sometimes the answers to these and similar questions will confirm pastors in what they are already doing. At other times they might demand radical changes in practice. It is not always a good thing for pastors to drop their ministry of counselling individuals to undertake social and political action, but it is always a good thing for them to see as clearly as possible what social and political implications their particular kind of care has. This goes some way to preventing them from unwittingly colluding with practices or values which might be at considerable variance with Christian and secular ideals and values like justice and peace. The theory and art of loving, to use Lambourne's words, must be set in the context of the theory and art of social and political justice.

The broadening of vision and analysis is the first requirement. The second is the ability to be flexible and live with very uncomfortable tensions. Once pastoral care is seen in its social and political context, it is automatically complicated. Co-existing with all this complication and the many alternatives it may suggest is not always a happy experience. One tension is that between the needs and interests of the individual and those of the community. Philip Wogaman, an American ethicist, suggests that Christianity is concerned for both and that where decisions are made which exclude awareness and concern for either something has gone wrong.[40] In the past pastoral care has emphasized the individual and lost sight of the community. It must now redirect its attention to the community and society, but without losing sight of individuals who remain supremely important ends in themselves.

Related to this tension is that between personalist and political values. Halmos suggests that there is a seemingly irreconcilable clash between the values which tend to be honoured in personally focussed care – mutuality, particularism, aspiration to value neutrality, tentativeness, lack of certainty and rejection of violence

– and those found in the socio-political dimension – segmentaliza-
tion, one-sidedness, universality, partisanship, forcefulness,
cognitive certainty, and implicit violence.[41] These values may
often openly conflict when it comes to making decisions about the
nature of pastoral care to be offered. Similarly, tensions and
difficulties arise in trying to sort out what goals should be served in
pastoral care. Pastors may have to choose between spending their
time, say, visiting individuals or attending meetings which might
lead to beneficial structural change in society. At such meetings
there may be difficult choices about whether to work for long-term
or short-term goals. The choice of the former may lead to more
suffering for people in the immediate future. In fact these
dilemmas are not new, but if pastors are more self-conscious about
them they will seem sharper. The point is that pastoral care must
not try either to shirk or resolve these tensions. Pastoral care must
be done within them and it must be prepared to be flexible and
responsive in different ways, according to different circumstances.

In addition to flexibility which allows both individual and
socio-political concerns to be taken into account and acted upon, it
is important that some attempt should be made to sort out
priorities. Individual pastors or groups of pastoral carers cannot
take on board every social or political issue which comes their way.
It is vital that certain issues or areas of concern be given priority
over others if anything useful is to be done. The process of arriving
at priorities is discussed in Hessell's book *Social Ministry* and I
refer the reader to that source for more information.[42]

These considerations raise the question of limitations of time,
energy, ability and motivation among pastoral carers. Different
people have different talents and abilities and not all pastors have
much aptitude for the social and political dimension described.
They have entered pastoral care because they are interested in
helping individuals and they perform most effectively in one-to-
one pastoral relationships. They are more like therapists, people
who want to help people within the limits of the present social and
political context, than politicians, people who want to change the
situation radically. It is very important that the gifts and talents of
pastors should not be distorted for the sake of dogma, in this case
the notion that pastoral care ought to be socially and politically
aware and committed. The idea of the body of Christ where each
person complements others in terms of ministry makes it possible

for not all pastors to feel compelled to become social activists. At the same time it should allow for others to be encouraged in a primarily social pastoral care. The key thing is to try and fit the right pastor to the appropriate pastoral context. Condemning the kind of pastoral care which is exercised by pastors with very different talents, methods and concerns must be avoided.

Pastoral care which takes the social and political dimensions of human existence seriously should probably adopt a bias to the poor in the pastoral situation. This is a principle taken from the theology of liberation but is also found in other sources of Christian theology. Wogaman, for example, suggests that in ethical decision making there should be a presumption made in favour of the underdog.[43] The thinking behind Wogaman's suggestion rests not so much on the intense concern expressed for the powerless in the Christian tradition but on the observation that in contemporary society those who have least in terms of class, status and power are most likely to be ignored and trodden upon, often inadvertently. The answer to this is to make a general assumption that those who find themselves socially and economically at the bottom end of society need more interest taken in them and their perspective taken more seriously than the wealthy and powerful who usually have the means to represent their own interests and obtain the services they need. Although it is doubtless true that all members of society need pastoral care, some need it more than others if they are even to begin to explore their human potential. It should be remembered that some of the poorest people in society do not necessarily live in inner cities. The elderly are one group who are much deprived of all resources and a bias to them could take place in most parishes.

Some people will be unhappy with the idea that pastoral care should be biased towards the poor. They might raise important questions: If pastors are determined to take sides sometimes in society, does not this mean that they can no longer be bridge builders and reconcilers? There is no easy answer to this. It does have to be said, though, that in practice neutrality often disguises a very real bias towards things as they are and so is in fact partisan: 'Political neutrality, as the Marxists know well, really favours one side rather than another and far from being neutral is unavoidably partisan.'[44] This unavoidable bias is illustrated by the psychiatric hospital chaplains mentioned above who believed that they were being neutral in their individualistic psychologically-informed pastoral care but were in some ways tacitly legitimating the perpetuation of very unacceptable conditions. As to reconciliation, this is often misunderstood or mistaken for simple conciliation. Conciliation takes place when fundamental injustices remain but all is peaceful due to one group successfully dominating another. True reconciliation only takes place when there is liberty, justice and equality for all the parties involved. For this reason, it is often necessary for there to be open conflict so that liberation can take place for oppressed groups: 'Liberation has to take place before reconciliation of the two sides is possible – without liberation there is not reconciliation but conciliation.'[45] The implication of this is that conflict and partisanship may be necessary in pastoral care, not for the sake of hating oppressors, but for the sake of helping to present all people perfect in Christ to God.

Another objection to social and political commitment of a biased kind might be that this alienates some people from pastoral care. It is certainly true that where a direct political stance is taken on an issue by a pastor some people may want to disown it. On the other hand, pastors may find that they reach all sorts of new people who hitherto have felt that the church had nothing to give them and no interest in them. Active social and political commitment is both alienating and attractive. If channels of communication are kept open and it is clear that a bias to one form of political commitment arises primarily from love and conscientious commitment rather than hatred and the desire to offend, alienation can be minimized.

The final feature of a socio-politically aware and committed pastoral care to mention is an obvious one. If pastors wish to influence social and political structures effectively, they will probably have to work with members of other, non-Christian groups. This presents its own problems and tensions with which many will be familiar. The fact remains that God does work outside the church as well as within it, and Christians working alongside those of different faiths or no faith may find it a stimulating experience which may in fact form part of Christian mission. Christians working for freedom and justice in South America alongside secular groups have found it sobering, challenging and inspiring. The kingdom of God cannot be built by Christians alone.

Conclusion

In many ways, politics and pastoral care are inseparable. As I
write, this truth is being embodied in the actions of Archbishop
Desmond Tutu in South Africa. The Archbishop describes
himself as a pastor not a politician. Yet his concern for the people
of South Africa has necessitated his becoming centrally involved in
the political struggle for liberation in South Africa. Archbishop
Tutu shows that there are times when simply binding up the
wounds of hurt individuals is not the main issue. Socio-political
involvement is necessary. At the same time, Archbishop Tutu
never forgets or despises the individual. He has put his own body
between a black police informer and the crowd of angry people
trying to kill him. Good pastoral care, awareness of the social and
political dimension and a willingness to be committed politically
cannot be divorced without the possibility of collusion with evil,
sin and sorrow. The point is made forcefully by the parody which
follows based on the Gestalt Prayer. Gestalt is a type of individual
psychotherapy based on the teaching of Fritz Perls who wrote the
original prayer.

> I do my thing and you do your thing. I am not in this world to
> live up to your expectations and you are not in this world to live
> up to mine. You are you and I am I, and if by chance we find our
> brothers and sisters enslaved, and the world under fascist rule,
> because we are doing our thing – it can't be helped.[46]

Chapter Six

The Bible and Pastoral Care

The Strange Silence of the Bible in Pastoral Care

The Bible is essential to Christianity. It is the main link between contemporary Christians and their founder and his first followers. No service of corporate worship is complete without readings from the seminal collection of documents. The churches in the Protestant tradition owe their existence to the assertion of the primacy of scripture, while scholars in all traditions have come to spend more and more time on the study of biblical texts. There is a burgeoning biblical studies industry throughout the world and few candidates for the ministry of any mainstream denomination escape critical biblical study with the minute textual dissection which it demands. The Bible is appealed to and consulted in all matters of Christian life. It is regarded as authoritative and indispensable. No one, then, could say that it is not important; but if they were relying on the contemporary literature of pastoral care, they might well draw the opposite conclusion. The fact is that pastoral theologians seem to have almost completely avoided considering the Bible. A handful of American works exist on the subject, but there is no significant British work on the use of the Bible in pastoral care.[1] There is an almost absolute and embarrassing silence about the Bible in pastoral care theory.

On the practical level, use of the Bible in pastoral care is equally confused. After a training of several years in biblical studies, pastors seem largely unable to integrate the findings of liberal literary-critical approaches with their ministry. Some of them reject the use of the Bible pastorally altogether; the insights of psychology or sociology seem of more use than a complicated and problematic collection of ancient texts whose message is all too culturally specific. Others appear to undergo a sort of 'post-ordination regression' whereby they forget or supress their critical knowledge of the Bible and take congenial texts at their face value. Biblical words are wrenched out of their context on an *ad hoc* basis and are used to amplify pastoral consolation or challenge. Pastoral fundamentalism creeps into the care of even the most well-educated and sophisticated. So, for example, the words of St Paul describing his afflictions as a missionary in the very hostile environment of the first-century Mediterranean countries are used to give heart to nominal Christians suffering from personal misfortune in the present century (cf. II Cor. 4.7–12); those attending Anglican funeral services are invited to be comforted by words written by St Paul at a time when he believed that most Christians would not die before the return of Christ anyway in some of the most obscure and difficult passages in the New Testament (cf. I Cor. 15.20–26, 42–44, 53–58; I Thess. 4.13–18). The incantation of words which derive magical power from their unintelligibility and their derivation from a sacred text has a long history in religion. It is, however, doubtful if this kind of uncritical usage can be applauded as being consistent with the intellectual integrity expected of liberally-educated pastors today. The first task is to look more closely at the factors lying behind the strange silence about the Bible in pastoral care.

The first and most obvious reason for the relative neglect of the Bible in pastoral care theory and practice is that the Bible is not itself much concerned with this area. Pastoral care is largely a product of the post-biblical church. At best, there are some parts of the Bible which may be deemed to relate tangentially to contemporary problems, but a great deal of this literature is of a completely different kind, e.g., history or narrative. The Bible is not a handbook of pastoral care (or of anything else, for that matter). When it is used as such it is usually distorted because some overtly 'useful' passage or text is taken out of context. The peripherality of pastoral care in the Bible is disappointing and frustrating. It is annoying to turn to an apparently relevant part of the Bible such as the promisingly-named 'pastoral epistles' only to find that they offer little of immediate significance or benefit to the twentieth-century pastoral situation.

The nature of theological education and the way in which biblical studies are approached are also significant. Theological study over the last century or two has gradually fragmented and become more specialized.[2] Biblical study has refined its own methods and skills which are largely historical and linguistic so that the Bible may be understood as much as possible upon its own terms and may be seen against the background of the culture and concerns of the people who wrote its constituent texts. This minute, historical, critical and analytical perspective has yielded many benefits, but it has also had the effect of making it very difficult to integrate specific textual insights with broad theological concerns, or with Christian life in general. Whereas at one time Christians believed that they could use the Bible to give them information about everything, the analysis of modern biblical scholarship leaves them in doubt as to whether the Bible can give information about anything. Critical scholarship disintegrates the text of the Bible for the sake of analysis but no reintegration takes place within theological education. Small wonder then that pastors are baffled by what they should do with the Bible when they enter upon ministry. It is as if the meaning of the book had actually come to pieces in their hands.

The historico-critical approach to the Bible has created problems for the use of that text not only by its methods but also by its findings. I want to spend some time at this point giving a resumé of those findings with a view to amplifying this assertion to prepare the way for giving a properly critical account of the use which is made of the Bible by contemporary pastoral care theorists. I shall attempt to summarize, in very general terms, some of the main ideas which seem to be shared to a greater or lesser degree by contemporary liberal theologians like James Barr, Peter Hodgson, Edward Farley, David Tracey and Dennis Nineham. It may rightly be objected that justice is done to none of these distinguished thinkers individually by a summary of this kind. For the purposes of the present work, however, it is necessary to condense and coalesce views which do share many features in common. It should also be admitted that the views of these writers do not command universal support amongst theologians and Christians generally, but it is these views which are widely accepted amongst liberal pastors and biblical studies teachers and it is these people's approach to the Bible and pastoral care which is of central concern here.[3]

One of the most important assumptions to be questioned by the historical and critical approach to the Bible is the so-called 'scripture principle'. This principle embodies the notion that

> scripture contains a unique deposit of divine revelation – a deposit whose special qualities are due to its inspired origins, and which is to be handed down through the ages by an authoritative teaching tradition.[4]

This way of looking at a written text originated in Jewish attitudes to the Torah, but was adopted by Christians in their attitude to the collection of writings which we now call the Bible. For at least 1500 years Christians found it quite unexceptionable to assert that the Bible was directly inspired by God and as such it was to be regarded as uniquely authoritative and relevant to all people at all times. Not only was the content of scripture inspired revelation, the actual text came to be seen as holy since it was the vehicle of revelation. Several implications follow from such a view: first, there is the danger of putting the Bible in the place of God (bibliolatry); secondly, revelation is situated firmly in the past not the present; thirdly, the Bible itself becomes immutable over time – it cannot be changed.

The scripture principle has been challenged at many different levels by modern biblical criticism. It has been queried whether all of the Bible is equally inspired and revelatory; people tend to see the Gospels as very inspired, but can the Wisdom literature with its meticulous instruction about everyday life and behaviour be seen in the same light? Should some events like the Exodus, where God is portrayed as saviour, be taken on a par with events like the Flood where he is seen as punisher? Such contradictions and variations in biblical literature make any simple notion of direct and plenary inspiration difficult to maintain.

The idea of divine inspiration is also threatened by a number of other findings. The first of these is that the biblical writers make no claim themselves to direct divine inspiration. Nor do they see the scriptures which they used themselves as in themselves holy or directly revelatory. As a devout Jew, Paul undoubtedly gave great respect to the writings which now form the Old Testament, but he does not seem to have regarded them as sacred in themselves. Neither he, nor any other New Testament writer, would have seen their writings as the production of inspired and authoritative holy

scripture. The witness of the biblical writings themselves, therefore, questions the validity of the scripture principle.

These questions are amplified by, for example, the recognition
that the content of the Bible is in many respects not absolutely
unique. Much of the Old Testament literature is paralleled in the
literature of contemporary Middle Eastern cultures, while New
Testament writers like Paul drew on the conventional wisdom of
their time in regard to ethical issues. By the same token,
recognition of the somewhat arbitrary way in which books came to
be included in the canon of scripture has questioned the value of
some of the canonical literature; can an epistle like III John really
be held to have more intrinsic value than an extra-canonical book
like I Clement, also written in the formative years of the church?

The compilation of the canon was the work of a human
institution, the church, and not directly the action of God. If there
is one thing which contemporary biblical scholarship has made
clear above all others, it is that the Bible is the work of human
hands. Methods of criticism like redaction and form criticism have
exposed the reality of the historical human situations and needs
which shaped the concerns of the biblical writers. This, together
with the factors mentioned previously, has led to a complete re-
assessment of the nature of divine inspiration. Although once it
may have seemed reasonable to hold a doctrine of direct divine
inspiration of scripture (God→Revelation→Scripture) so that the
Bible could be seen as part of the doctrine of revelation, many
scholars now maintain that the biblical literature is only indirectly
inspired. It is a record of human responses to revelation recorded
by the community of faith, not revelation itself. Thus it must be
situated within the doctrine of the church (God→Revelation→
Tradition→Scripture).[5] This view implies that revelation and
inspiration are diffuse, indirect and take place over a long period of
time involving many individuals and communities.

At the forefront of liberal critical scholarship the scripture
principle has been largely abandoned but elements of the principle
continue to haunt the church and other areas of theology,
including the theory of pastoral care. It is because of its subliminal
pervasiveness that so much has been said about it here. It is now
possible, however, to summarize some of the other relevant
important findings, challenges and questions which have emerged
from biblical scholarship.

The facticity of the Bible has come under considerable pressure. It is now widely accepted that biblical authors did not write what we would regard as accurate historical accounts of events. Instead, they wrote history-like narrative which had inbuilt interpretations, biases and theological presuppositions. The discrediting of the Bible as a trustworthy historical record of events is one of the factors which has led many interpreters to see the Bible as essentially great literature comparable with the poems and novels of our own time. While the biblical writings do not give a literal historical record, they do give a profoundly truthful and eternally relevant account of aspects of the human condition. They are accurate and inspired in the same way that, say, the poems of T. S. Eliot may be said to be truthful and inspired. The student of the Bible who adopts this point of view does not pay too much attention to facts in the text, but tries to get beneath the events described to appropriate the deep and universal verities therein.[6]

The Bible has also been subjected to theological criticism. Some theologians, for example, are now suggesting that the simple theories of divine intervention and causation which dominate the literature of the Bible are untenable in the modern world where causation is perceived to be a very complex process and God's action is thought of as being indirect rather than direct (the classic case here would be the way in which people now see creation). The biblical writers saw God as king analogous to rulers in their own social order. The intellectual climate has changed radically and such views of God are now challenged as being anachronistic and outmoded.[7]

Recently, the diversity of the nature and purpose of the various writings which compose the Bible has been highlighted. At one time, it was fashionable to refer to '*the* biblical view of x' or to talk of biblical theology in the singular. The Bible, however, contains many different types or genres of literature (poetry, narrative, law, wisdom, etc.) written in very diverse circumstances over many centuries. It is therefore unrealistic, indeed impossible, to make its writings speak with one voice unless a great deal of editing, distortion and suppression of inconvenient elements also takes place.[8]

The cultural relativity and distance of the Bible from our own time has been emphasized by many scholars. The more it has been studied, the more it has become apparent that there is an enormous gulf between the essentially rural and simple society inhabited and addressed by the biblical writers and our own. For Christians of the first century demons were part of life and the coming of Christ in glory was imminent; two thousand years later it is very difficult for modern people to relate easily to such a world view.[9]

The diversity of biblical perspectives and the cultural distance of the scriptures from the present day have pointed up the need for interpretation. The science of hermeneutics is not new; it has always been necessary to interpret scriptural texts to make them relevant to contemporary needs and situations. In earlier generations, elaborate methods like allegorization were used to unfold the meanings of texts, especially those which did not seem to have an obvious meaning. Contemporary scholars generally do not resort to those methods, but talk instead of instituting a conversation between the two horizons provided by the text and the pre-understandings of the contemporary reader. The idea is that a real dialogue should take place in which new meanings come into being and the two horizons merge to produce new understanding. Interpretation of this kind is rigorous and controlled. It proscribes simply taking a text at random and using it to buttress views adopted for quite other reasons. Being faithful to a text using this kind of hermeneutic method does not mean repeating its words verbatim, but allowing its meanings to transform and be transformed by the interpretative process so that new meanings of contemporary relevance and integrity emerge.[10]

Biblical scholarship has had an enormous impact on the authority attributed to the Bible. Once it is seen as a humanly produced document which is not inerrant and which has no direct divine inspiration, its status as a sanctified authority in Christian life comes into question. Many critics believe that the scriptures can still be regarded as authoritative, however. This is not because they contain the words of God or have any divine mandate, but because the church has chosen, and continues to choose to make them central in its life. The authority of the Bible is given to it by the Christian community. It is a functional, *de facto* authority and, as such, it is not absolute. Scripture helps to shape the people of God; it is their book. It has an indispensable authoritative role in the community, but it is not the only authority.[11]

There are many Christians who still adhere to the scripture principle, whether they would articulate it in that way or not.

These people may be characterized as fundamentalists or biblicists. They continue to maintain the uniqueness of scripture, its
absolute divinely-bestowed authority, and its use as a direct and
literal guide to the will of God who has revealed himself directly
therein. The Reformation principle of *sola scriptura* (scripture
alone) is magnified in this tradition. It has already been suggested,
though, that this approach to the Bible has many problems. Critics
of the fundamentalist position argue that factors other than
scripture must be, and in fact always have been, consulted in the
lives of individual Christians and of the community of faith. These
include the presence of the living Lord in the community; other
aspects of the Christian historical tradition (for example, the past
experience of the church); the use of reason; contemporary, non-
theologically derived insights into the nature of reality; contemporary experience; and, finally, the mind of the community of
faith filled with the Holy Spirit. These critics also point out that
where it is claimed that scripture alone is being used as the sole and
ultimate source of information and guidance, all sorts of undesirable and unacknowledged things may occur. Often selection of
biblical passages and themes is based on extra-scriptural presuppositions; for example, scripture itself does not seem to be
overwhelmingly or exclusively concerned with individual salvation, but many fundamentalists dwell on passages which reflect
that interest to the exclusion of others. It has been pointed out that
Jesus himself did not feel bound by the dictates of scripture, that
he was creative and responsive in his obedience to God. Those who
would follow his example, and biblicists would certainly claim to
do this, should therefore not be bound by a book; especially not by
the Bible which itself does not at any point require that kind of
adherence by its readers. Lastly, by way of criticizing the
fundamentalist position, it has been pointed out that it can lead to
the absolutization of one particular time and set of stories, the
biblical events, so that the present time is relativized and the
contemporary promptings of the Spirit are ignored. It is not the
job of Christians living in the twentieth century to respond to God
in exactly the same way as those living nineteen hundred years ago.
As long as they believe that God is present and working in the
world and church today there is no need for them to resort to the
sacred text of scripture as the exclusive medium of divine
revelation. It is inappropriate for Christians to ignore the Bible

completely, but it is also wrong for them to be absolutely bound by it. A careful and discriminating dialogue is required which transcends the blind slavery of textual literalism and the cavalier neglect of some liberalism.[12]

The nature and place of the Bible in Christian life and theology is more controversial and problematic than it has ever been. It is against this rather confused background that an assessment of the use of the Bible in pastoral care theory and practice can now take place.

The Use of the Bible in the Theory of Pastoral Care

The next few pages are devoted to an examination of the ways in which some contemporary pastoral care theorists use the Bible in their work. Three important preliminary points need to be made here. First, all but one of the theorists considered here (Campbell) focusses on pastoral counselling in particular rather than pastoral care in general. This can be accounted for by recalling that in North America counselling has often been regarded as forming the totality of pastoral care. It is a somewhat remarkable observation, however, if one considers that the Bible really has very little direct concern with using the skills of listening (which are the main constituents of good counselling) to help troubled individuals. This suggests that contemporary writers may be trying to stretch the Bible a very long way to make it relevant to their concerns. It also brings up a crucial consideration which should be borne in mind: To what extent do pastoral care theorists relate the Bible to pastoral care in such a way that it preserves the autonomy and integrity of each of them? The insights of biblical criticism, especially those concerning the difficulties of interpretation, indicate that it is very difficult to relate the Bible to any modern situation without either subordinating the texts to the interests of the situation or, conversely, trying to make the latter fit one's own version of the meaning of the text. The former is a danger for liberals, the latter for biblicists.

The second point is related. Although it is quite clear that some pastoral care theorists have tried to take the Bible and critical biblical scholarship seriously and have attempted to understand scriptural texts on their own terms, none of them actually discusses at any length or depth their view of the status, authority, inspiration and usage of the text. Hermeneutic principles also remain implicit for the most part. It will thus be necessary to try and point up these implicit understandings where this seems relevant and useful.

The point about failing to be explicit about theories of the Bible in writing about pastoral care could, and should, be applied to pastoral practice as well. It is certainly intrinsically interesting to look at the way in which pastoral theologians use the Bible; hopefully, some of their perceptions may be of direct use to pastors. The greatest value of this kind of survey may, however, be in alerting practitioners to the confusion and issues of integrity which may come into play in using the Bible in pastoral care.

Five main approaches to the Bible in pastoral care theory may be discerned. At the risk of distorting or caricaturing them, each has been given a short label which encapsulates the main thrust of the approach. The five approaches are:

1. The fundamentalist or biblicist approach
2. The tokenist approach
3. The imagist or suggestive approach
4. The informative approach
5. The thematic approach

Each approach is closely linked to the work of one main author.

1. *The fundamentalist/biblicist approach*   It has just been said that pastoral care theorists fail to make their position with regard to the status and usage of the Bible clear. This is true for the most part, but it is emphatically not the case where the fundamentalist approach to the use of the Bible in pastoral care is concerned. The inclusion of this approach here will throw into relief the more liberal positions of the theorists who are discussed subsequently.

Perhaps the most well-known biblicist theorist of pastoral care is the American Jay E. Adams. In his many popular writings Adams advocates what he calls 'Scriptural Counseling':

Counseling that is truly scriptural is (1) motivated by the Scriptures, (2) founded presuppositionally upon the Scriptures, (3) structured by the goals and objectives of the Scriptures, and (4) developed in terms of the practices and principles modelled and enjoined in the Scriptures. To put it simply, scriptural counseling is counseling that is wholly scriptural.[13]

Adams rejects the use of non-biblical insights and resources in counselling altogether:

> How can Freud, Rogers or Skinner – men who loathed the Bible and Christianity . . . help wayward, suffering, sinning parishioners to repent and grow in grace?

Instead, he asserts the complete adequacy of the Bible which he defends as the handbook that God has given to his ministers to perform their task adequately:

> If God has assigned the task of nouthetic confrontation to ministers as part of their life calling and He has given the Scriptures to them to equip them fully for this life calling, then it follows that the Scriptures, while treating other matters as well, adequately furnish all that ministers need to counsel.[14]

In Adams' view, the Holy Spirit is *the* counsellor and the counsellor of counsellors. The Spirit is the author of the scriptures and works directly through their divinely-inspired words.

The positive aspect of Adams' work, and that of writers like him, is that it corrects the tendency to completely neglect the Bible in pastoral care theory, even if it does this in rather an extreme way. It is right that the Bible should have some critical, questioning and corrective role in any Christian caring. This said, however, it is difficult to have much sympathy with Adams if the liberal perspective outlined above is adopted. Clearly he falls for the scripture principle hook, line and sinker. In doing so, he distorts both the nature of scripture and the nature of contemporary pastoral care. It has already been seen that in the historic Christian community elements other than the Bible (e.g. reason, experience, contemporary insights derived non-theologically) have been regarded as important for guidance. Adams appears to reject all these wholesale. In doing this, the reality of God's revelation and work of creation is confined to a collection of ancient texts which can only be regarded as directly relevant to pastoral counselling by a considerable stretch of the imagination. It might be hoped that Adams' attention to the work of the Holy Spirit in counselling would liberate him from his bibliolatry. Instead, he chooses to imprison the work of the Spirit in a book. The presence of the living Lord in church and world relativizes the importance of scripture – scripture itself bears witness to this. But in Adams' theology, contemporary experience is made relative and subordinate to the scriptural text. Perhaps one should say, 'some scriptural texts', for like many others who adopt so-called biblical approaches Adams is actually rather arbitrary in his selection of texts, interpretations and principles. An example of this is his selection of the term 'nouthetic' to describe the counselling he advocated. This draws on the Pauline term *'nous'* meaning, loosely, 'mind'. Adams, then, believes that the purpose of counselling is to change people's *minds*. Arguably, however, much if not most of scripture is not concerned with changing the rational conscious part of people. What is called for is a transformation of a person's whole being and behaviour in obedience to the presence of the reality of God. For Paul himself the *nous* element of a person needs to be subordinated to the Spirit, *pneuma*. Counselling which claims to be based on Paul's theology would be better entitled 'pneumatic counselling'![15]

Similar criticisms can be made in regard to Adams' use of scripture generally. While Jesus and Paul, for example, were flexible and creative in their own responses to scripture, taking it seriously, but refusing to be legalistic, Adams cleaves to the letter of the text. The Bible then becomes authoritarian, normative and oppressive in its demands. A good example of this stultifying and dangerous literalism is to be found in Adams' treatment of Proverbs 22.15 which the author believes legitimates the general use of corporal punishment for children.[16] Proverbs is given considerable prominence in Adams' writing because it provides so much concrete guidance. The author is apparently untroubled by the complications introduced when it is suggested that the spirit of the New Testament with its message of love radically relativizes the more specific teaching of the Old Testament.

Finally, and most ironically, it is almost certainly the case that Adams is guilty of introducing non-scriptural concerns and presuppositions into his work. It is the contemporary prominence of secular counselling which has prompted Adams to undertake his own work, not the interests or dictates of scripture. In this sense, scriptural counselling is profoundly unscriptural in its very essence. Perhaps not surprisingly, Adams' approach has more in common with some contemporary judgmental, cognitive theories of counselling than it has with the creative God to whom much of the Bible bears clear witness.[17]

Many of the criticisms made of Adams' theories can be applied *ad infinitum* to other biblicist writers. Lawrence Crabb, for example, though more liberal than Adams in some important respects, insists on claiming the authority of the Bible for his principles of counselling although he does very little to back up this assertion from scripture. In fact, he refers very little to the Bible in his text, *Basic Principles of Biblical Counselling*. When texts are cited, this is done without any reference to the writer's original purpose, the context of the quotation cited or the detailed meanings of the words in it.[18] The Bible is taken as self-evident final authority. Scripture is used by biblicists like Crabb as corroboration for essentially extra-scriptural concerns and perceptions. The fact that this is not acknowledged, and may even be denied, damages the integrity of the Bible and that of pastoral care. It can also have quite drastic consequences for those seeking care who find themselves subject to 'inspired' pastors, untrained in counselling methods, who use the authoritative texts of the Bible to buttress their own presuppositions and prejudices in confronting the needy with their sin.

Finally in this section, some space must be devoted to consideration of biblicist attempts to see Jesus as a counsellor. Adams is fond of calling Jesus 'the Wonderful Counselor'. At a more sophisticated level, writers like Duncan Buchanan who accept the validity and value of secular counselling theories and methods as well as the difficulties raised by modern biblical scholarship still try to portray Jesus as a skilful counsellor from whom modern Christians could and should learn. In many ways, Buchanan's *The Counselling of Jesus* is sensitive, judicious and enlightened; it is an attempt to deal sympathetically with counselling and human need in the contemporary world without losing Christian distinctiveness. Nonetheless, it is haunted by the scripture principle and a simplistic view of the imitation of Christ.[19]

It is very difficult to know what Jesus was and did in his earthly life. This is the conclusion of modern attempts to find the historical Jesus. Some scholars have suggested that Jesus was a political revolutionary, others that he was an apocalyptic preacher. Until recently, no one has seriously suggested that he should be regarded as a great counsellor in the sense of being one who spends a great deal of time sitting and listening to troubled people. In their eagerness to maintain that scripture and the life of Jesus contain all the information needed for Christian life today, biblicists are tempted into eisegesis whereby some aspects of Jesus' ministry are emphasized to suit contemporary needs and interests. A good commentary on this tendency is found in Anthony Thiselton's discussion of Cadbury's book, *The Peril of Modernizing Jesus*:

> Cadbury begins by reminding us of some of the more obvious ways in which an interpreter can become guilty of anachronism in thinking about Jesus. For example, phrases such as 'the kingdom of God' have been used to describe modern humanitarian ideals of creating a better world. These are then understood in this way when they are heard on the lips of Jesus. Some of the actual examples of modern biographies of Jesus cited by Cadbury almost defy belief. For example, in a book called *The Man Nobody Knows* Bruce Barton interpreted Jesus from the viewpoint of an advertising expert. 'Jesus exemplifies all the principles of modern salesmanship. He was, of course, a good mixer; he made contacts easily and was quick to get en rapport with his "prospect". He appreciated the value of news and so called his message "good news". His habit of early rising was indicative of the high pressure of the "go-getter" so necessary for a successful career'.[20]

Of course, Buchanan is not nearly as crude as Bruce Barton, but the passage cited makes an important point.

If the scripture principle is discarded, if it is realized that the truth must be gleaned from many different sources not just one, if it is believed that Jesus continues to guide his church through his living presence, and if it is clear that modern Christians are supposed to reincarnate Jesus' spirit of obedience and responsiveness to God rather than exactly and slavishly to replicate his actions, then there is simply no need to find a primary source for the legitimation of counselling in the life of the earthly Jesus or any other part of the Bible. From the liberal point of view, the biblicist quest to ground pastoral care and counselling minutely in the text of scripture is ultimately futile and unnecessary. Though it has its illuminating moments, it can distract pastors from the word revealed in many different places by a Lord who is not buried in the pages of a book, but is alive and working in the whole contemporary created order.

2. *The tokenist approach* Tokenism, at its worst, may be characterized as the indiscriminate use of parts of scripture to add an air of religious respectability or legitimation to theories or practices undertaken on other grounds. The tokenist user of the Bible in pastoral care theory is not interested in wrestling with different biblical perspectives and original meanings which might challenge or inform assumptions; the confirmation and corroboration of those assumptions is sought from convenient and congenial excerpts of text. The Bible is such an important aspect of Protestantism in particular that it is easy to see why pastoral theologians in this tradition have an almost knee-jerk desire to include scriptural texts in their work where possible. The trouble is that specific meanings and contexts of biblical writings are ignored and the difficulties of interpretation are more or less dismissed. The words of the Bible are taken at their face value and press ganged into an approving chorus for contemporary concerns.

Perhaps the most notorious example of tokenism of this kind is to be found in the work of Howard Clinebell. On the flyleaf of *Basic Types of Pastoral Counseling* (1966) appears the following quotation from Isaiah: 'And his name will be called Wonderful Counselor' (Isa. 9.6). Not only is this quotation simply a fragment of a verse which contains several other countervailing images of the Messiah, it also, by implication, suggests that Isaiah's counsellor was a specialist in personal therapy. The counsellors Isaiah had in mind were, in fact, political advisers and governors of the nation. Clinebell uses this quote to baptize a work which is thereafter based exclusively on secular theories of counselling. This usage may help to obtain respectability for his book in religious circles, but it is certainly not respectful of the Bible.

In the revised version, *Basic Types of Pastoral Care and Counselling* (1984), the quotation from Isaiah remains but there is a whole chapter on the biblical bases for pastoral care and counselling. In it Clinebell enthuses about the value of the illuminative, informative and guiding functions of the Bible in pastoral care. Pastoral care should be integrated with biblical insights because, he argues, this roots it in the wholeness-nurturing truths of the Western spiritual tradition; it generates healing and growth-facilitating attitudes in carers; biblical images communicate profound truths; and the wisdom of the Bible critiques, corrects and enriches psychological understandings of wholeness.[21] He asserts that the six dimensions of wholeness with which he is concerned can be rooted in the Bible. A non-dualistic understanding of persons is found in Hebrew traditions; the cognitive aspect of persons is affirmed by injunctions like that in Mark 12.30 which demands that God shall be loved with all one's *mind*; wholeness in relationships is rooted in biblical ideas of *shalom* (peace) and *koinonia* (fellowship); the wholeness of ecological relationships can be anchored in the creation stories of Genesis and in Jesus' 'closeness to Mother Nature'; corporate aspects of the exodus narrative as well as Jesus' concern for the ordering of social life give a mandate for concern with institutions; the groaning of the whole creation described in Romans 8.19 offers a rationale for wholeness in the entire universe.[22] Jesus is regarded by Clinebell as the model of 'a growing, fully alive, love-filled person', while the kingdom of God is symbolic of the new age of caring and communal justice and social transformation, based on a wholeness-making relationship with God.

Despite the much vaunted centrality of the Bible in *Basic Types of Pastoral Care and Counselling*, it can still be argued that Clinebell has not changed his tokenist spots. No real attempt is made to appropriate the results of critical biblical scholarship. The strangeness and distance of the Bible, though acknowledged, is minimized. The attempts to base the various dimensions of wholeness in the Bible only really show that these dimensions are not wholly alien to some parts of scripture. The biblical writings are used corroboratively rather than as truly originative points for constructing a theology of wholeness. Perhaps the most important clue to Clinebell's use of the Bible is that, having asserted its illuminative, informative and guiding functions, the remainder of the book makes almost no reference to scripture at all and draws, as did its predecessor, almost exclusively on secular counselling theory. Of course, on the liberal critical views of the Bible expounded above, there is no reason at all why the Bible should be central in determining the nature of pastoral care and it is positively desirable that secular insights and concerns should be prominent. The fact remains, however, that Clinebell asserts an importance for the Bible which he then largely ignores. He must therefore be suspected of tokenism and of the employment of scripture for essentially cosmetic effect.

3. *The imagist/suggestive approach*   Some pastoral care theorists overtly choose to select particular themes or images from the Bible in order to uncover or illuminate the nature of pastoral care. One such is the British writer, Alastair Campbell. In *Rediscovering Pastoral Care*, Campbell carefully selects three biblical images. Shepherding is expounded from the scriptural material in both parts of the Bible relating to shepherds. The image of the wounded healer considers the life and work of Jesus and Paul. New Testament texts also throw up the image of wise folly.[23]

Campbell is clearly aware of modern biblical scholarship and uses some of the insights of critical textual study to construct his images to great effect. But there are problems and limitations with Campbell's approach, too. For one thing, he does not discuss his view of the Bible and its authority or the degree of normativeness which should be ascribed to particular scriptural texts. One suspects that in many ways Campbell regards the Bible as a collection of great literature much like the other great literature of our culture (e.g. that written by Shakespeare or Eliot, both writers Campbell is fond of quoting to illuminate the human condition). As such, it contains symbolic truths of lasting value. If this inference is correct, it must immediately be said that there is nothing intrinsically wrong with pastoral care theorists mining the resources of the Christian tradition for illuminating images, especially when the claims made for those images are not exorbitant; nowhere does Campbell claim that the images he has selected are the most important ones in the Bible or that they should be regarded as normative. It has to be recognized, however, that there are possible limitations and criticisms of this kind of use of the Bible. This is especially the case when an author fails to discuss the place and authority of the Bible.

The fact that images are taken from the Bible may give them a power and authority which they would not be accorded if they came from some other source. It is possible in this circumstance that the Bible is being used once again to legitimate ideas derived from other sources. Secondly, there are many, many images in the Bible. Campbell's approach begs the question as to which images should be selected. To some extent, it may also give a false impression of homogeneity. Perhaps images like the wise fool, the courageous shepherd and the wounded healer need to be placed alongside very different images which are less congenial like that of the risen, powerful ascended Lord in glory. There again, selecting specific images from a text prescinds from the problem of specific context and meaning to emphasize some very partial aspects of that image. Images selected in this way may therefore be over-simplistic or incomplete making them misleading as well as illuminating to some extent. And what of the theological, informational and doctrinal content of the texts containing these images? Undoubtedly these elements are present in the biblical contexts of the images. All of which adds up to a note of caution in the use of images which claim a degree of biblical origin. Sundering images from scriptural text can throw pastoral care theory helpfully into relief; it can also lead to partial blindness and unhelpful distortion resulting from over-simplification.

4. *The informative approach*   The best way of characterizing the approach of the distinguished American pastoral theologian, Donald Capps, to the use of the Bible in pastoral care is that it is informative. Capps has devoted a good deal of his considerable literary output to relating the Bible and pastoral care.[24] His most important work on the subject is entitled *Biblical Approaches to Pastoral Counseling*.[25]

In *Biblical Approaches to Pastoral Counseling* a positive attitude to the Bible is prominent from the outset:

> The question is not whether the Bible has a role in pastoral counseling, but what is the nature of this role.[26]

Capps is fully aware of the problems raised for the relationship between pastoral care and the Bible by modern methods of biblical criticism. He recognizes that both the Bible and pastoral care are pluriform and diverse and so there can be no simple solution to their relationship. He suggests that there are various ways of applying the fruits of biblical studies to counselling. The counselling practices of biblical figures, for example, could be analysed and then used by contemporary counsellors. Biblical treatments of theological problems, like the problem of evil which emerges in counselling, could be utilized in care situations. Capps himself, however, opts to explore the particular forms of genres of biblical literature to elicit their significance for pastoral counselling. Before embarking on this exploration in detail, Capps reviews the use of the Bible in modern pastoral care literature and sets out some important principles. He suggests that the Bible must be used with discrimination and that its usage should not violate the normal principles of counselling. It must be recognized that the Bible has several different uses in counselling, e.g. comfort, diagnosis and instruction, and that the context and setting of counselling vitally affect the usage of particular biblical material. It is equally important to recognize that different types or genres of biblical material will inform the counselling process in different ways. Bearing these presuppositions in mind, Capps goes on to explore the way in which three genres of scriptural literature might inform three different types of counselling situation. He outlines the use of wisdom literature (Proverbs) in educative premarital counselling, the use of parables in marital counselling; and the use of psalms in grief counselling. An account of the last category will suffice to give an impression of Capps' approach.[27]

Capps limits his treatment of the relationship of the psalms to grief counselling to the so-called psalms of lament.[28] He first points out that the words of these psalms can have a useful role in helping grieving people to explore their feelings, especially their negative feelings. This can bring new insight into their situation and infuse new spiritual energy. Using these psalms for discussion or reflection in counselling allows the communication of acceptance and concern as well as permitting clarification and judgment which comes through the acknowledgment of negative feelings (these psalms are full of feelings of anger and desolation) and the expression of contradictory feelings. But, Capps maintains, the very structure of the psalms of lament as it has been exposed by biblical scholars can itself directly inform and shape the grief counselling process; 'the lament can shape the counseling process by forming our experience of grief'.[29] This is consonant with the original purpose of the psalms which were intended to rehabilitate and restore sufferers and to provide a form for experiencing suffering. The six-fold form of the psalm of lament which proceeds step by step from complaint to praise is outlined and related to the contemporary counselling process. First, there is an address to God. This is necessarily often implicit in pastoral counselling. Next comes complaint – the ventilation of negative feelings of guilt and anger which has a cathartic effect. Catharsis is followed at the third stage by the confession of trust which may not necessarily be verbalized in counselling but is necessary for healing to proceed. At the fourth stage, that of petition, the psalmist/client makes articulate and explicit her needs. The pastor helps in the expression and clarification of these. In the psalms of lament words of assurance come next. In counselling, the client experiences support and relief from these petitions while the counsellor assures that God hears and gives support. At the last stage the psalmist offers a vow to praise which is paralleled in the counselling situation by the client experiencing a response to her petitions and starting to hope while the counsellor clarifies the grounds for hope and praise.

The advantages of this model are clear. First, it relates grieving to explicitly religious sources. Secondly, it gives a clear structure to the grief process which contrasts very favourably with the amorphousness of secular theories of grieving such as that of Kubler Ross which excludes any religious dimension and simply talks of a vague and general movement towards gradual acceptance. Thirdly, it makes the objectives of grief counselling clear. It, fourthly, clarifies the roles of counsellor and client. Finally, it allows the grief process not to be rigid or forced.

Capps deserves admiration and respect for his determination not to neglect the Bible, for his willingness to undertake detailed study of the Bible using modern critical methods and to relate the findings of that study to pastoral counselling, and especially for beginning to use the Bible as a real source of critique in regard to the assumptions of contemporary pastoral care. He cannot, however, escape some criticism. The use of critical scholarship in Capps' work disguises the fact that he, like most other liberal theorists, completely omits any discussion of the nature and status of the Bible and its place in the modern world. Is the Bible to be regarded as great literature, a source of real information, or as directly inspired? No answer to these questions is directly forthcoming, but clearly Capps inclines towards a high doctrine of scripture, akin to the scripture principle, if the following is typical of his thought: 'The proverbs within the Bible represent a treasure of human experience that has claim to *divine sanction.*'[30] This perhaps explains why Capps goes to such lengths to relate the two very different worlds of the Bible and pastoral counselling; like the biblicists, he may believe that the Bible has things to say which are in some sense truer, more unique or more important than those which come from secular sources. If this were not the case, there would be no need to exalt biblical patterns over others in pastoral counselling.

Capps is surely right to make good and imaginative use of the
biblical literature as a source of interesting, original ways of
looking at pastoral care. His failure to discuss the nature and status
of the book and his usage of it leads to its being implicitly ascribed
great unquestionable authority; if you read the Bible critically, you
really can find the answers to all your pastoral situations, even if it
is not as simple and direct a process as the biblicists believe. The
determination which Capps shows to relate the Bible directly to
pastoral counselling mars his fine work in that it forces him to
identify neat categories and correlations in both the Bible and
pastoral care. It strains credibility to imagine that the Bible
contains ready-made models for contemporary pastoral counselling, given that it is neither a counselling manual, nor the container
of all that is or can be known about human relations with God.
Where the impression is given that the Bible easily relates to
pastoral counselling, there is always a real danger that violence and
distortion is being done to one or other of these elements – if not
both.

5. *The thematic approach*   A thematic approach to the use of the
Bible in pastoral care is proposed by William Oglesby. His book,
Biblical Themes for Pastoral Care is written for those who stand
between the two poles of complete rejection of the Bible in pastoral
care or using scripture as a comprehensive book of rules.[31] The
Bible can be valuable for pastoral care, Oglesby claims, because it
provides evaluatory principles and acts as a stimulus to ministers
in clarifying the means whereby the pastoral role should be
fulfilled. Being fully aware of the findings of critical scholarship
and the need for interpretation, Oglesby suggests that the best way
to use the Bible is to discern its underlying themes and purposes
and then apply these to pastoral care.

Four main themes are identified as underlying and informing
the whole of scripture:

> it is clear that the Bible in all its diversity of form and style deals
> essentially with God as creator, redeemer and sustainer, and
> with wo/man as creature, sinner, and new creation as a
> consequence of response to grace by faith. In a word, the
> essence of biblical revelation is encompassed in its central theme
> regarding who God is and what He does, the nature of
> humankind and her/his tragic flaw, and the way God acts for and

with humankind toward reconciliation and restoration, i.e., *God*, *humankind*, *sin*, and *salvation*. Throughout, from beginning to end, the Bible deals with one facet or another of this quadratic emphasis, which draws from and informs the whole of Scripture.[32]

Oglesby believes that all parts of the Bible should be read in the light of the whole so that an interpretation of scripture by scripture takes place. The fact that the Bible is not a homogenous whole is acknowledged. Having identified four major themes, however, Oglesby does not dwell on these; he turns instead to five important sub-themes relevant to pastoral care. These are (a) initiative and freedom, (b) fear and faith, (c) conformity and rebellion, (d) death and rebirth, (e) risk and redemption.

Oglesby's exploration of the theme of initiative and freedom can serve as an example of the way in which he uses biblical themes in relation to pastoral care. An underlying theme of the Bible is the way that God constantly takes initiatives to achieve reconciliation with humanity; Oglesby particularly cites the ministry of the Old Testament prophets and of Jesus himself. Yet, God's action is never coercive or restrictive of human freedom; it must always evoke a free response. Having identified this tension, Oglesby explores the implications of it for pastoral visitation. Pastors must always be prepared to take initiatives in their ministry, but imitating the divine action they must also be willing to withdraw if their initiatives are not acceptable or appropriate.[33]

Oglesby's work using the Bible is outstandingly interesting and creative. Scriptural themes are used to great effect in illuminating pastoral care and posing questions for it. At no point does Oglesby claim that the Bible has all the answers or that his own selection of biblical themes is the only possible one. Nevertheless, his approach is not above some criticism. Like all the other authors with an essentially liberal and critical standpoint on the Bible, Oglesby omits any direct discussion of the nature, authority and place of the Bible except for one footnote where he writes:

What follows, and indeed the entire argument of the book, is based on the conviction that the Bible is authoritative in faith and practice . . . I understand the Bible as the source to which we turn as theologians for an understanding of the true meaning of our life and work in the belief that God who is the ultimate source of all authority reveals himself through the Scriptures.[34]

This statement begs as many questions as it answers; How, and why is scripture to be regarded as authoritative today? In what way is God revealed therein – directly or indirectly? One is left with the impression that Oglesby operates with a very 'high' doctrine of scripture whereby much can be attributed to it as a source of true information about contemporary life and pastoral care. That position in itself is not indefensible, but Oglesby does not take the trouble to defend it adequately.

The Bible is a book which came into being in, and has served, a community. Oglesby seems oblivious of this and one of the possible consequences is that all the biblical themes he deals with are related to the problems experienced by individuals. This is surely a distortion of the corporate concerns of many of the biblical themes he deals with. It often seems that Oglesby's selection of particular themes has been determined by non-scriptural concerns arising from his own interests in pastoral practice. Once again it must be acknowledged that there is nothing inherently wrong in using present needs as criteria for the selection of biblical themes or the beginning of scriptural exploration. It can be misleading, however, if this procedure is not made explicit. In *Biblical Themes for Pastoral Care* it is not. The suspicion that Oglesby is not always scrupulous in allowing the Bible itself to throw up priorities and questions for pastoral care is underlined by the fact that the themes he identifies are not all equally prominent or well-supported in scripture. The theme of freedom and initiative is certainly present in many parts of the Bible. Arguably, however, that of conformity or rebellion is more minor; Oglesby has a great deal more difficulty in justifying its use with textual citations from the whole of the Bible. The citation of texts is also problematic in Oglesby's work. At the beginning of the book he argues strongly that individual texts cited in a piecemeal, a-contextual fashion should be abandoned in favour of looking at wider underlying themes. Yet throughout his book he constantly quotes individual passages to reinforce the points he is making. Usually he does this without citing the countervailing texts which would open up the critical conversation of the interpretation of scripture by scripture. So, for example, in dealing with the theme of initiative and freedom he cites Revelation 3.20 to give biblical sanction for pastoral initiative; 'Behold, I stand at the door and knock; if anyone hears my voice and opens the door I will come in to him and eat with him and he with me.' There are other passages in the New Testament which would query this approach, notably the notorious injunction in the parable of the great feast given by the master to his servants when the invited guests have failed to attend: 'Go to the open roads and the hedgerows and *force people to come in* to make sure my house is full . . .' (Luke 14.23 Jerusalem Bible, emphasis added).

It may seem churlish to make these minute criticisms of a very bold and imaginative piece of pastoral theology. They are not unimportant, however. Perhaps their main value is to emphasize the fact that there is still a great deal of work to be done on relating the Bible and pastoral care together in a way which embodies critical integrity. The task is an essential, but not an easy one for pastoral care theorists.

Using the Bible in Pastoral Practice

It is necessary now to begin to try and develop some of the implications for pastoral practice from what has been learned of the nature of the Bible by modern biblical scholarship.

The first point is to draw out the significance of the original corporate ecclesiastical context and use of the Bible. The Bible is the church's book. It was compiled by and for groups of believers and its main historical use has been in corporate public worship. Smart writes, 'No part of it (with the possible exception of a few passages) in its origin was intended for private consumption. It is distinctively a public book.' He goes on to criticize the devotional use by individuals of the Bible rather harshly: 'The Bible is marching orders for an army not bedtime reading to help one sleep more soundly.'[35] These remarks may be somewhat exaggerated, but they do serve as a warning to those who would individualize and personalize the message of the Bible in order to apply it simply and directly to pastoral care. The biblical writings do not form a handbook of personal pastoral care, nor can individual passages of them be used as a spiritual bromide in every pastoral situation. The Gideon Bibles placed in many hotel rooms and beside hospital beds contain a list of passages suitable for consultation in times of particular emotional need. It is doubtful whether this usage can really be respected if the original purpose and integrity of scripture is to be preserved. (The practice can, of course, be defended if the scripture principle is adhered to, but that is not the concern here.)

This is not to deny, however, that the Bible has a place in pastoral care. The main role it performs is to shape and form the consciousness and character of the Christian community and the individuals who comprise it. Pastors and those in their care are in a constant dialogue with the text of scripture, particularly liturgically. This crucially affects who they are and what they do. Growing up into the perfection of Christ involves a lengthy conversation with the text that stands at the heart of the worshipping community. But this interaction is a long-term, gradual and indirect matter which embraces the totality of scripture in all its pluralism and not merely texts congenial to moments of intense personal need. It may well be that, if members of a Christian community have been steeped in scripture, they will be able to use a common vocabulary of biblical words and images in pastoral care situations. The scriptural words and texts cited may also provide useful material for pastoral diagnosis and may tell a pastor a great deal about a person's way of seeing themselves and the world (curiously, the texts a person selects and finds meaningful may say far more about them than about God). These are, however, by-products of living in and being affected by a community which is formed in part by non-specific ongoing interaction with the texts of the Bible. The Bible's primary role in pastoral care on this understanding, then, is one of contributing to the vital task of Christian formation. This is a background function as far as meeting specific pastoral crises or needs is concerned.

What is known of the original nature and purpose of the Bible as the book of the Christian community suggests caution in using parts of its text as analgesia for needy individuals. This point is underlined by acknowledgment of the cultural distance and strangeness of much of scripture. Many parts of the Bible clash with, and challenge contemporary ways of seeing the world, the attribution of illness to demon possession being but one example. It is important to retain the sense of distinctiveness and distance regarding the Bible if it is not to become domesticated by selectivity and individualization:

Make (the Bible) primarily devotional literature for private use and . . . it is subjected to an intensely individualistic interpretation and thereby silenced at the most incisive points of its message.[36]

The point is clearly made if 'pastoral' is substituted for 'devotional' in Smart's quotation. The cultural distance and strangeness of the Bible must be allowed to challenge and perplex pastors and those they care for. Perhaps it is as well that St Paul's obscure words about resurrection continue to be read at funeral services if after all they continue to remind those involved in pastoral care that they can never fully understand the Bible or apply it for their own ends.

It was noted earlier that, on almost any subject, there is no one view or theology in the Bible. Pluralism and diversity reign. This, too, has implications for pastoral situations. Where a pastor is tempted to buttress a perspective on, say, suffering with a biblical text which implies that God uses suffering to educate or discipline his people, there is also a need to take into account other texts which give contrary views. The witness of the synoptic gospels to Jesus' ministry, for example, suggests that he saw suffering as a fruitless evil. There is a real danger in citing biblical texts of only presenting one side of the biblical picture. The pluralism of the Bible reflects the pluralism of religious experience and of perceptions of life generally. It should be recognized and welcomed by pastors and they should be very careful of laying down *the* biblical line on any matter in pastoral care.

This leads on to the problematic nature of biblical authority in contemporary liberal thought. It was suggested that the Bible should now be regarded as authoritative because of its functional usage in the church rather than because it is directly inspired by God. It was also proposed that the Bible could not be regarded as being the only or supreme guiding factor in Christian life; experience, tradition, reason and other factors also have a large part to play. These perceptions should liberate pastors from any notion that they must always appeal to, or quote scripture in their pastoral care. They also warn of the potential dangers of quoting scripture. The direct quotation of scripture may add an authority to the utterances of a pastor which they do not really possess or deserve. Contemporary pastoral judgments or opinions should rest upon their own merits and not on an invisible platform of scriptural authority. It is all too easy to co-opt a biblical text to bolster one's own point of view; those who say that you can 'prove' anything from scripture are right. If the person who is being cared for is both ignorant of the detail of the Bible and in awe of its supposed divine authority a direct appeal to scripture can be very damaging. There is no doubt that many people live in the sure and certain knowledge that they have been condemned by scripture, and if by scripture, by God too. Some homosexual people have felt this way, for example. Equally, there is no doubt that some pastors rejoice to make them feel so, disguising their own moral judgments by selective and sometimes distorted use of some of the words of scripture. Such examples show the real dangers of leaning on the absolute authority of the Bible.

The Bible needs constant re-interpretation if it is to be related to contemporary needs and situations. It was noted previously that sophisticated modern interpreters call for a merging of the two horizons formed by the text and the interpreter's own pre-understandings so that new and authentic meanings come into existence. Interpretation is not repeating the words of a text verbatim in each new situation, it is finding new words to convey the contemporary meaning of the text as it emerges from the critical hermeneutic dialogue. The implication of this in pastoral care is that being faithful to the Bible does not necessarily mean that pastoral encounters have to be bedecked with multiple quotations from scripture. Biblically faithful pastoral care is not a matter of including lots of words from the Bible at every opportunity, but of re-expressing new meanings in different words appropriate to contemporary situations. Sometimes the actual words of a text may be helpful in a pastoral encounter, sometimes not. Sometimes the use of actual biblical words can even be a betrayal of the need to interpret and make relevant.

In any case, the pastor needs to be very careful that she does not fall into one of two traps. The first is that of escaping from the immediacy of honest personal encounter in pastoral care by hiding behind the words of a biblical writer. It is tempting, if one feels inadequate, to want to do, or say, something helpful and the Bible may seem a useful resource for finding the right words. Unfortunately, the right words for relieving the pastor's uneasiness may be the wrong words from the point of view of conveying immediate and honest personal care to a needy person. The second potential trap is that of failing to realize that a text may mean one thing to the person who selects and quotes it, and quite another to the person at whom it is quoted. It is not unknown, for example, for pastors to choose a text which they hope will hearten a person because it treats of hope in God or having faith. If someone is feeling very depressed, such a quotation from an authoritative book may have quite the opposite effect from that intended; the person being cared for may be made to feel further away from God and more inadequate than ever because they do not possess the faith or hope of the biblical author.

There can be no hard and fast rules for the use of the Bible in pastoral care so that it respects the integrity of scripture and those cared for are helped on a human level. The observations made above suggest that caution and discernment are certainly needed if what we know of scripture is not to be distorted and those who receive pastoral care are not to be damaged. Knee-jerk quotation of scripture at all times and in all places obviously needs to be avoided and it is of the utmost importance that pastors should recognize and reflect upon the way they do in fact use the Bible.

At the risk of falling into a biblicist trap, it might be suggested that pastors could do worse than to emulate the attitude to scripture of Jesus and Paul. Both men had their character and perception profoundly moulded by the Old Testament writings and were deeply respectful of them. At the same time, neither felt exclusively bound by the words of a sacred text. Each felt free to use his own words and experience to modify the perceptions of the past in obedience to the spirit of the living God in the present.

Interlude

No one in Western society today needs to be told of the influence that technology has on everyday life. Not everyone, however, is very conscious of the values which underlie technology and the large effect that they have on our everyday consciousness and assumptions. These are some of the assumptions upon which technology operates. First and foremost, it is rational and logical. Next, it depends on very detailed and specialized knowledge of a highly complex nature. The existence of this kind of knowledge brings with it the need for experts or specialists with that knowledge. A third aspect is that of componentiality; each process can be broken down into constituent parts (a necessity in, say, looking at an industrial process). At the same time, the component parts of a machine or technological process must be related to each other and seen as part of a whole. Technological activity is, fourthly, goal centred; it is orientated towards the production of some desired end or goal. A corollary of this is a fifth aspect, that of purposeful activity directed towards the desired goal. Achievement of the goal set and the means used to reach it can, sixthly, be measured using objective means. In this way, the effectiveness of the use of resources can be ascertained. A final aspect of technological rationality is that when a problem occurs which impedes or halts progress towards the desired goal, it can and should be analysed and understood. When this has been done, and the knowledge needed to solve it acquired, the problem can be resolved.

Underlying these assumptions which govern the maintenance and use of technology in society are three further, but implicit, notions. First, the supreme importance and value of rationality. Secondly, a belief in progress; things can and should be done and when they are, it is a sign that the world is advancing. Thirdly, that human beings, aided by knowledge and tools, have the capacity to move in a technologically progressive direction.[1]

All this may seem a very long way from the subject of pastoral care, but the sort of thinking which informs technology and industrial production shapes modern consciousness profoundly, even that of people who have nothing to do with the main processes of industrial production. Technological assumptions and understandings overflow into everyday life and shape human activities like care. To give one example: Peter and Brigitte Berger point out that the family is now often seen as a technical problem needing the attention of highly qualified professional workers if it is to be able to function. It is seen almost as a machine which people like marriage counsellors or social workers are competent to 'run' while the members are merely unqualified assistants![2] Perhaps it is not for nothing that professionals like family therapists regard the family as a 'system', borrowing that term and many accompanying notions from science, especially computer science. Other contemporary therapies have a similar bias. Gerard Egan's skills approach to counselling, which is widely influential in the UK as well as in North America, not only emphasizes the acquisition of expertise and skills, but also pays great attention to setting goals for the counselling process and to measuring progress against those goals.[3] Many contemporary therapies emphasize the solving of problems and this too might be seen as the product of ratio-technological thinking impinging upon care.[4] Most modern caring techniques and organizations share the technological optimism about progress, the triumph of rationality and knowledge over problems and difficulties, and the human capacity to accomplish this.

Pastoral care literature from the liberal tradition has recently become critical of unacceptable aspects of modernity. Oden, for example, warns against taking contemporary therapies and their underlying ideologies as normative.[5] Nelson Thayer strongly rejects the aspects of technological rationality which concentrate only on objectivity and measurement in favour of allowing space for the transcendent and inner elements of human experience to be seen as constituent elements of reality.[6] Nonetheless, most writers fail to criticize the fundamental norms and assumptions of the ratio-technical world view described above. At the same time, many practitioners display a voracious appetite for learning new ways of helping people in pastoral care. At the bottom of this lies a fundamental sympathy with the technologically mediated view of the world. This is entirely proper and it has been very productive in terms of broadening pastoral techniques and understandings. If such a sympathy had not existed, pastoral care would never have been able to adopt the techniques of counselling, for example. But not all aspects of ratio-technical thinking are equally acceptable or theologically defensible. Many, in fact, are very much open to question, particularly the assumptions about progress, the freeing power of reason and the capacity of humans to bring about their own salvation. I shall return to these and similar criticisms soon. Here, I simply want to emphasize the fact that most modern pastoral care literature falls unwittingly and unconsciously into the trap of adopting fundamental culturally-based assumptions about the manipulability of the world and the humans within it which are based on the ratio-technical thought forms which pervade the Western world. So Regis Duffy, for example, in advocating the adoption of a disciplinary model of pastoral care assumes that if a goal is sought and particular means are used, a certain result can be wrought by pastoral carers through human means. A mechanism is described and this can then be used for desired ends.[7] Donald Capps suggests a particular use of the Bible to attain particular goals in pastoral care. The end, the means and the result are clearly stated and can be steadily and effectively worked towards.[8]

The only aspect of ratio-technological thinking which does not play such a large part in contemporary pastoral care literature is that of measuring end results. While techniques are advocated with eloquence and fervour, ranging from the pastoral care of systems to apophatic prayer, no means are suggested whereby the effect of these methods might be measured and assessed; their results are therefore unknown, or can only be known subjectively. The cynic might suggest that to adopt ratio-technical devices while having no means of measuring their potential for good or ill is to keep the stone of the fruit while throwing the flesh away.

Much pastoral care literature and practice in the middle part of the century was dominated by techniques culled from psychotherapy which helped pastors to do their jobs better. Although much modern pastoral care literature is more critical, theologically informed and sophisticated, it still follows in the basic mould of ratio-technological optimism which was much more crudely expressed in the counselling-dominated literature which dwelt on technique. The underlying ideology is the same – use these ideas or this technique and the desired goal can be identified, rationally sought after, and finally achieved. It is still just a matter of getting the right understandings or tools to attain the desired end. To be fair, it has to be acknowledged that the pragmatic nature of pastoral care itself contributes to the need to suggest apparently relevant and workable techniques and concepts. There is no point in writing a book which simply outlines the human condition and gives no guidance as to how it might be improved. There are also honourable exceptions to the general trend. Thayer's work has been mentioned. More important examples are the American Catholic Henri Nouwen and the British Presbyterian Alastair Campbell. Both of these authors play down the importance of technique or even understanding to focus on the person of the pastor and the intimate nature of the pastoral encounter.[9] Goals, measurement by objective means, purposive activity and rationality play a subordinate role in their approaches which focus far more on being than on doing. Before considering the dangers and limitations of the ratio-technological approach and its assumptions further, it is, however, important to point out the real values and benefits which it confers on caring activities.

First, the prominence of reason has been significant for it militates against mystification. The human mind can be applied to human situations and this is a precondition to their being changed. Obviously, the acquisition of specialized knowledge about the human condition can have enormous advantages. The rise of experts with a great range of specialized knowledge, too, can be seen as a positive gain. People are not limited by their own lack of knowledge. The ability to be able to break situations or phenomena down into constituent parts while relating these parts to one another, componentiality, is another means by which human situations can be understood and made manageable rather than being overwhelming. The identification and pursuit of goals in care has given it a sense of direction; no longer is the caring process directionless and rudderless. The notion that care and its effectiveness can be measured and evaluated is also important as potentially it can prevent wasted or misguided effort (there is, however, a real problem here, as has already been hinted, for caring activity is difficult to evaluate and measure by any very objective measure).

The most obvious manifestation of ratio-technological influence in care, problem solving, also has substantial benefits. At its best, the identification of problems, or areas where problems and difficulties may occur, serves as a trigger for the input of analysis and resources which may result in satisfactory solutions being found, distress being alleviated and human misery minimized. The underlying optimism of the ratio-technological outlook is also important. It suggests to people that their situation can be looked at and understood to some extent objectively and that they can actually have some hope that human effort and expertise can bring about desired change. In other words, instead of being overcome and defeated, positive things can be done.

These points can be made more concretely if an example is taken. One hundred years ago, comparatively little was known about the way in which marital relationships work. People experiencing marital difficulties at that time would have had little knowledge or expertise to draw on and may have felt doomed to suffer mutely in confusion and bewilderment (as indeed many still do today). Now there is a vast amount of knowledge about the way marriages function. Rational analysis has de-mystified many of the problems which can occur in marriage and often expert caring facilities are available to help people at times of stress and crisis. Intellectual effort and expertise has removed many of the obstacles to hope and there is some possibility that people can work towards the kind of relationship which they would like. The belief that things can and will be sorted out satisfactorily is a direct benefit of ratio-technological thinking in care generally and pastoral care has experienced similar advantages. Contemporary pastors are in a much better position to make positive interventions and to make them in a more effective way.

But there are real dangers and disadvantages resulting from this kind of development, too. In the first place, rationality has its limits. People have other aspects and facets to their lives than the rational and they do not conform to systems and laws, nor are they prone to acting predictably at all points. It may be very useful pragmatically to make generalizations about how people will, say, develop and mature as Donald Capps does in his book *Life-Cycle Theory and Pastoral Care*.[10] Not everyone, however, fits very well into that categorization. Ultimately, people are a mystery, both to themselves and to those who care for them and they cannot simply

be understood objectively. Imaginative, intuitive and receptive
knowledge is required to understand them, as well as knowledge of
general principles. It is misguided to allow neat objective intellectual formulae or plans to obscure this, especially in the religious
community where mystery should stand at the centre and not be
subordinated to rationality.[11] The objective analysis and measurement of causes and effects in caring situations can miss out badly
on subjective and personal elements of great significance, not least
those of religious experience itself.[12]

This kind of criticism can be carried over to the problem-solving
mentality adopted by many pastoral carers. People, and indeed life
itself, are not problems to be solved, they are mysteries to be
loved.[13] In an eloquent paper, 'On not solving the problem', John
V. Taylor writes

> What the Church should be saying is: This problem/solution
> view of life is a distortion of reality as we actually experience it.
> The universe is not a vast examination paper. Frustration and
> evil and pain can't be packaged as problems, nor does human
> happiness consist simply in eliminating them. Salvation is not
> the same as solution.[14]

Taylor believes that Christians have been far too heavily influenced by the technological world view and attitude to problems and
condemns the way in which this makes people too dependent on
experts and colludes with the fantasy that people have no
limitations. He highlights the fact that often the solutions to
problems are in fact worse than the problems themselves and goes
on to suggest that, actually, humans need problems and questions
more than they need answers and solutions:

> man needs problems more than he needs solutions. This is
> because he is a being with immortal longings and an indelible
> ideal and he suffers his greatest harm whenever, for a while,
> success sends him out believing that his ideal has been reached
> and his longing satisfied.[15]

Over-attention to problem-solving can also mean that situations
which do not actually have solutions are liable to be neglected.
Chronically ill and mentally handicapped people, for example, are
not going to get 'better'. If the caring services and agencies like
medicine concentrate only on those areas of life where solutions or

satisfactory outcomes are possible, those who need greatest attention because of the ongoing nature of their disability may be left hopeless and without support.[16]

Criticisms can also be levelled at the notions that caring activity should be goal-centred, purposeful and effective. The adoption of goals prompts the question, Who should choose goals? It is often professionals and experts who define objectives and goals which are carefully selected to fit in with their own knowledge, expertise and abilities. Writing from a social work context Wilkes states,

> When the emphasis is on conscious, planned change it is not possible to stand back and let things be. Activities are goal-orientated, task centred, and purposeful and social work intervention, more often than not, is based on control and on approval in terms of what is socially acceptable.[17]

Measuring effectiveness is very important in a technological society where it is important that effort and financial resources should be accurately targeted, but when it comes to care there are real difficulties. Who is to say whether care has been effective and well-delivered? Any criteria which might be used to evaluate success are likely to be arbitrary and may be illusory, for success like progress is a relative term which can only be very crudely applied to human beings and human relationships in their particularity. Dykstra points out that, theologically, effectiveness is a very dubious criterion to be applied to Christian service. He questions the assumption that 'we do not consider a service to have been rendered to someone unless that service changes that person's condition in a material way.'[18] He suggests that there is a 'diabolical dynamic' bound up with seeing service and, by implication, pastoral care in this way. Rendering such service requires power and this produces a class of powerful masters who are different from those who are served, who define the goals which service will aspire towards, who have a high view of their own ability to serve, and who may abandon a particular kind of necessary service if it does not seem to be producing the results which they desire. Dykstra calls for service which has at its heart not effectiveness but personal presence, simply being there and becoming vulnerable and compassionate as an equal human being rather than aspiring to be a skilled professional expert who can manipulate the lives of others, ostensibly for their good.[19] No doubt Dykstra would sympathize with the approaches of Nouwen and Campbell to pastoral care which focus strongly on the kind of person the pastor has become rather than on her professional knowledge, expertise and skills.

Implicit in many of the points made so far is an underlying attack on over-optimism and the groundlessness of the belief inherent in the ratio-technological approach that human beings have the capacity to make things progress for the better using rational methods. The fact of the matter is that the best efforts of human beings are often deeply flawed in their outcomes. Human beings are not in any simple way perfectable. The tools which are used to try and perfect them are inadequate and the outcomes of interventions in the lives of others are unpredictable and frequently undesirable. In this century there are many examples of attempts to plan or manipulate human groups. Some have been successful in their own terms but many have come to nought or have enjoyed indifferent success. Failure to solve the provision of appropriate educational facilities at the right moment and the development of high rise flats to solve the housing problem are two conspicuous examples of the flawed and unpredictable nature of outcomes from the best laid rational planning. At the personal level, evidence that counselling has any beneficial effect on people is equivocal. Despite all the training and expertise that goes into training counsellors, there is the real possibility that at least some clients are damaged by this activity.[20] There is no doubt that some situations, personal or social, should be left as they are, without the benefit of professional intervention and that the possibility of human irresponsibility should be recognized.

The charge brought against caring based on ratio-technological optimism here is, in theological terms, that it fails to take seriously enough human sin and evil in the world. Insofar as pastoral care has taken this optimism on board it, too, is guilty of failing to take these factors into account. This is a serious accusation. It must be said, however, that there is also a temptation to be over-pessimistic and passive here. It is one thing to recognize that human efforts are limited and that there are problems with the ratio-technological assumptions implicit in modern pastoral care. It is quite another to conclude that it would be better if these assumptions were completely absent, for they have led to considerable developments in this area. The trouble is that they have remained implicit and that this has led unwittingly to a rather facile and over-optimistic view of pastoral activity being promulgated. What is needed is a critical viewpoint which is neither over- nor under-optimistic. Just because human efforts can be destructive even when they are well-intentioned does not mean that they should not take place. Just because outcomes are unpredictable does not mean that plans should not be made and desired goals sought. To become pessimistic about all human pastoral endeavour might be an invitation to passivity and despair; this does not do justice to the fact that we really do have knowledge, insight and skill which can be applied to the human predicament. A realistic viewpoint which recognizes and encourages human endeavour with its goals, purposive activity and desire to change things (surely part of developing the full potential of humans as co-creators with God who are not merely passive pessimistic spectators in life) while realizing that there are substantial problems with the whole matter of shaping human activity and destiny is required. In pastoral care we cannot shape a utopian destiny for ourselves or other people, but this does not exonerate us from trying all the resources of skill, knowledge and expertise at our disposal. We will be helped in our endeavour if we realize that the nature of our situation is such that the most we can hope for using our own efforts is modification and not transformation. This is a realistic overall goal which takes into account sin and evil, as well as the need to take responsibility for our own time and place. It allows change while not insisting upon it and it suggests that assessment of goals, purposes, methods and effects should be carefully considered before well-intentioned but heavy-handed and short-sighted intervention of any sort is entered into.

Having examined the strengths and weakness of what has been designated the ratio-technological approach which underlies much of even the most recent pastoral care literature as well as contemporary pastoral practice, the last two chapters in this book amplify and extend the kind of criticisms outlined above in a somewhat tangential but positive and creative way. This is done by selecting two themes which are common in human experience, and indeed in pastoral practice, which in many ways stand completely outside and beyond any kind of reason or technological manipulation; failure and laughter.

Given the sort of mind-set which has determined the shape of contemporary pastoral care, it is not surprising that neither of these topics has been much explored by writers in the field. Failure is the antithesis of the optimistic, progressive ratio-technological project whereby a human activity like pastoral care can be planned, efficiently executed and improved so that a better world can be brought into being. Yet all pastors have known the sharpness of failure in their best laid plans and at the points of their greatest strength and expertise. Failure is part of the human condition as well as the Christian tradition, and realism in pastoral care demands that it should be recognized and taken more seriously. It is a phenomenon which exposes and shames, making clear the limits of human limitation. The ominous silence which surrounds it is an indicator of the threat it poses to the highest and best hopes and aspirations, even in a religious tradition which could be said to be founded on one of the greatest failures of history.

The unpleasant, negative, vision-shattering nature of failure is perhaps enough to explain its neglect in contemporary pastoral care. The neglect of laughter is more difficult to explain, for surely laughter is a vibrant, positive and enjoyable thing. Or is it? The trouble is that laughter is anarchic. It sits light to rules, plans and conventions. In allowing people a distance from their immediate situation it can be a subversive force shattering reason, system building and intensity of commitment. Totalitarian rulers engaging upon serious and rational plans to improve the lot of the masses have always feared the jokes and wit of those same masses whose own survival may itself depend on the kind of distance created in their situation by laughing. That which can be laughed at cannot be taken as absolute. Perhaps, then, there is a threat from laughter to ratio-technologically informed pastoral care, planned and exercised with the best possible motivation by earnest pastors. Those who write about pastoral care or practise it do, after all and, sometimes, above all, want to be taken seriously!

Failure and laughter go to the root of what it is to be human. They also lie close to some of the most important insights of theology. Failure is a place where people are most aware of the senselessness of sin and evil. It is a condition from which they most want to be saved. Laughter as its counterpart provides an experience of grace, hope and creative possibility as well as profound human solidarity. Pastoral care which does not embrace these themes is theologically and practically emaciated and impoverished. In its rationality and earnestness it may well be deadly for pastors and those they care for. It may also be simply ridiculous. Laughter and tears lie at the heart of pastoral encounters and relationships. They must find a much more prominent place in fundamental thinking and writing about the nature of pastoral care as well.

Chapter Seven

Failure in Pastoral Care

In modern achievement and success orientated secular society failure has replaced sin as the greatest evil to be avoided. Failure brings in its wake that most terrible of feelings, shame, a sense of complete exposure and vulnerability. It enters the lives and activities of most, if not all people at some time or another and it is frequently encountered in the helping relationships of pastoral care. It is common for someone who has sought pastoral counselling to say at some point, 'I am a failure'. That confession in itself brings out one of the grimmest features of failure; for it is felt as a total experience of one's whole being. One does not *have* failure or fail in parts; one *is* a failure. While most pastoral carers would probably agree with Jean Vanier when he asserts the inappropriateness of applying terms like success and failure to human life and experience in the following quotation, few escape some kind of evaluation according to these categories in their own lives and work:

In questions pertaining to life, there is no real success, only growth.

Vanier himself goes on,

I believe I learned more through my mistakes and failures than through the successes.[1]

The omniprevalence of failure in society is, however, rarely acknowledged as a phenomenon which afflicts pastoral care. Those who are cared for may fail and feel guilty or ashamed, but a reading of modern pastoral care literature leaves the impression that the efforts of pastoral carers are only rewarded with success. Most books are written in an optimistic tone which suggests that, if only the ideas and techniques contained in them are faithfully noted and applied, the pastor's care will become more and more effective and beneficial. This seems strangely at odds with the reality of pastoral ministry where failure is a frequent and uncomfortable element for many people much of the time:

> A pastor was lamenting to a colleague the fact that he seemed to be totally unable to help a particular person who had come to him for counselling. In fact, the person, had ceased coming to the appointments which had been arranged. The colleague offered this remark, 'It is often like that. You lose some and you lose some and you lose some, then you gain one.'

The disparity between the perception of failure in pastoral care and the almost total lack of consideration of its possibility in the literature on the subject is similar to the contrast drawn by Norman MacCaig between the neatness of life in the circus and the chaos and despair of real life outside:

> *Big Top*
> In the circus so many things
> don't happen. When last did anyone fall
> from those flying trapezes? When last
> was the sword-swallower carried off
> on a stretcher? And always the elephants
> toddle off holding each other's tails.
>
> Such expertise, such perfection
> can't compare with the show going on outside,
> where a man bleeds
> on his bed of nails,
> the high wire's always breaking
> and only the clowns keep time
> with the Universe going *oompah oompah*
> over the broken tiger cage,
> the fire exploding in a corner
> and the crowds panicking towards exits
> that aren't there.[2]

If failure is such an integral part of existence in general, and of pastoral care in particular, why has it been so ignored by pastoral care theorists? It would be gratifying to be able to suggest that one reason for a lack of prominence for this theme is that it is peripheral or irrelevant in pastoral care. Perhaps pastoral care really is mostly blessed with success and seldom fails or harms anyone. This seems unlikely. But even if it were so, it would be a depressing answer, for that which has no power to inflict harm or to fail has no power to do good or succeed either. Pastoral care should not be ineffectual bumbling which has no effect for good or ill on anyone. Here, then, is one case of pastoral failure:

> Two ex-psychiatriac hospital patients were living together and had had a baby. Sadly, the child died within a few weeks of its birth. The parents were very upset and, although not church-goers, they decided they would like it to have a Christian funeral. A local vicar took the service. He was an elderly man, but the parents found it difficult to forgive the fact that he had conducted the service in a perfunctory manner and had got the name and the sex of the child wrong throughout, despite their attempts to interrupt and correct him.

This case and others like it can leave no doubt that pastoral care has the capacity to fail, and indeed damage, if there was any doubt about the matter before.

Two other reasons for the neglect of failure in pastoral care have already been hinted at. First, failure runs counter to optimistic ratio-technological assumptions upon which much pastoral care theory rests. It cannot and does not form part of any plan for a better future where sin and sorrow are to be minimized or alleviated. Secondly, failure provokes feelings of extreme shame, exposure and vulnerability in those who feel they have failed. Like the stigmatized disease, cancer, failure is not a topic to be talked of loudly or openly. Failures with which one has been personally associated often remain painful memories and, though they may be learned from, they can seldom be easily talked about in the success and achievement orientated culture which pervades the church as well as the society which surrounds it. It is, then, very difficult to deal openly with failure in a public way.

A further, and perhaps more significant reason concerns the slippery nature of failure, its measurement and definition. Failure is a relative concept together with its correlate, success. One person's failure may be another's success. This brings out a further point, namely the subjective nature of failure. It is true that if goals have been established and are not met, then some kind of objective measure of failure may be held to have occurred. Similarly, harm caused to people might be used as another objective measure. But, ultimately, there is a great deal of subjectivity involved in assessing failure. This leads to some very interesting consequences. In the first place, it is very difficult for people to assess their own success or failure. Secondly, people's own evaluation of their success or failure may be wildly at odds with the evaluation of others; hence the phenomenon of people condemning themselves as failures while being celebrated by others for the very thing they think they have failed at. Thirdly, people are often ignorant of their real failures in relation to other people, while they may chastise themselves for failures which have had no harmful effect on them. It is certainly true that it is what people *think* they have failed at which discomfits and shames them, not any objective measure of harm done or offence committed. The whole business of failure in pastoral care is complicated by this subjective aspect. Those who are cared for are mostly too polite or too angry to tell pastors where they feel that they have been failed, while pastors feel sure they have failed when no failure has actually taken place. The nightmare for all pastoral carers is that they will never really know when they have failed and let people down. Pastoral carers from time to time fail others, fail themselves and fail God. Most tragically of all, perhaps, often they do not fail anyone, but they *think* they do; from a subjective point of view that is just as bad as any objective failure. The sense of failure is often more significant and potent than failure itself.

Failure and Sin

It is useful to compare and contrast sin and failure, for this throws the concept of failure into greater relief while it also demonstrates the real similarities and connections between them. Perhaps a further reason for the neglect of failure in modern pastoral care theory can also be discerned here. Despite living on the verge of nuclear disaster in a world riven by poverty and strife, sin is out of fashion in liberal pastoral care! The emphasis still lies on the essential goodness and acceptability of human beings rather than on their capacity for sin and evil. While this hopeful vision of human potential has been a necessary corrective, it does perhaps lead in part to an averting of attention from the fallen aspects of human existence of which failure may be seen as one.[3]

In some lights, sin and failure have many similarities and parallels. Indeed, in many respects it is tempting to see failure as simply a particular manifestation of sin, the human condition of being separated from or at odds with the loving purpose of God. Most obviously, sin and failure can produce strong feelings of guilt and shame. Both sin and failure harm people, the self and others. There is a mixture of objective and subjective in perceiving both failure and sin; both are often primarily in the eye of the beholder, but the beholder can be beheld and judged to be sinful or a failure. It is often difficult to discern whether sin and failure are relative or absolute things. People may believe that they sin or fail, but there is often room for argument as to whether their perception is right. In the case of both sin and failure, it is frequently very difficult to appreciate their full dimensions and gravity. Sometimes people ridiculously over-estimate their sin or failure, but they may equally under-estimate it. Human beings often have some responsibility for their sin or failure, but there is also a sense in which factors come into play which are not within human control. In theological terms this might be characterized as a sort of calculus of evil which is operant to the extent that even when people are trying to avoid sin or failure and are applying their very best efforts, they may find themselves deeply bound up in them. This perception leads to a related point; it is often when people are giving of their best efforts and are trying to be most loving and directed towards God's purposes that they find themselves most deeply embroiled in sin and failure. It is almost as if there is some perverse law here which dictates that people's best efforts and aspirations may lead to the worst and most harmful effects. The closeness of the relationship between sin and failure is confirmed by the fact that they can often be mistaken for each other. Worldly prosperity and rewards were seen as signs of righteousness and divine approval in the biblical world while afflictions could be regarded as signs of sin. A residuum of this attitude continues today as can be illustrated by this quotation from former UN Secretary General, Dag Hammarskjold:

The courage not to betray what is noblest in oneself is considered, at best, to be pride. And the critic finds his judgement confirmed when he sees consequences which, to him, must look very like the punishment for mortal sin.[4]

There are, however, significant differences between sin and failure. In the first place, failure is always unintended while sin may be deliberate. If a person sets out to fail, they in fact succeed in failing and therefore they do not fail at all. Secondly, sin may be regarded as desirable at times whereas failure is never so regarded. Sin is presumably always wicked and harmful in some way but failure is not necessarily so. Failure to achieve or perform some actions may damage no one, but sin is always damaging to someone, at least to some degree. Curiously, it seems that people can actually sin quite cheerfully and without much sense of guilt or shame. The running sore of world poverty, for example, leaves most Western Christians relatively untroubled in regard to their own life style. Failure, on the other hand, when it is perceived as such, always produces strong negative feelings of shame, guilt and regret. Another strange feature of the difference between sin and failure is that while it must always be undesirable and abhorrent to be a sinner or to act in a sinful way, sometimes being a failure or failing may be regarded as admirable. Some of the greatest Christians in history are venerated because they had the courage to fail. This brings out a very important difference between sin and failure, the fact that sin is always related to morality and correct action while failure does not necessarily have any moral connotation at all. These significant differences can be made more concrete if the example of Jesus is cited. Many Christians would assent to Jesus being called a failure because of his untimely and cruel death on the cross. At the same time, however, they would claim that he was sinless. Interestingly enough, of course, the reason he was crucified and became a failure was because the rulers of his day regarded him as a sinner. So the confused relationship between sin and failure is in fact exemplified in Jesus himself.

Failure and sin share many common characteristics, not least the fact that failure may be the result of sin and can have evil effects while sin may be regarded as a flaw or failure in the order of the universe and the lives of the people who inhabit it. In many circumstances sin and failure may amount to the same thing and it may be unnecessary or extremely difficult to distinguish between them. The vicar in the case study failed and also sinned as far as the onlooker is concerned, although he may have regarded himself as having done neither. Despite the difficulties involved, it is desirable where possible to discern the differences between sin and failure both theoretically and practically. If this is neglected, all sorts of errors may arise and these may have a directly harmful effect on people. Failures may be taken too seriously and regarded as morally culpable while sin and evil go unnoticed and uncorrected. People may feel the needle of guilt in relation to their failures when it is really only appropriate to those aspects of failure which are bound up with sin and evil.

Awareness of Failure in Pastoral Care

As indicated already, failure has been little considered in the literature and theory of pastoral care despite its prevalence in practice. A partial exception to this general rule is, however, to be found in the image of the wounded healer as a model for pastoral care. This image was first suggested by the Catholic writer Henri Nouwen in a book of the same name.[5] In this, as in his other books, Nouwen has been much influenced by the richness of the Christian mystical and spiritual tradition. This is perhaps significant for that tradition is all too aware of human inadequacy, the tragedy of life, and the impotence of human beings to make their way towards God and the kingdom of heaven. Nouwen's original conception of the wounded healer has been developed by Alastair Campbell who has a similar interest in the interior and symbolic life which is to be found, for example, in modern poetry which so often seems to have a much better grip on the realities of existence in all its joy and sorrow than the books which form the literature of contemporary pastoral care.[6] While neither Campbell or Nouwen dwell specifically on the component of failure in the ministry of pastors as wounded healers, it is clearly at the heart of the image. The basic notion contained therein is that as by the wounds of Christ we have been healed; so it is the weaknesses, vulnerabilities, griefs and sorrows of the pastor which enables her to come close to others and minister to them. The hard, yet joyful lesson to be learnt is that good, and indeed successful, Christian ministry which follows in the steps of its founder is born not from skill, power and knowledge but from the experience of inadequacy, rejection and sorrow transformed by the love of God and then offered to others.

The wounded healer image presented by Nouwen and Campbell is a valuable corrective to facile ratio-technological optimism in pastoral care. A similar kind of awareness is found in the poems of R. S. Thomas, an Anglican vicar in Wales for many years. Thomas's poems embody his own awareness of standing within a secular contemporary desert where the whole enterprise of Christian ministry is problematic and often seems futile and doomed to fail:

> *The Priest*
> The priest picks his way
> Through the parish. Eyes watch him
> From windows, from the farms;
> Hearts wanting him to come near.
> The flesh rejects him.
>
> Women, pouring from the black kettle,
> Stir up the whirling tea-grounds
> Of their thoughts; offer him a dark
> Filling in their smiling sandwich.
>
> Priests have a long way to go.
> The people wait for them to come
> To them over the broken glass
> Of their vows, making them pay
> With their sweat's coinage for their correction.
>
> He goes up a green lane
> Through growing birches; lambs cushion
> His vision. He comes slowly down
> In the dark, feeling the cross warp
> In his hands; hanging on it his thought's icicles.
>
> 'Crippled soul', do you say? looking at him
> From the mind's height; limping through life
> On his prayers. 'There are other people
> In the world, sitting at table
> Contented, though the broken body
> And the shed blood are not on the menu'.
>
> 'Let it be so', I say. 'Amen and amen'.[7]

For a more specific awareness of failure in care, though, it is necessary to look outside the church to social work writer Bill Jordan. In his brilliant book, *Helping in Social Work*, Jordan is brutally frank about his failures in caring. Many pastoral carers will resonate to passages like the following which are as relevant to pastoral care as to that exercised by secular institutions:

> From the start, I recognised that social work, even with the best of intentions, could as readily be unhelpful as helpful. It was clear to me that every attempt to influence a person in trouble entailed a risk of making things worse for him, and that social work often did just this. Far more painful for me was the gradual recognition that often it was when I minded most about my clients, tried hardest or liked them best that I did them most harm. The risks of damage were highest where the investment was greatest.[8]

Failure is a terrible and poignant experience wherever it arises in human life. It is particularly tragic and difficult to cope with and recognize in activities of care which are explicitly devoted to the nurture of growth and the relief and alleviation of sin and sorrow for others. Failure in altruism is a uniquely cruel experience.

The Nature of Failure in Pastoral Care

The first prerequisite for failure in pastoral care is the desire to succeed. Success and failure are correlative evaluatory terms; where no success is aspired towards, or worked for, there can be no failure. But wherever people have longings, goals, purposes or aspirations, failure, or at least relative failure, enters into the picture. Some critics have been very hard on the whole notion of success and failure, particularly from the perspective of the Christian theological tradition. They point out that the prominence of the idea of success is not to be found in the Bible and indeed that the concept has only relatively recently attained its current importance in Western society generally. For Shakespeare success meant progression, as in one season following another.[9] This sort of observation which relativizes the contemporary dominance of success is useful but it is unlikely to have a great impact when success is such an important part of our upbringing and self-understanding:

Life in the Western world today tends to be success-oriented; from childhood we are exposed to influences which raise our expectations of ourselves or project on to us the expectations of others.[10]

But criticism of success-oriented society with the damaging experiences of failure it engenders, valid though it may be in many ways, should not be allowed to obscure the fact that the hope of success with its goals has an enormously positive and stretching role:

> when expectations grow from truth they can be very creative. If we had no expectations and no one else expected any good of us either, we would sag and stagnate. Either we would never grow, or we would collapse under the struggles of life. Expectations can stretch us challenging us to grow and to change, to try and to leap.[11]

Pastoral care is surely a place where much must be hoped for, and hopes must be set high. Where pastors have no experience of failure in their ministry, it may be a sign that they have aimed low or have neglected to aim at all. The parable of the buried talent springs to mind here as well as the popular proverb, 'nothing ventured, nothing gained'. The trouble is that where much is ventured for the sake of the people of God the searing pangs of failure inevitably ensue. This daunting paradox is an integral part of pastoral care.

Implicit in the above is the notion of risk. Any creative enterprise demands risk. Those who care for others are engaged in a particularly risky task for people are not predictable and their lives cannot be lived for them by others, however well intentioned. Good parents know that they have at some point to trust their children to live their own lives and to let them go. It is often difficult for pastors to take a similar attitude to those in their care. They want to protect the people they care for from the knocks of life and may be tempted to map out their lives for them in a paternalistic fashion. When they let them go, they may very properly fear damage and disaster ensuing and, if it does, they may well feel that it is they, not the people directly involved, who are responsible. At every stage in pastoral care risk is involved. The pastor takes risks in becoming involved with people, in becoming vulnerable to them and in trusting them to map out and live their own lives. At every point the devastating possibility of failure and rejection is present. Risk and attendant failure are not easy to live with. Unfortunately, the alternative is death, opting out of the dynamic movement of creation which might itself be thought of as God's risk.[12]

Of course, a great deal of risk would be eliminated if we could only see into the future and predict accurately the outcomes of situations and actions. Things never work out quite as they were intended or desired and there is always an element of surprise which may be pleasant or unpleasant. Perhaps the openness and unpredictability of the future should be seen as a sign of grace. It is very hard and very strange grace, however, when the pastoral carer finds that well-founded hopes and predictions are confuted by disaster and failure. Here is a small example of an unpredictable outcome to a pastoral situation:

> A psychiatric hospital chaplain had been called to a ward to see a very depressed young woman who had been talking of committing suicide. She was worried about whether, if she took her own life, she would go to hell. The chaplain tried to reassure her of God's love and acceptance and eventually prayed with her and blessed her. He was shocked when at the end of the encounter the woman thanked him for coming and said she could now take her life with a clear conscience and no fear. He had completely failed to communicate to her the value of her continuing to live! (In fact, the woman did not commit suicide after all – yet another unpredictable aspect of the situation at the time.)

The ethical theory of Utilitarianism which depends on predicting the results of particular actions so that they maximize pleasure and minimize pain suffers similarly from the sheer unknowability of the future and painful consequences which were completely unforeseen often result from plans and actions designed to maximize pleasure.

Sometimes failure in pastoral care occurs because the wrong expectations, hopes, goals, or methods have been applied to a situation. There is a degree of subjectivity in assessing the appropriateness of these so there is always scope for argument, but there are occasions on which it becomes clear that the wrong direction was taken and so failure was inevitable, and in some cases perhaps even desirable. A controversial but well-known case surrounds the death from cancer of the prominent English evangelist, David Watson. Right up until the moment he died many Christians believed that Watson would receive full bodily healing and so would survive. Their hopes and expectations were shattered by his death, but arguably these had been wrong in the first place. Instead of counting on God acting in a particular way they should have relied on him in a less mechanistic way which allowed God to be God and would also perhaps have allowed Watson to make a rather different preparation for his death. As it happens, his eventual death may be seen to have accomplished far more than a supernatural cure, for it has deepened and complexified the thinking of many faithful people about the nature of healing. Sometimes, then, pastoral care is wrongly directed and so it fails. When this happens it can sometimes be a merciful, if unwanted and uncomfortable, deliverance.

At a more practical level, failure in pastoral care can be the result of the lack of skills, resources or appropriate attitudes. At the moment when a person may need highly skilled counselling, for example, the pastor may discover that she just does not possess the skill which is required to make an appropriate intervention. On another occasion she may have the requisite qualities but then she may not have the time to use them. Many complex motivations go into the desire to help and care for others. A lot of these can be very dysfunctional. David Brandon, a social work writer, points out the temptation to want to deprive those cared for of their autonomy, the desire to manipulate and control others, the pathological need to give rather than to enter into mutual encounter in care, the refusal to learn from what he would call 'clients'. To these features might be added the refusal to listen.[13] Brandon characterizes these features as 'hindering' clients which must be taken as a form of failure when the task of carers is to enable:

> Hindering is rarely examined in relation to helping. In our hearts we know we frequently offer little assistance to people and even, sometimes, hinder them.[14]

Closely related to the lack of appropriate resources and attitudes in pastoral failure is the lack of knowledge about self and those who are cared for. For a mixture of reasons pastors often fall into performing what Jordan calls 'naive helping' which is based on instinctive response rather than on deep knowledge of the self. To be sure, Christian history is scattered with examples of saintly people who have in actions great and small helped the poor and shown great spontaneous love and compassion to those around them for the sake of the kingdom of God. It is now quite clear with our knowledge of psychology, however, that instant responses based only on intuition are not always helpful to people in the long term. They may, for example, simply replicate the responses of the helper's parents and be paternalistic or distorting.[15] This is an example of a situation in which pastoral care based on naive kindness may have unwittingly contributed to the long-term misery of a particular person:

> Rose was an unhappy woman in her early thirties. She had been unemployed for many years because of a chronic disease. She attended church some miles away from where she lived and always came to services where there were few other people in the congregation. That was the limit of her active involvement. This did not stop her from knowing a large number of local clergy whom she went to see often and with whom, she maintained, she had very intimate relationships. In fact, each of the clergy concerned found her a difficult person and dreaded seeing her, for they found her false expectations of their relationship with her very difficult to cope with and did not believe that her visits did them or her any good. Despite this none of them was frank with her on this matter and rather than tell her how they felt or that they would no longer see her they simply tried to make themselves inexplicably unavailable after a time.

Personal insecurity and immaturity on the part of pastors in this case so that they could not offer honest and challenging care to Rose but preferred to maintain an image of being kind helped to imprison her in her dysfunctional behaviour patterns. While she needed the costly bread of real help, she was given the stone of weakly smiling superficial toleration and kindness. She was failed very badly by her pastors. This kind of example underlines the importance attached by Campbell to pastors being a particular kind of person, and not only being the holders of specific offices or possessors of particular skills.

Pastors are human and imperfect. So are the people they deal with:

> We fail because we are weak, wounded, confused and inconsistent. We each have particular built-in weaknesses, flaws that seem to be part of the very stuff of our characters. We fail to do and we fail to be. We fail in the good we try to do, and we fail to love. At the deepest level of our life is sin: we fail God.[16]

It would be extremely odd if such a profoundly human activity as pastoral care were not shot through with failure. But ultimately perhaps the real tragedy of failure lies in its being ignored, glossed over or disguised. This is the failure to come to terms with failure which in itself may distort and warp pastoral care more than any single failure can by making it seem profoundly inhuman and therefore un-Christian. Teilhard de Chardin reminds us that

> The great objection brought against Christianity in our time, and the real source of the distrust which insulates entire blocks of humanity from the influence of the Church, has nothing to do with historical or theological difficulties. It is the suspicion that our religion makes its followers *inhuman*.[17]

History's Greatest Failure

This is how Maria Boulding characterizes Jesus: 'Jesus himself is history's greatest failure.'[18] At a later point in her book *Gateway to Hope*, which explores the whole phenomenon of failure from a religious point of view, Boulding suggests that, 'The Word was made failure and died among us.'[19] Boulding argues that failure goes to the heart of being human and that Jesus has plumbed the very depths of failure and redeemed it in his own flesh. This, in her view, gives enormous hope to all those for whom failure seems an overwhelming defeat, to all those in fact who seek to be human and to follow that same Jesus Christ. Pastors may well be heartened to read Boulding's own words on this matter:

> If you have ever been sickened by the crumbling of some enterprise into which you had put all your best effort and the love of your heart, you are caught up into the fellowship of Christ's death and resurrection, whether or not you thought of your experience that way. God has dealt with our failure by

himself becoming a failure in Jesus Christ and so healing it from the inside. That is why we can meet him in our failure: it is a sure place for finding him, since he has claimed it. So central is failure to the Easter mystery that a person who had never grappled with it could scarcely claim to be Christ's friend and follower.[20]

There is room for dispute as to whether Jesus' life and death did unequivocally manifest the signs of failure. Some would argue that in his short ministry he was actually remarkably successful and that he had accomplished what he had set out to do which led in due course to the foundation of a church which has endured for nearly 2,000 years. As always with success and failure, there is a great deal of room for different interpretations and evaluations. It does seem difficult to believe that the man dying on the cross and beholding the desertion of his friends and followers could regard himself as a great success. The disciples themselves certainly seem to have been shattered and disillusioned by the apparent failure of the servant Messiah, who they had hoped would rule the world. Even more daunting for them was the fact that they apparently had to accept their own failure before they could enter into their mission of preaching, teaching and healing for the sake of the kingdom of God. Rowan Williams writes movingly of the way in which Peter receives forgiveness and a vocation in the moment of realizing that he has failed utterly and so has to repent:

> the memory of failure is in this context the indispensable basis of a calling forward in hope. Peter, in being present to Jesus, becomes – painfully and nakedly – present to himself: but that restoration to him of an identity of failure is also the restoration of an identity of hope.[21]

The motif of failure as an integral part of the ministry of Jesus and his followers, while never identified using this modern term, also seems to pervade the apostolate of Paul, who speaks of death being at work in his own body for the sake of others and gives a long catalogue of his sufferings and rejections for the sake of the gospel:

> We are in difficulties on all sides, but never cornered; we see no answer to our problems, but never despair; we have been persecuted, but never deserted; knocked down, but never

killed; always, wherever we may be, we carry with us in our body the death of Jesus, so that the life of Jesus, too, may always be seen in our body (II Cor. 4.8–10 Jerusalem Bible).

Paul's own account of his sufferings and failures is reinforced by reading of his ministry in the book of Acts where being ignored and rejected by hostile audiences (not to mention some people in the church itself) seems part and parcel of the apostle's life. Once again, it is difficult to see Paul as a great success from many points of view.

It would be a mistake to suggest that experiences had by Jesus or his first followers and not even formally designated 'failure', our modern term, should always be normative for ministry today. Nonetheless, the biblical witness should be taken into account and interrogated by modern pastors. It would certainly put a question mark against the pastoral care of anyone who found that they never experienced the turmoil, anguish and failure which characterized the ministry of Jesus and the first Christians. Most pastors do not experience a smooth pastoral ministry replete with unproblematic success. Failure for them, as for the first apostles is integral, and in this way their pastoral care may bear the marks of Christ. For these pastors the biblical witness is illuminating, inspiring and, above all, enormously encouraging. If failure lies at the heart of Jesus' own life and work there is hope for Christian pastoral care which fails, though that hope may be difficult to discern and retain at times. The price of attaining it is facing up to failure.

Facing up to Failure: Attitudes

If pastoral care is to be creative it will inevitably involve the possibility of failure at every turn. This is a hard and unwelcome truth about the nature of reality which may lead some carers towards the option of trying to take no risks so that pain and trauma can be avoided. Perhaps everyone at some point will be tempted to do this. It would certainly be difficult for anyone who has faced failure in their own life or ministry to condemn others for trying to evade it. This is true not least because there is no docetic failure or simple appearance of failure. Some early Christians called Docetists believed that Jesus only appeared to suffer on the cross and was actually somewhere else when his human body was being tortured. Orthodoxy has always denied this claim; God really did suffer in Jesus, it maintains. When people are tempted to minimize the anguish and extent of failure they should remember that there is no mere appearance of failure. It is a total experience involving the whole personality in a sense of exposure, vulnerability and shame.

Even in situations where failure could not have been avoided or where it might bring about some long-term greater good, the immediate feelings and perceptions are distressing and unbearable. It strikes at the core of the person so that she feels she *is* a failure. All too easily, failure in a particular area of life can lead to a sense of being a complete failure in all aspects and areas. The burden of a real sense of failure is heavy and intolerable. It is an overwhelmingly real experience to those who bear it. Their plight is exacerbated by feeling that they have to bear it on their own because others are not interested, would not understand, and might well condemn, as the 'failed person' does herself. Loneliness and isolation accompany failure and add to its destructive power. If that were not enough, it should be remembered that, while it is possible to sin boldly, it is seldom possible to fail gloriously. 'Most of our failures are unheroic and unglamorous', writes Boulding.[22] It is their triviality, unintended nature and consistency which so often grinds the carer down.

In the light of reflections like these, it is not surprising that some people want to opt out of thinking about failure or undertaking activities which are prone to it. A second option also exists for Christian pastors, that of idealizing or seeking failure as a way of supposedly replicating the ministry of Jesus. 'If Jesus was a failure,' the argument might run, 'when I fail I am surely doing Jesus' work.' This is a kind of Christian masochism which can serve as an excuse for all kinds of passivity and incompetence in pastoral care. Maria Boulding describes the danger of seeking a cult of failure, and has these strong words to offer on the subject:

> There was no cult of failure in Jesus' life and there should be none in ours. He rejoiced in his strength and intelligence and used them to the full; he tried his utmost to succeed. So should we.[23]

Failure in pastoral care is inevitable. It is neither to be sought nor avoided but, ideally, to be recognized, faced up to and learned from.

Facing up to Failure: Practice

Failure is failure is failure. The point of this tautology is to emphasize the fact that, for the most part, there is no easy way of dealing with the sense of failure, whether subjectively or objectively perceived. It cannot be efficiently rationalized, minimized or wished away. It can, however, to some extent be faced up to, understood, accepted, put into proportion and, above all, shared. It must be acknowledged from the outset that this process is not an easy one. It demands much courage for a person to begin to come to terms with their failure, whether in pastoral care or elsewhere. The fundamental reason for this is the close association between failure and shame.[24] The shamed person desperately seeks to hide herself away from exposure and vulnerability, to forget or elude the cause of this hardest of emotions to bear. The temptation to contain the causes of shame within the self and then seek to hide that self away from public gaze is tremendous and instinctive. If this is done though, there is no prospect of learning, healing or redemption of shame and the failure which brings it about. The suggestions for beginning the process of coming to terms with failure offered here are made in full awareness of the difficulties that any person who feels they have failed would have in trying to implement them. The only excuse for their inadequacy is that they are perhaps better than making no proposals at all.

The sense of failure derives much of its power from remaining hidden (or half-hidden) and untalked about. The psychotherapeutic movement in this century throws a great deal of light on the way in which that which is repressed or excluded in the mind can effectively 'haunt' people's lives in such a way that they actually suffer quite considerably. The first proposal is, therefore, that pastors should find ways of talking about their failures with someone else. This gets things out in the open and begins the process of coming to terms with failure and seeing it in some kind of perspective. Boulding suggests that the Christian church should be a place 'where people fail, and are seen to fail, and are forgiven.'[25] It may sometimes be difficult to recognize this as a description of the average Christian congregation where success seems as well ensconced as a fundamental aspiration as anywhere else in society. Despite this, many pastors are in a privileged position to know how many Christians carry round with them a deep sense of failure about some aspect of their lives. This means that, contrary to first impressions, there may be a considerable fund of understanding and empathy in the Christian community upon which the pastor may draw in times of failure. Sometimes a pastor's willingness to share her own failure may inspire and enable others to be open and honest about theirs. (In this sense, acknowledging failure may be a liberating act of pastoral care for others as well as for the self.) It is sometimes possible for a pastor to be able to talk about her failure in a public way, say in a sermon. More often it will be shared with particular individuals or groups who may not be part of the pastor's charge, at least initially. Pastoral supervisors, consultants or spiritual directors are useful in this role. Whoever is talked to, the process and end result is to begin to accept and understand one's own failure by virtue of being accepted and understood by another person who will be unlikely to condemn to the extent that one condemns oneself. However real and awful a failure may have been or still be, sharing with another person may well reduce its subjective horror and overwhelming magnitude, even if this does not happen immediately. It is right that pastors should seriously consider this option, for it is what they would hope people in their care would do in similar circumstances and the pastor who refuses to place trust and confidence in others when it comes to very intimate matters can hardly expect others to do the same. It is a case of do unto yourself what you would want and expect others to do with you.

Being open and honest about failure with another person, preferably on a regular basis, is part of, and sometimes a preliminary to, coming to self-knowledge and understanding of the self. Mention has already been made of the importance that writers like Nouwen and Campbell attach to pastors becoming particular kinds of people who know themselves and have come to terms with their strengths and weaknesses in such a way that they can put themselves at the service of others. Nouwen's term for this service is 'hospitality'.[26] When a pastor has faced up to things inside herself and been honest about her own reactions, space is created which can then be offered to others. Most people cannot come to terms with themselves and particularly with what they take to be their unattractive and negative aspects on their own. A good way of coming to terms with failure, then, both before and after any specific episode is to be receiving ongoing support and supervision alongside any particular request for help. Amongst other things, this kind of support will reassure pastors that they have good points as well as bad, strengths as well as weaknesses, and that they are actually capable of success as well as failure.

Sharing failure with other people either in crisis or in the context of ongoing support leads to another point, the need for objectivity and analysis. It was noted above that the sense of failure can be very subjective and may bear little relation to the perception of others about the situation. Pastors may torment themselves about having failed dismally when others may think they have done nothing of the sort. Although telling someone else that they have not in fact failed is unlikely to relieve them emotionally or subjectively in any immediate way, it can be very helpful if a chance is provided for people to explore why they feel themselves to have failed. It is vital that people should be encouraged to become aware of the expectations and emotional factors which make them believe they have failed. In many cases, people will know exactly how and why they have failed and they will be judging themselves according to very legitimate expectations either of their own or of others. But sometimes people are living by illegitimate expectations and become involved in complex and destructive webs which are entirely dysfunctional for them and those in their care. Sometimes, for example, pastors may feel entirely responsible for any misfortune which may afflict any member of their congregation. This attitude contains a good deal of parentalism in it and such pastors need to re-draw the boundaries of responsibility. Occasionally, congregations wish to have a scape-goat for everything that is going wrong and can end up blaming the pastor for it all. Here again the notion that the pastor who feels a failure in this situation really is a failure needs to be challenged. Often pastors may perceive themselves to fail because they have too high expectations of themselves which are in fact unreasonable. If they can become conscious of these they can change them and may be able to do what they do do better as a result. Some pastors simply feel bad about themselves and everything that they attempt to do. They have a sense of failure about specific things only because these act as a kind of 'peg' for a generic sense of guilt, shame and unworthiness. Once again, close analysis of the realities of the situation concerned and the boundaries and expectations which surround it can begin to liberate people from a very painful experience which may be inappropriate to reality. Intellectual clarity does not in itself bring a sense of healing and forgiveness, but it is a necessary accompaniment to it, not least because it may suggest ways in which a failure may be rectified or avoided in the future.

The Value of Failure in Pastoral Care

Christian explanations are sometimes rightly criticized for being superficial and over-optimistic. There is sometimes a tendency towards saying that suffering is a good thing (it is just that humans do not understand why it is good) or towards the idea that, at the very least, a silver lining is to be found in every cloud, however thick or black. Failure often causes suffering and one must therefore be very cautious about presenting it in a facile way as a positive thing in disguise. The only people who can be facile or optimistic about any form of suffering are usually those who are not experiencing it themselves. Let us be quite clear, then, that failure is not a thing to be talked of easily, to be desired, sought or celebrated. It comes unbidden and unwanted into pastoral care and may be extraordinarily damaging and destructive to the legitimate and desirable hopes and efforts of individuals and institutions. Having said this, however, it must be acknowledged that positive byproducts may flow from failure if it is faced up to and learned from. There is a danger of advocating a kind of 'Protestant work ethic' of suffering whereby people must always 'make' something of everything that happens, however awful, rather than rejecting it or protesting against it. Nonetheless, it is worth cataloguing some of the more positive things which might be learnt from failure in pastoral care. We are stuck with failure in pastoral care whether we like it or not. We might as well do something with it.

First and foremost, the occurrence of failure in pastoral care emphasizes its profoundly human nature. Pastoral care is exercised by and for humans and it is in no sense exempt from failure. All humans fail and pastors fail too; there is the basis for a profound and necessary mutuality here which reflects God's action in Jesus Christ:

God has dealt, and still deals, with our human disasters not by some omnipotent gesture from afar, but by coming down into it with us and transfiguring it from within so that its whole meaning is changed.[27]

From the secular world of social work Jordan writes of his own painful journey from expert professional detachment and aloofness to an equal involvement with people based on weakness and failure:

> I have been forced to re-examine my concern for the underdog. My identification and championship were from a position of strength and achievement. However much of an underdog I might have felt, my performance belied these feelings, so I often appeared to be fighting battles that were not my own. I have only slowly learnt how much harder it is to be brave and committed to the unfortunate from a position of weakness and vulnerability. It has taken me even longer to learn to share with others the things about myself which I regarded as most inadequate and blameworthy. Yet I now feel, through having allowed others to know about my failures, more secure, honest and realistic in my relationships with clients who feel ashamed and despised.[28]

If it is fully experienced and faced up to failure can actually humanize pastoral care and give pastors a greater mutuality with those in their care who experience the wounds of failure in other contexts. Failure can heighten the sensitivity, compassion and awareness of pastors so they are actually more effective with, and available to, those in need. In a sense, then, it is a gateway to mutual hope both for carers and those cared for, and gives a firm base for mutual solidarity.

The experience of failure in pastoral care can be a valuable teacher for the pastor. Maria Boulding speaks rather alarmingly of 'creative disintegration' whereby the norms, goals, standards and ways of acting are challenged by failure. This is often a very necessary process which brings change for the better and personal maturity in its wake, though disintegration in itself is an upsetting and unpleasant experience. Again, Jordan alludes to the creative teaching power of failure:

> I have also learnt from specific mistakes. I could not escape the links between things I had said or done at certain times and various bad consequences for my clients. I found that by

looking these mistakes directly in the eye, by seeing them as they were and acknowledging them as my own, I could change, and do better.[29]

For pastors as much as anyone else, change must often be forced by crisis and failure rather than by positive desire.

Failure can deepen the religious and spiritual life of the pastor and produce a greater awareness of the need to depend upon God as well as upon knowledge and skills. Failure exposes the limits of human ability and achievement. Sometimes nothing humanly can be done to rectify the effects of failure. For example, a person may leave a particular neighbourhood, die or break off relations with a pastor or congregation. At moments like these all the pastor can do is to commend the situation to the forgiveness and love of God. Sometimes, apparently miraculously, the most futile and morbid situation can be redeemed, but it may not be the particular pastor who has failed who can redeem it. The more aware pastoral carers become of the harm they can do as well as the good, the more they become acquainted with human lostness in pastoral care as in other activities, the more they will need to place themselves in the presence of God both in personal prayer and by taking part in the liturgy of the community of failure when it meets together to offer mutual support and encouragement to the lost.

Ultimately, the positive fruits of the experience of particular failures are to be found in the difference it makes to the pastoral care which is offered to other human beings. Many of the most enabling and helpful pastors are so because they bear in their own personalities the marks of deep failure experienced, faced up to (usually very painfully) and finally, at great cost, offered up to God and to the service of their fellows. Usually they are not famous, or even well known, but the humiliated and rejected recognize the one who was despised and rejected within their ministry and unerringly seek them out for help. One such pastor, a Jewish rabbi in fact, is Lionel Blue. Blue is an exception to my general description, for he is very well known from his work in broadcasting. In his talks on the radio he conveys very clearly a personal experience of life which contains much suffering and failure, caused to quite a large extent by a chronic mental disorder, manic depression. Blue's failures and sorrows, honestly faced up to, have been transmuted in faith so that while he speaks very personally of himself and his own experience in a curious way he speaks for us all. He has used the valley of the shadow of failure and death as a well, and so brings the water of life and hope to many.[30] Nouwen might have been writing of him when he said

> When (the pastor) is able to deny himself, to be faithful and to understand the meaning of human suffering, then the man who is cared for will discover that through the hands of those who want to be of help God shows his tender love for him.[31]

The last words on failure, however, must go to Maria Boulding. First, a word of caution:

> If we cannot endure failing and being weak, and being seen to fail and be weak, we are not yet in a position to love and be loved.

Finally, some very hopeful words for all those who have experienced failure in life generally or in pastoral care in particular:

> Christ has gone down into the deepest places of our failure and claimed them as his own, and now there is no possible failure in our lives or our deaths that cannot be the place of meeting him and of greater openness to his work.[32]

Chapter Eight

Laughter and Pastoral Care or, The Importance of Not Being Earnest[1]

> Men will confess to treason, murder, arson, false teeth or a wig. How many will own up to a lack of humour?[2]

The capacity to have a sense of humour and to be able to laugh is greatly valued in our own culture. But the significance of laughter as a fundamental feature distinguishing humans from animals was made in ancient civilizations. To be human was to be rational – but also to laugh. It is probably not overstating the case to say that laughter is one of the things which makes life worth living. For happy people their laughter is icing on the cake of good fortune. The laughter of unhappy and suffering people may be the only thing that keeps them going. For everyone, laughter has gracious and unbidden qualities similar to those ascribed to the Holy Spirit. Where it enters in, lives and situations can be transformed and transfigured, even if only temporarily, and the richness of new life in solidarity with others seems possible. Laughter, like love, cannot be commanded, contemplated or preserved. It fills the moment of its entry and involves the whole person, body, mind and soul while apparently having no very clear purpose by way of relieving any biological or physical need:

> laughter prevents the satisfaction of biological drives, it makes a man equally incapable of killing or copulating; it deflates anger, apprehension and pride. The tension is not consummated – it is frittered away in an apparently purposeless reflex . . .[3]

Like the gifts of the Spirit, laughter seems to have enormous and ambivalent power to build up and break down, to humiliate and to heal. It has been called God's 'oddest and most healing gift'.[4] It is universally available, mostly enjoyed, sometimes feared and usually amplified by being shared. Frustratingly, but perhaps fortunately, it is little understood and eludes organization and analysis. The question, 'What's in a laugh?' is certainly a pertinent one which could and should be asked more often in relation to life in general and pastoral care in particular with illuminating results. (A complementary question which might be more appropriate to some circumstances would be, 'Why is there no laughter here?') Even so, any answer will be only partial. Laughter remains a tantalizing enigma in the midst of ordinary everyday experience. It is a sign of transcendence so common that most of the time it is regarded as unremarkable and simply ignored.[5]

Laughter in Pastoral Care: The Example of Lionel Blue

Like failure, laughter is so much a part of human experience that it is difficult to contemplate anything approximating to good total pastoral care which finds no place for it. Unfortunately, so far as one can tell, the Christian tradition and the pastoral care which accompanies it have found it very difficult to accommodate laughter and the humour it betokens in any very direct way. Howard Clinebell suggests that it is a good thing for pastors to laugh regularly, seeming almost to prescribe it as a sort of medicine or spiritual keep-fit technique in describing it as 'internal jogging' which reduces stress.[6] Alastair Campbell goes some way towards rescuing this dimension in pastoral care in his image of the wise fool.[7] Campbell starts with Paul's notion that Christians should be fools for Christ's sake if they are to be truly wise (cf. I Cor. 3.18). Christian fools in Paul's sense are not hilarious entertainers or wits, but more outsiders to the world in which they live and its assumptions. They are simple in a child-like sense, and so expose insincerity and self-deception. In a sense they are foolhardy, disregarding self-interest for the sake of selflessness and loyalty to a higher master (Campbell draws parallels with the Fool in King Lear here). But they are also prophetic, using wit and laughter to expose underlying inconsistencies, vanities and wrongs in the established order and so showing it in a clearer light. Campbell builds on Heije Faber's image of the clown as a model for ministry in suggesting that pastoral care must be expert yet spontaneous, immediate and simple, loyal and vulnerable and able to join in prophetic divine laughter at itself and the world.[8]

Campbell's exposition is helpful and suggestive, but it manages to be both a bit over-serious and yet not to take the place of laughter in itself seriously enough![9] To find a full-blown example of laughter exploding into care, however, I turn now to the Jewish tradition and Rabbi Lionel Blue.

Lionel Blue is a rabbi of the Reformed synagogue. He is a prolific writer on many subjects to do with religion as well as on cooking, a subject which he believes goes to the heart of Judaism.[10] During a life which sounds difficult and unhappy in many ways, Rabbi Blue has been involved both in giving and receiving counselling and psychotherapy.[11] Blue is not best known for his care of individuals though, but rather for the care he has exercised for thousands of listeners to his three minute 'Thoughts for the Day' on Radio 4 on Monday mornings. Typically these short talks follow this format: (i) Blue's own personal experience – he often discusses in a very personal way his own weaknesses and failings which he regards as the seeds of his ministry. Strangely, this seldom seems exhibitionistic, and what is most particular to him often seems to strike a chord in others. (ii) A story drawn from the Jewish tradition. (iii) One or more Jewish jokes. Sometimes Blue includes a recipe; at one time he was given to beginning or ending his broadcasts with the phrase, 'Don't take it too heavy!'

Dust and Ashes

Here is a story about the Jewish Day of Atonement, the most solemn and serious fast in the Jewish Year. As the service was about to begin, a hush came over the assembled congregation. The venerable rabbi held out his hand for silence. Instead of going to his pulpit, he approached the Holy Ark with tears in his eyes. He flung open the doors and prostrated himself before the scrolls with their white mantles, the symbols of purity and repentance.

'Lord,' he said in a strained voice, 'have mercy on me, for I am only dust and ashes.'

After his confession the congregation watched him as he arose and took his place at the reading desk. He opened his prayer book, and was about to commence the solemn service.

But before he could do so, the cantor of the synagogue said gently, 'Wait!' He too approached the Holy Ark, and following his venerable rabbi in all things, gently opened the doors of the Ark, and prostrated himself humbly before the scrolls.

'Lord,' he said, 'I too seek mercy, for I too am just dust and ashes.'

In the silence, he took his place at the reading desk, and signed to the rabbi that the service could begin.

But there was yet one more confession to be heard, from the humblest servant of the synagogue. The beadle moved forward from the door with tears in his eyes. And while the congregation watched, moved and astonished, he too climbed the steps to the Ark with bowed head. He opened its door lovingly, and also prostrated himself, and spoke piously and gently.

'Lord,' he said, 'have mercy on me, a sinner, who is but dust and ashes.'

The rabbi breathed deeply and turned to the cantor. 'Look,' he said, 'who presumes to think he is only dust and ashes!'

I don't know how this story takes you, but it certainly pricked me, and as I laughed I could feel all my pomposity and ecclesiasticism oozing out of me. The humour deflated me as effectively as hours of agonising on my knees. The funny thing is that when I try to remember my sins, all I end up with is my foibles. It takes a joke to hit me below the belt, and take the stuffing out of me.

It's very easy in religion to miss the point, to get so interested in the symbols and signs that you forget what they are supposed to symbolise or what the signs are supposed to point to. Tapping your chest or your bosom during a confession can be fun, very unlike the stab of piercing pain that comes with real loss.

In the scriptures, yours and mine, God is jealous or wrath or loving, but He hardly ever laughs, and doesn't wink. Nor is there any official blessing for jokes, even those which purge you. So I will have to make one up: 'Blessed are You, Lord our God, King of the Universe, Whose love is manifest in laughter.'[12]

Blue's talks are often hilarious, the hilarity being an inevitable part of the humanity and caring which come through them in a very personal way to people who are not Jews and are physically many miles away from where Blue is himself. People in the slough of despond and sadness find their load lightened, feel cared about, and burst out laughing. One is reminded of the words of Isaiah quoted by Jesus in Luke chapter 4:

> He has sent me to bring the good news to the poor,
> to proclaim liberty to captives
> and to the blind new sight,
> to set the downtrodden free,
> to proclaim the Lord's year of favour (Luke 4.18–19).

With the laughter comes an authentic experience of pastoral care which makes present life endurable and new life possible. Why should this be so?

The reason lies in the fact that Jewish humour arises from the profound suffering of the Jewish people over many centuries. Unhappy people listening to Blue's talks instinctively sense that the humour in them does not circumvent or minimize misery, but embraces it. Blue himself suggests that there is not a great deal of humour in scripture; it is a late-comer to Judaism which begins with the worldly defeat of the Jews when the Temple was destroyed in 70 CE. Subsequently, it has allowed Jews to live with the objectivity of God's demands without becoming rigid, bitter, or dour, while purging the failure and depression which have so often threatened Jews facing privation and persecution in hostile environments like Nazi Germany:

> The humour of the Jews is not merely light relief, it is extremely profound. It takes the bitterness of the human heart, and reduces kings, emperors and dictators down to size . . . In Jewish jokes Hitler is not a hated figure but a pathetic one. The joke . . . is the vehicle of compassion. It is in humour that God comes close to the Jews, and through them to all men.[13]

It seems sad and puzzling that Christianity appears to have missed out to a large extent on the gifts of humour and laughter in pastoral care as in other areas. Blue himself suggests one reason for this. It is that Christianity in its understanding of the awful suffering of the cross transforms defeat into victory; 'The tree of shame was made the tree of glory; and where life was lost, there life has been restored.'[14] It may be that humour and laughter are primarily the heritage and possession of the defeated and marginalized while those with a 'victorious' view of the world and their fate are denied it. Nonetheless, the response to Blue's talks suggests that followers of the crucified God are increasingly aware of their own suffering and defeat in a chaotic world where they find themselves on the edge. Perhaps one of the real gains from secularization and the decline of glib certainty about the meaning of suffering and eventual victory will be a greater receptiveness to the gift of laughter proferred by the Jews. The liberating power of Blue's humour is badly needed in Christian pastoral care. It is to be hoped that, in at least this respect, we may be grafted on to the stock from which Christianity sprung two millennia ago.[15]

Laughter and Christianity

God laughs twice in the Bible. In Psalm 2 verse 4, 'He that sitteth in the heavens shall laugh; the Lord shall have them in derision.' This is an unpromising start for humour and laughter in the Judaeo-Christian tradition, for here divine laughter is that of hatred and contempt, without humour of any kind. In many ways the Bible deserves its reputation as a very serious book. It is true that it contains some satire and irony, even some riddles and amusing stories, but for the most part it is unrelieved by any kind of wit. Faced with this appalling fact some scholars have tried to redeem Jesus from the general solemnity of the Bible, arguing that many of his sayings and stories have a teasing, ironical, even witty flavour to them. It is difficult to believe that the human face of God seen in Christ never cracked with smiles or laughter. Nonetheless, there is no record that it did and this has helped to create a religion where humour and laughter have at best a very subordinate place. 'Jesus did not laugh,' the tacit argument seems to run, 'therefore neither should we.' This kind of assumption reached its unfortunate zenith in the thinking of the Reformers of the sixteenth and seventeenth centuries.[16]

But if Christianity has not placed humour and laughter in the foreground they have been a steady background murmur. Paul's allusion to Christians as fools has already been mentioned. One of the first representations of Christ in art is as a crucified human figure with the head of an ass, possibly reflecting the early Christians' awareness of the absurdity of their claims and position.[17] A long tradition of 'perfect fools' stretches the length of Christian history. These were not comedians or jokesmiths so much as those who gave up everything for Christ and lived on the margins of society and its conventions as a very serious sign of contradiction.[18] They were idiots mainly in the sense of being like the insane, outside the main structures of worldly life. Then as now, insane people were sometimes thought to be funny, but more often despised, rejected and feared. Some of those who stood in the tradition of folly do seem to have had a sense of humour, fun and laughter, St Francis of Assisi and his followers being the most obvious examples.[19] This is shared by some of the mystics of the middle ages. Dante talks of hearing choirs of angels singing praises to the Trinity in such a way that 'it seemed like the laughter of the universe' while Julian of Norwich's writings are full of references to rejoicing, delight and even being merry in the presence of God.[20] Meister Eckhart locates joyous laughter in the Godhead itself in the following, rather enigmatic, words:

> The soul gives birth to the person of the Word 'when God laughs at her and she laughs back'; the Son and the Father thus delight in each other 'and this laughter breeds liking and liking breeds joy, joy begets love, love begets the person (of the Word), who begets the Holy Spirit'.[21]

From the Reformation onwards laughter and humour were almost completely eclipsed in Christian writing, but a substantial revival of interest in them occurred in the optimistic and somewhat anarchic period at the end of the 1960s when theologians became fascinated with concepts of play and joy. Harvey Cox became interested in the concept of the feast of fools in which he describes laughter as 'hope's last weapon' against the calculated utilitarian seriousness which threatens to deliver the world up to an apocalyptic end.[22] This theme is taken up by Moltmann who believes that play and laughter are the necessary prerequisites for liberation:

> it is possible that in playing we can anticipate our liberation and with laughing rid ourselves of the bonds which alienate us from real life.[23]

More recently, Hardy and Ford describe basic Christian existence itself as 'a laugh', sharing in the logic of intensification, overflow and abundance which underlies a praising universe whose purpose in creation is to create joy.[24]

These recent attempts to integrate laughter into Christianity are refreshing and welcome, but often uncritical and peripheral to the main Christian tradition.

With token exceptions, none of the writers mentioned actually discusses the nature of humour and laughter. Humour and laughter are regarded as self-explanatory and unequivocally good and desirable. Only in an essay by Reinhold Niebuhr published in 1946 have I been able to find a detailed theological assessment of the nature and, most significantly, the limitations of humour and laughter.[25] Niebuhr believes that fundamentally humour arises from the incongruities of life and it is appropriate for dealing with proximate and relatively small inconsistencies, frustrations and evils. It becomes a dangerous and bitter thing when it tries to cope with the great inconsistencies and incongruities of the universe which really should be dealt with by faith alone. So, for example, to laugh at death is to laugh at life and make it trivial and meaningless; to laugh at sin or evil may be an important and necessary preliminary sign of self-transcendence, but ultimately these things are tragic and need to be wept over and amended. Niebuhr points to the Nazi concentration camps as a stunning refutation of the idea that insufferable forms of tyranny can be ameliorated by laughing the tyrant out of court, as many hoped they might. There is nothing to laugh at in the cross where the incongruities of good and evil, justice and mercy meet. Humour should therefore be a preliminary to faith and not a substitute for it, or it runs the risk of corrupting people and allowing the *status quo* of evil to remain intact:

> Insofar as the sense of humour is a recognition of incongruity, it is more profound than any philosophy which seeks to devour incongruity in reason. But the sense of humour remains healthy only when it deals with immediate issues and faces the obvious and surface irrationalities. It must move toward faith or sink into despair when the ultimate issues are raised. That is why there is laughter in the vestibule of the temple, the echo of laughter in the temple itself, but only faith and prayer, and no laughter, in the holy of holies.[26]

It may be felt that Niebuhr is in danger of falling into the rut of Protestant pessimism and gloom which characterized his Reformed forebears but at least he poses important questions about the nature of humour, its relationship to faith and for example, joy, and prevents any facile euphoria about the place of laughter in religion.

It is now appropriate to consider the factors which may make humour and laughter problematic for Christianity and for Christian pastoral care. The first was touched on by Blue. Christianity is a religion which turns defeat into triumph while humour is often the property of the defeated and marginalized. The second factor has been raised by Niebuhr; there really is not a lot to laugh about in the tragedy of the cross. Thirdly, it could be said that there is not a lot to laugh about in the state of the world. 'How can I play in a strange land,' Moltmann asks,

> in an alienated and alienating society? How can we laugh and rejoice when there are still so many tears to be wiped away and when new tears are being added every day?[27]

Christian pastors are only too well aware of this kind of feeling.

The non-rational nature of humour and laughter is the fourth factor. Since the Enlightenment the best efforts of Christian theology have gone into trying to make this religion credible in a rationally ordered world. The non-orderly, unpredictable nature of humour hints of a different kind of order from the utilitarian ratio-technological one and may therefore be seen as a threat not least in pastoral care with its serious attempts to bring order out of chaos:

> The fool . . . belongs to 'a society shaped by belief in a Divine order, human inadequacy, efficacious ritual'. Consequently, there is no place for him 'in a world increasingly dominated by the notions of the puritan, the scientist, and the captain of industry; for strange as it may seem the fool in cap and bells can only flourish among people who have sacraments, who value symbols as well as tools.'[28]

Perhaps the sheer physicality of laugher is another problematic factor for Christianity. Humour may originate in the mind, but laughter manifests itself in the body and can even physically disable people for a while:

Spontaneous laughter is produced by the co-ordinated contraction of fifteen facial muscles in a stereotyped pattern and accompanied by altered breathing.[29]

Historically, Christianity has been vulnerable to 'spiritualizing' tendencies which have tended to exalt the mind or spirit over the body. Laughter, on the other hand, is a firmly embodying experience.[30]

Finally, it may be that the associations of laughter and humour with aggression make it difficult for Christianity to cope with.

Humour frequently depends on doing others down or triumphing over situations rather than on happiness or joy. When laughter breaks out in the Old Testament, for example, it is often derisive and gained at the expense of enemies. Koestler suggests that there is always 'an impulse, however faint of aggression or apprehension' in humour and that laughter emerges from the past 'with a dagger in its hand'. It could be that Christians sense this apparently negative aspect of humour and instinctively try to avoid it for the sake of peaceful and forgiving fellowship. Perhaps the balm of laughter is eschewed because of its potential barb.[31] This point highlights the importance of seeing the ambivalent and sometimes negative aspects of humour rather than demanding that it should immediately and uncritically be assimilated into the Christian religion or pastoral care.

It is high time that a much closer look was taken at the nature of humour and laughter as disclosed by psychologists, biologists and others. Combined with the theological considerations above, this will eventually allow some informed remarks to be made about the place of these elements in pastoral care.

The Nature of Humour and Laughter

The experience of laughter is universal and commonplace, yet theology has almost completely ignored it. It is a consolation in these circumstances to find that other disciplines have given it almost as embarrassingly little attention. Humour and laughter remain a perplexing enigma to behavioural scientists, although a certain amount of theory does exist as to their nature and function.

Laughter is confined to the human species and appears to be biologically redundant, serving no very obvious function in preserving or propagating the human race, unlike most other aspects of human behaviour. In a sense then it is a 'luxury' which is only available to a species which is biologically secure. Laughter springs from an interaction between mental apprehension and the physiology which lies at the bottom of all emotional reactions; this means that its causes and course are extremely complex and difficult to identify. It seems likely that there is a very close connection between laughter and the other 'luxury' reflex enjoyed by humans, weeping. Both have a physiological component which is located in the adrenal system as well as being directly affected by the perception of the mind. When people say that they have to laugh or they would cry, they seem instinctively to be expressing the connection between these two apparently contrary reactions.[32]

There is no single explanation for the existence and function of the laughter reflex, but three main groups of theory have been advanced. The first of these emanates from Freud and is favoured by writers like Koestler. It focusses on the notion that laughter is a way of relieving or dissipating emotional tension that has been aroused by some kind of threat mobilizing the sympathetico-adrenal system. Crudely speaking, the idea behind this is that adrenalin is released into the body because some kind of danger or attack is perceived. When the suspected attack does not take place and so physical defence is not required, the pent-up emotional force is dissipated in laughter, an explosion of harmless physical activity. A simple example of this kind of response is, say, being thumped in the back while walking along the street. One's first instinct may be one of fear and defensiveness, even outrage. If, however, it becomes apparent that one's 'attacker' is in fact a friend trying to greet one, then smiles and possibly laughter can defuse the situation and dispose of unwanted aggressive responses, thus maintaining the friendship. Theorists in this tradition suggest that at a very sophisticated level humour and laughter are always a by-product of self-assertive/defensive-aggressive associations of this sort. 'A drop of adrenalin' is always required to trigger of the laughter reaction, however subtle or affectionate the laughter may be.[33] Weeping likewise allows physical relief of redundant physio-logical response, but in this case emotion drains away rather than exploding. In this kind of theory, then, laughter and humour allow an indirect and socially acceptable way of expressing oneself when direct aggressive expression would be inappropriate.

A second line of theoretical reflection on humour and laughter has suggested that humour arises from a sense of superiority, or perhaps the relative degradation of others. When people become aware of being more favourably disposed than their fellows then they exult in their own superiority and laugh at those who they think to be inferior to themselves. This theory is well, if unpleasantly, encapsulated in a sentence by the seventeenth-century philosopher Thomas Hobbes:

> The passion of laughter is nothing else but sudden glory arising from a sudden conception of some eminency in ourselves by comparison with the infirmity of others, or with our own formerly.[34]

The third main group of theories about the causes of humour and laughter is the most popular among modern psychologists. It prescinds from aggression or superiority lying at the heart of the matter to suggest that it is incongruity which gives rise to humour and laughter. It is when different frames of reference or expectation collide with each other that a situation becomes humorous. Thus it is funny when the person slips on the banana skin not primarily because they hurt or humiliate themselves (reasons which might be given by relief or superiority theorists) but because the person expects and is expected to walk straight on and unexpectedly finds him or herself on the ground. More sophisticated examples of incongruity occasioning laughter are to be found in every good TV comedy programme.[35]

These are the three main theories, but there are others. Laughter has been attributed to triumph, relief from anxiety, agreement, sudden comprehension, embarrassment and scorn, while it has been seen as the product of situations as diverse as humorous, social, ignorance, anxiety, derision, apologetic and laughter in response to tickling.[36] Opting for any one theory is somewhat arbitrary and they are probably all relevant, though perhaps at different times and in different situations. The theories focussed on aggression or superiority, for example, encapsulate important points about the way in which humour and laughter are often used to attack or defend. The theories of incongruity and superiority enshrine another important truth about humour, namely that a sense of distance or perspective is required for laughter to be possible. One cannot laugh at oneself unless one can, so to speak, stand outside oneself to see that self as another might see it. Laughter and humour as distancing mechanisms are enormously important, hence their value as survival techniques for people like the Jews or as tools of criticism in totalitarian régimes. Laughter gives an 'as if' perspective:

> The laughter that occurs in everyday life is a response to what makes us angry, frustrates us, dismays us, disillusions us, and causes us pain. This anger is as Wittgenstein says 'not a mood but a way of looking at the world.'[37]

I want to pause at this point to underline the fact that laughter and humour, as accounted for above, often have very substantial negative connotations. They arise in response to difficult or frustrating situations. This contrasts strongly with the way laughter is talked about in the context of Christian theology where it is more often associated with joy and fulfilment rather than endurance. If there is laughter in heaven, surely it does not arise from aggression, defeat or frustration. It may have something to do with triumph over sin and death (there are connotations of superiority and relief here) and the incongruity of what was expected and what has happened may also be relevant, but the laughter of the theologians really seems a different species to any which has been considered by the scientific theorists. I therefore want to distinguish the laughter of delight which flows from a sense of well-being and being loved. This kind of mirth can be seen in children and particularly in babies. The beloved child in whom its parents delight seems, at least sometimes, to laugh just because she is alive and secure. It is true that babies are not angels and are self-assertive and aggressive so they may need to dissipate these emotions in laughter if they are to maximize parental interest and the sustenance they need to grow. Nonetheless, the laughter of children cannot betoken much self-awareness or perception of incongruity because of their lack of mental development and it sometimes seems to betoken sheer joy and delight in existence. It has very little to do with humour, jokes, or perspective. In many ways, then, it is this naive or primal laughter which flows from an immediate unreflective and total awareness of loving and being loved which is idealized and sought after by the theologians reflecting on the relationship of a loving Father with his children. It is unambiguously good and desirable, the consummation and outward sign of loving intimacy which totally involves rather than distancing. Something of its essence is sensed by Helen Merrell Lynd:

> Humour that arises from the enjoyment of the predicament of others may betoken a cynical self-interest which can be a warping experience for the observer as well as for the person observed. This is not all of laughter. 'When you laugh,' says Turgenev, 'you forgive and are ready to love.'[38]

The existence of primal, or naive laughter highlights another very important and obvious fact, namely that there is not always a connection between laughter and humour. The two things tend to be conflated (as has been the case here) in a way which is confusing and unhelpful, but they do not have to be talked of in the same breath. After all, laughter can simply be a response to the physical stimulus of being tickled. No humour need be involved there at all. An important corollary of this observation is that the presence of laughter does not necessarily imply that something amusing or funny is happening.

Laughter is a reflex, but it is not a simple reflex. It is under the control of the higher nervous centres and is affected by consciousness. This means that while it is sometimes the case that people feel they cannot control their mirth, for the most part they can. This leads to the possibility of either suppressing laughter or indeed contriving it. People do not have to laugh in any particular situation, however amusing; equally, they can force themselves to laugh if they feel they are required to do so (so-called 'false laughter').

The interaction of consciousness with physiological reflex response in laughter also means that it can be modified by a person's mood. It is possible to laugh cheerfully, but also dolefully, sadly, ruefully, angrily, vengefully and so forth. Laughter is often very subtly nuanced though this is seldom recognized or reflected upon consciously.[39] The laughter of each individual, in terms of both meaning and cause is also subtly nuanced. Different people laugh at different things for different reasons. It cannot be assumed that the meaning of laughter is a constant for everyone and interpretation is always necessary. A classic example of this arises when someone hears laughter and assumes it is directed hostilely at them. Another occurs when it is assumed that someone is laughing because they are amused or happy when for them it may be a way of avoiding bursting into tears or of expressing relief when a difficult or dangerous situation has been survived. The forms of laughter are varied too, ranging from the thin smile through to the belly laugh or even the falling fit. Some people laugh loud and long at the smallest thing, others may only permit themselves a polite giggle at what they may find extremely amusing. Social and cultural circumstances and expectations play a very large part in determining what the objects of humour and laughter should be and the degree of response which is appropriate to them. For example, it used to be acceptable in this country to laugh at the deformed and the insane. This would be frowned upon today. Similarly, it is expected that people will laugh when someone trips over deliberately in a pantomime, but if this happens on an important social occasion laughter would be regarded as callous. It is often noted that humour, what makes people laugh, varies from country to country. This is certainly true, and it is enormously important to be sensitive to the taboos which might exist around certain objects of humour in societies and cultures other than one's own if one wishes to convey a suitable attitude of respect and consideration.

This preliminary, and by no means exhaustive survey of the nature of laughter and its relationship with humour is a prelude to looking in a more practical way at the place of these elements in pastoral care.

The Value of Laughter in Pastoral Care

When laughter is associated with humour and the latter's possibilities for gaining a different perspective on a situation, it has enormous value in pastoral care. Of course, in a very real sense, the value of laughter cannot be measured, any more than that of happiness. Nor could laughter be programmed into pastoral care self-consciously, for it has the quality of an elusive and spontaneous gift. Nonetheless, it is possible to make some observations on the positive aspects of humour and laughter for carers and those cared for, in very general terms.

The first thing to point out is that laughter is distinctively human. Where laughter is heard, albeit that it may be low, angry or even insane, there can be no doubt that people are involved. The sound of laughter can remind pastoral carers and those for whom they care that they remain human and have the hope of human potential, however unlikely that may seem in any particular situation. When laughter and the humour it can betoken is entirely absent, there may well be cause of anxiety that a person or situation is losing contact with humanity. It is only slightly overstating the case to say that to lose one's sense of humour and the capacity to laugh is to lose at least part of one's soul. The same thing can be said of pastoral care in general; where all is given up to serious planning for people's good and to sober intense individual encounters, where there is no ghost of a smile, pastoral care may be in danger of becoming inhuman. There is much to weep about and despair of in the human condition. But there is much to laugh about too; the furrowed brow of concern needs at least occasionally to give way to the raised eyebrows of hilarity. Where people cannot laugh at all, and are gripped by despair, it is a signal that the best and most urgent kinds of pastoral care are badly needed to stand by and assist wounded humanity. This pastoral care might be bereavement visiting of a very depressed person or trying to alleviate unemployment with its attendant misery. There is much which prevents people from laughing today.

Laughter points to essential humanity in pastoral care and its absence can be an indicator of inhumanity and diminishment. Since laughter is often a thing experienced with other people and is usually enhanced if shared, it is also something which has the capacity to indicate and create greater mutuality in pastoral care. Of course, it is possible for laughter to be a sign of distance and contempt, but more often in sensitive pastoral care it bears witness to and generates real warmth, mutuality, sharing and solidarity. Humour can cement people together in a unique way, helping them to realize that they are not on their own in the situations they face. Indeed, the more threatening and awful reality may be, the more it may be possible for people to join together in laughter in the face of a common enemy.

By far the most important benefit conferred by humour and laughter in pastoral care is the sense of distance and perspective. It will be recalled that this lies at the heart of some of the main theories of laughter discussed above. Somehow, humour requires a step back from the situation in which one is involved so that the incongruities in it are seen. This is the process of 'seeing the funny side' of the situation, or even of the self and its actions. When people can take this step back, things come into proportion and can be seen in perspective a bit more easily. For those who are suffering or involved in deeply troubling circumstances, the advent of laughter can be a sign of great hope, for it means that they are in some way transcending themselves and their circumstances. It means that they have the problem or the difficulty, rather than the problem or difficulty having them. A sense of some control, or mastery, can at least be glimpsed through humour even if there is no prospect of easy solution or quick release from bad circumstances. It is certainly true that there are some situations which defy humour and laughter and where no distance is possible; severely depressed people, for example, are completely caught up in their own suffering and attempts to joke with or 'cheer them up' can be very misplaced. But many very serious situations do have their funny side which can be recognized and used to lighten them. It is possible, then, for problems and difficulties to be faced in a 'euphoric' rather than a 'dyphoric' mode. This does not minimize or seek to escape from harsh reality but allows it to be coped with more adequately and pleasantly.[40] Sometimes the perspective provided by humour allows people to change and grow; their past ways of behaving and responding seem literally ridiculous and so can be surrendered. At other times, it simply helps people to endure and retain their self-respect in overwhelmingly difficult circumstances. These remarks are summed up by the following comment on the Jews:

> For Jews, life is funny in every possible sense, but Jewish humour, born of accumulated anguish, actually takes life very seriously. It is an attempt to root out the meaning of experiences, to posit a certain control over them and exercise some independence from them, to penetrate the heart of suffering so as to rise above it, to save some sanity and to find just a little compensation. It bespeaks the poignance of Jewish life: the tears of laughter and the laughter through tears.[41]

At the level of the individual the humorous perspective seems to be able to accomplish results which no other approach can touch. In a very positive way it can liberate people from self-absorption. They can, as it were, stand outside themselves and in so doing become more open to others. It can do a great deal to set people free from two very destructive attitudes to themselves, pride and self- humiliation, allowing a more realistic and healthy humility or true self-acceptance to enter in:

> Sometimes humour can expose the fantasies which underlie my pride or my self-humiliation, rendering them vulnerable to an insight in which they lose their power over me – for a crucial moment at least . . . A sharp, penetrating joke can prick my pompous pretensions, bringing me down to earth. Or, alternatively, it can pierce through the prison walls of my somber self-abasement, jolting me into an initiative towards freedom.[42]

It is important to add the words with which Evans goes on:

> But the humour must be gentle and humane, generating a kindly chuckle at another of the funny foibles of humanity. If the exposure is too stark and savage, it may destroy me along with my pride, or shame me into deeper self-humiliation.[43]

The theologian Harry Williams believes that laughter is the beginning of self-acceptance and forgiveness, mirroring God's forgiveness and acceptance. It helps to get the self in proportion and opens the path to forgiving others:

> God, we believe, accepts us, accepts all men, unconditionally, warts and all. Laughter is the purest form of our response to God's acceptance of us. For when I laugh at myself I accept myself and when I laugh at other people in genuine mirth I accept them. Self-acceptance in laughter is the very opposite of self-satisfaction or pride . . . In laughing at my own claims to importance or regard I receive myself in a sort of loving forgiveness which is an echo of God's forgiveness for me.[44]

At their best and most positive, humour and laughter can be enormously enriching. They can reveal and reinforce a sense of humanity, rediscover a sense of mutuality, re-define and relieve even the most difficult situations, help reconcile people to themselves and others and help them to recognize the reality of situations and selves from a different angle. But there is a problem. Humour and laughter relativize; that is to say that with their 'as if' perspective they tend to de-bunk established ways of seeing and traditional authorities. There may be a difficulty here for those who exercise pastoral care in a very traditional perspective, for once they start 'seeing the funny side' in pastoral care they may find that all sorts of other areas also dissolve in ridicule and laughter. Some people would argue that this is one of the reasons why humour and religion are incompatible.[45] Religion is absolute and can only be seen in one way. When it becomes possible to see things from different (and perhaps irreverent) angles, the gods fall from heaven and things can never be quite so certain again. Pastoral care in this context cannot therefore simply 'use' humour and laughter; it will be transformed by it also and, like religion, it may find its pomposity pricked and its solemn good order destroyed for ever. There is a price to be paid for the entry of the non-orderly phenomenon of laughter into pastoral care.

It should also be remembered that laughter is an ambivalent thing and has a dark side which may manifest itself in pastoral care. Humour and laughter can be signs of callousness, cynicism, escapism and lack of involvement. They can be used as nothing more than an analgesic to take away present pain while distracting people from facing up to reality and seeking to change it. To the extent that laughter enables a relatively passive tolerance of the intolerable it must be regarded with grave suspicion in pastoral care. The fact is that, in themselves humour and laughter are not necessarily unequivocally good and desirable. Their value and appropriateness must be carefully assessed in each pastoral situation. With this warning in mind we can go on to look at the meaning and use of laugher in the individual pastoral encounter.

Listening to Laughter: What's in a Laugh?

It should be becoming clear by now that humour and laughter are very complex. In terms of the individual pastoral encounter this has direct practical implications. It is not enough to assume that laughter is a sign of happiness and well-being, though of course sometimes it is. Instead, the meaning of laughter must be discerned and interpreted. The questions must be asked: 'What is in this laugh? What is the meaning for this person of her laughter in the present context?' If laughter is carefully listened to and its significance is successfully elicited, it can cast a great deal of light on the situation of the person being cared for. People laugh for all sorts of reasons. Sometimes, far from expressing their true feelings, laughter can be used as a mask for feelings. In this defensive usage, the logic might run, 'I am laughing therefore I must be all right and happy. I do not need to look inside myself and I do not need help from anyone else. Everyone can see I am OK.' This kind of laughter can easily put a pastor off, making it very difficult to get beneath the surface and to offer help which may be very much needed.

Another kind of laughter is occasioned by feelings of embarrassment or shame. A person feels that some innermost thing has been revealed and in the absence of any alternative, such as running away, they may dissipate their tension in laughter which may well sound shallow and nervous. There is nothing amusing about being embarrassed, ashamed or anxious, so this kind of laughter has no particularly humorous connotation. In the same vein, it is quite common for people to direct scorn and derision at themselves in their laughter. They have stood back from themselves, but they despise what they see within or their own behaviour and their laughter becomes a way of directing hostile feelings towards themselves. There is nothing more painful than to witness a person cynically and vindictively making themselves the butt of their own bitter humour. It is almost a kind of self-mutilation and it is very important that pastors should not join in by laughing along with the person they are caring for. There is also a more defensive kind of laughter which is associated with self-mockery. The logic lying behind this is that if a person criticizes and mocks herself, this will prevent others from doing so. Holding oneself up as an object of ridicule may prevent others from criticizing, but it also keeps them at arm's length. Judgment and support are both pre-empted.

Not all laughter has these negative connotations, however. Mercifully, people do sometimes find things which are genuinely amusing in pastoral encounters and laugh at them. They may laugh at themselves in a genuinely accepting way. Often, laughter accompanies some new insight into the self or the person's situation – they see the funny side of things with its incongruities and limitations. When support and understanding is offered, there may be the laughter of relief from anxiety or the delight of solidarity. Sometimes it betokens a complex mixture of feelings. Types of laughter are endless, as are the moods which they indicate. People laugh joyfully, angrily, bitterly, nervously, and so on. The point is that it is absolutely necessary to discern the meaning of laughter for the person concerned if the pastor is to be able to help them. Sometimes it will be useful to ask a person what their laughter means to them, for they may not themselves appreciate its significance.

But it is not enough for pastors just to listen to the laughter of those they care for. They must also try to understand the significance of humour and laugher in their own lives, interactions and ministry. Some pastors pride themselves on their sense of humour and their love of a good joke. This may be a good thing, but is it always a good thing in every circumstance? For them, as much as for anyone else, humour can be a defence against being open about their real feelings which may be far from jolly and benevolent at times, or against having to take people seriously. Again, humour can be a form of disguised aggression against people. Many pastors feel constrained to be nice and kind to people under all circumstances but may inwardly harbour a sense of grievance against those who make demands upon them. One way in which they can express hostility in a relatively acceptable way is through humour. The trouble is that those who seek the pastor's care may well pick up the veiled aggression contained in jokes and wisecracks so trust is damaged. People seeking care may also very well be put off by someone who appears to laugh a great deal, whatever the circumstance. Laughter is an ambivalent communication and persons desiring care may be puzzled or worried by it, particularly if they do not know the pastor personally very well. People who are deeply distressed may find a laughing pastor difficult to approach as they may assume that he is unsympathetic to the sorrowful. They may even feel that they do not want to make her sorrowful! Pastors who have a sense of humour and laughter can also be seduced into trying to impress or amuse the people in their care with jokes and repartee. There is certainly a place for this at times, but it is an obstacle if the person cared for becomes no more than an audience. Lastly, it is sometimes possible for people who need care to deflect the pastor's attention from their needs by appealing to her sense of humour. It is easy for pastors to be drawn into a web of laughter which may be ultimately very unhelpful to the person being cared for who needs to face up to the real difficulties and opportunities of a situation. All this means that the pastor has to listen to her own laughter as well as that of those she offers care to. In doing this she will stand a better chance of making humour and laughter an appropriate and liberating aspect of pastoral care rather than an obstacle to it.

A pastor who tells jokes to those who come to her for help is using an unoriginal form of humour which is not specifically related to the present situation of the needy person. If she adopts a light-hearted bantering tone this may help some people, but it may make others feel rejected or belittled. By far the best way of engendering humour which is likely to be helpful in pastoral care, then, is to help the person seeking care to develop their own humorous perspective. This will not crush or attack her and will become a real part of her own view of the world. Pastors can encourage such a perspective by having one themselves and by trying to reinforce humorous awareness in those they care for. If they are willing to discover and disclose the incongruities in their own situation, this can create an environment of mutuality where those who seek care can also begin to experiment with humour and laughter. The key factor is that the person cared for is not made the victim of the pastor's wit. The pastor may be willing to make a fool of herself and reveal it to those in her care, she does not make them feel fools! The social worker, Bill Jordan, is a leading exponent of this 'humour by example' school:

> I believe that social workers have to be prepared to make fools of themselves from time to time, and to be made fools of by others . . . If a social worker spends his time trying to safeguard himself against being made to look ridiculous he is likely to limit his opportunities for giving real help to his clients. It is better to let the ridiculous happen, and then try to use it creatively; or failing that, simply to endure it.[46]

There is a real place for becoming a fool in pastoral care, for Christ's sake, for the sake of those who seek pastoral care, but also for the pastor's own sake. Pastors, after all, have just as much right to be foolish as the rest of the human race. If they can give up their claims to professional earnestness and intensity, a difficult thing to do for people who sometimes want to be taken very seriously indeed, their care might be enriched, the burdens of those they care for might be lightened – and pastoral care might be a lot more fun.[47]

Conclusion: Contemplation, Laughter and Pastoral Care

It is a curious fact that very saintly people often seem to possess a very fine sense of humour as well as very real compassion for other human beings. Those who spend a great deal of time in the solitary, difficult and sober business of prayer can often appear to be more involved, sensitive and humorous than those who never pray and remain firmly involved in the humdrum activities of everyday life. So, for example, a person like the Cistercian monk Thomas Merton fled the world into a monastery but paradoxically became more involved in, and compassionate towards that world by campaigning for peace in his writings. At the same time as he became more involved in passionate struggle for world peace, Merton managed also to cultivate a sense of compassionate but humorous detachment about himself and even about the things he thought were most important. In a way, as he grew older he took himself and the world in which he lived both more and less seriously.

It is not an accident that deep spirituality or contemplation can be associated with a humorous outlook on the world. Contemplation consists in coming to see the nature of reality through God's eyes. It puts a different perspective on life and throws its tragedies, but also its incongruities, into relief. In contemplation, as in humour, a sense of distance and perspective is created and so laughter can burst through. But the laughter of the contemplative is a particular kind of laughter. It is not a sign of ironic detachment, or contempt for creation, or people. It is more the laughter of delighted recognition and acceptance which springs from the knowledge of God as loving Father. This kind of laughter betokens simultaneously the possibility of intense involvement but also detachment. It puts failure and success into their correct proportions and resists totalitarian fanaticism and utilitarian benevolence without belittling human efforts to change and create a better future.

Humour and spirituality are inextricably intertwined in Christianity but modern pastoral care has often seemed to lack both, to judge from much of the material reviewed in this book. In the thick of its intense and proper battle against dehumanizing sin and sorrow, pastoral care can easily lose any sense of perspective. Perhaps it is this which has led to its being seen by some people as no more than social work undertaken by a religious agency. In the end, the thing that Christian ministry distinctively has to offer people is not good works or righteous actions, but a way of seeing reality: 'To contemplate is to *see*, and to minister is to make *visible*'.[48] Christian pastoral care badly needs to rediscover the possibility of involved detachment based on the perspective gained by trying to see the world through God's eyes and so seeing reality as it is. The outward sacrament of this rediscovery will be the sound of laughter. This is as it should be, for Christianity embodies the truth of the resurrection. And what is resurrection but

> a laugh freed
> for ever and for ever.[49]

Paradoxically, it may be that it is only when pastoral care gains the perspective which allows it to see itself as a joke – a bad joke even – that it will be beginning to take God and reality seriously.

Towards a Critique of
A Critique of Pastoral Care

Perhaps the most flattering compliment which can be conferred upon a book which is intended for the use of students amongst others is that it should become the subject of an examination question! I was, therefore, delighted to learn that an ingenious pastoral studies teacher had asked some students to write a critique of *A Critique of Pastoral Care*. This is a question which I have stolen for my own examination papers. It can also usefully form the basis for constructing this Afterword which attempts to comment on developments in pastoral care theory and practice which have (or have not occurred) since 1987, to evaluate critically some aspects of the original chapters of the book, and to provide additional updated bibliography. My overall intention here is to assess critically, and partially to expand, the original book. I wrote most of the chapters of the book in such a way that they could be read as self-contained essays on particular topics. The most convenient way to proceed is therefore to comment on each of them in turn, briefly outlining new practical and theoretical developments, questions and significant contributions to the topic under discussion.

Introduction

At the conclusion of the Introduction I stated that *A Critique of Pastoral Care* was primarily addressed to practising pastors and students in training courses for ministry. While recognizing the increasingly important place given to non-professional or lay people in pastoral care the book was oriented towards professionals or quasi-professionals. I drew attention to the lack of recognition of women's role in pastoral care by stating that I was going to use the feminine forms of pronouns.

I have subsequently come to regard the stances expressed on lay pastoral care, and pastoral care for and by women, as defective. This is largely the result of a deepening encounter with feminist thought and practice, of which more anon. The norm for thinking about care must now be that of the ordinary non-trained, non-professional person. Most people are primarily cared for, not by professionals or organizations such as churches, but by their families, friends and relatives. Often, they do not need highly specialized skills or a particular attitude on the part of their carers, but they do need constancy, availability and appropriateness. While there clearly is a role for professional or paid carers designated and trained as such, it is a mistake to see this latter kind of care as the norm. Indeed, regarding it in this way is a usurpation of power and significance which leads to an ideological distortion of reality.

The reality is that, throughout history and especially today, most caring is undertaken by women, the majority of it unpaid and often unrecognized. One of the most important tasks for pastoral care theory and practice is to recognize this fact and to help others to recognize it, including women themselves. One of the most heartening developments in pastoral care is the beginnings of a feminist critique of pastoral care and the growth of feminist consciousness about the giving and receiving of care. It now seems vital to me that professional males who designate themselves as official 'pastoral carers' should cease to see their caring as exemplary or paradigmatic and should instead privilege the knowledge and care of lay people and particularly women.

The professionalized view of the pastor and the adoption of the encapsulated role of pastoral carer may now be a considerable obstacle to learning in mutuality from the real experts who might value recognition and support for what they do, but should probably be spared professional ideas of what care should be. I have come increasingly to believe that any book about care for professionals should start with the views and experience of non-professionals who must become the subjects not the objects of care. It is a tribute to my own blindness, and to that of other professional pastoral theologians, that it would be very difficult to know where to begin on this task as informal, unpaid, care finds little official articulation or hearing![1]

This perception of the importance of privileging 'lay' care and perspectives over professional pastoral care is one which has emerged from encountering feminist thinking. It is, however, in some ways a corollary of the need to adopt a bias in pastoral care towards the unheard and unseen (outlined in chapter 5 above) and of the need expressed right at the end of chapter 8 to develop right ways of seeing and making visible in pastoral ministry.

What is Pastoral Care Anyway?

The necessary if frustrating debate about how pastoral care should be defined is destined to continue. Here, again, it would be very good to see non-professional carers getting involved and helping to shape the discussion, though it is easy to see why it might be of absolutely no interest to them whatsoever!

An important new 'official' definition of pastoral care is to be found in the *Dictionary of Pastoral Care and Counseling* recently published in North America:

> *Pastoral care* is considered to be any form of personal ministry to individuals and to family and community relationships by representative religious persons (ordained or lay) and by their communities of faith, who understand and guide their caring efforts out of a theological perspective rooted in the tradition of faith.[2]

There are several noteworthy features of this definition as against my own (on p. 13 above). First, it emphasizes the essentially personal nature of pastoral care (this appears to significantly exclude non-personal activities aimed at improving the human condition, e.g., interventions in social policy). Secondly, it implies that pastoral care is only done when the people who do it can be seen as representative of religious communities (possibly restricting pastoral care to being an official or semi-official activity). Thirdly, it allows for communities of faith actually to be pastoral actors (a welcome corrective to individualism in care). Fourthly, it gives a decisive place to the cognitive theological perspective rooted in a tradition of faith (this might disqualify from pastoral care those in the community who have little or no theological perspective or faith rooting.) Lastly, and most interestingly, the definition does not include the word 'Christian' anywhere, thus suggesting that members of non-Christian faith communities can be engaged in pastoral care (Is this a case of making Christian pastors of all people of good will?).

The questions which I raised in my original discussion of the definition of pastoral care could all be raised here again in relation to this new definition. Is it too specific or too non-specific? Is it normative or descriptive? Should it be regarded as permissive or prescriptive? My conclusion to an inconclusive debate is that it is probably useful to consider critically a wide variety of definitions in trying to come to understand what pastoral care is. However, it is not necessary to adopt any one to the exclusion of others, particularly if doing so limits one's ability to discern and affirm practical pastoral care in whatever form when it is actually being performed.

Stepping Westwards

One of the aims of *A Critique of Pastoral Care* is to introduce British readers to some of the recent North American literature on pastoral care. The book was written at the end of a decade in which a major developmental change had occurred in the theory and practice of pastoral care, particularly in the USA, the source of much of the energy and innovation in this area. That change was the critical detachment of pastoral care from the therapeutic or counselling paradigm in which much of this activity had been framed since the 1950s. The 1980s saw the development of many diverse perspectives, insights, theories and methods for pastoral care; many of these have continued to grow and develop. Because we are broadly in a phase of evolution rather than revolution in our understanding of pastoral care, and many of the major North American innovators like Donald Capps and Don Browning are still pursuing tracks first adopted in the 1980s, the account of the US literature given in *A Critique* still remains largely timely and relevant.[3]

If we step westwards again now, some of the main recent developments in the theory and practice of pastoral care in the USA can be summarized under the following headings:

1. *Recovering the religious and theological tradition*   One of the most apparent effects of pursuing the secular counselling paradigm as *the* model for pastoral care was a loss of contact with theology and the specifically religious tradition. This tendency has been most vigorously redressed by theologians Tom Oden and Don Browning. Oden's dillusionment with contemporary therapies popular within the American pastoral care movement and his turn to recover the historical wisdom of the specifically religious pastoral care tradition of Gregory the Great and others was noted above (pp. 27–8). Subsequently, Oden has continued his voyage 'back to the future', which some might regard as somewhat idiosyncratic or misguided, through a series of dense volumes in the series, 'Classical Pastoral Care'.[4]

If Oden's response to the gap between Christian theology, the Christian tradition and pastoral care has been to pursue the resources of the past, Browning's has engaged more actively with the theological resources of the modern world. Browning, it may be recalled from chapter 4 above, attempts to situate pastoral care within the wider quest for practical theology, i.e. normative, action-guiding theology which focusses round practical action and within which Christian action and thinking can be situated. Within this quest, pastoral theologians, using the revised critical correla-tional method, become critical practical theologians of care (see further pp. 36ff. above). In his most recent book, Browning has extended the scope of his work beyond pastoral care to present the challenge that all theology is essentially practical theology because it is practice-laden in its origins and content.[5] This represents a fundamental, if complex and obscure act of self-assertion on the part of practical and pastoral theology to the mainstream of contemporary theology. Whether or not this will prove fruitful for pastoral care itself remains to be seen, though the quest to give a public and critical account of the fundamental values of Christian communities and their disclosure in human encounters is likely to have broad and important implications for this activity. The attempt seems a noble one, though it is not matched by much apparent enthusiasm on the part of 'non-practical' theologians.

2. *Rediscovering the Bible and the use of hermeneutic methods*
   Donald Capps continues to explore the relationship between the Bible and pastoral care (more will be said about his contribution when I comment on chapter 6 below). An additional feature which

is of growing significance (initiated by Capps himself in *Pastoral Care and Hermeneutics*) is the attention now being given to using hermeneutic methods of various sorts in exploring contemporary pastoral events and situations.[6] Two manifestations of this tendency can be cited. First, Charles Gerkin in his book, *Prophetic Pastoral Care* argues that images and metaphors drawn from the Christian tradition can be used to question the underlying myths and narratives which form the intuitive moral common sense of ordinary people and so to transform them imaginatively.[7] Drawing on the hermeneutic theories of Gadamer and Ricoeur, Gerkin proposes that pastors should have the role of being prophetic interpreters and guides of the Christian tradition who have the job of engaging contemporary world-views and situations with the images, metaphors and insights of that tradition. From a slightly different standpoint which starts more directly with experience rather than the Christian tradition, John Patton has tried to evolve more sophisticated means of theological reflection on pastoral encounters.[8] The need to find better ways of interpreting both the Christian tradition and present day pastoral situations is proving of growing interest in contemporary pastoral theory.

3. *Recognizing the corporate, communal and socio-political dimensions of pastoral care*   Using counselling as a paradigm pulled pastoral care away from its context within the ecclesiastical and wider community and colluded with a sense of a-political individualism, deeply consonant with North American society. It has been difficult for American pastoral care theorists and practitioners to engage deeply with the corporate, communal and socio-political dimensions of their activity and there is not a great deal of evidence to suggest that this is a central concern. However, Howard Clinebell has initiated an International Pastoral Care Network for Social Responsibility and there continues to be some writing on the subject.[9] Attempts to relate contemporary pastoral care to the Christian tradition and to church as opposed to therapeutic life represented by the works of Browning, Capps and Oden discussed above show awareness of corporate and communal dimensions. The social and political continue to be rather elusive however; Gerkin's *Prophetic Pastoral Care* contains little of the anger and trenchant social criticism that one might hope for from a book which claims to stand in the tradition of the classic prophets of the Old Testament.[10]

4. *Re-siting pastoral care within the horizon of values and ethics* Although one of the main features of Christianity from an outsider's point of view might be its emphasis on values and morals, these aspects were largely ignored in the pastoral care movement until Don Browning began critical and constructive work in this area. Browning has pointed up the values implicit in all human activity, and the dangers of uncritically accepting the values of secular counselling into pastoral care, which should have its own self-conscious value system based in the church, itself a community of moral discourse. Browning's value critique of the basis of Christian action and belief continues in *A Fundamental Practical Theology*. His concern for ethics and values has been taken up by a number of other authors, notably Noyce and Bondi. From a Catholic perspective, Richard Bondi considers the place of ethical leadership and communal value formation for ministers in the church community, while Gaylord Noyce is concerned to help ministers to become more effective moral counsellors with those who seek their help.[11]

5. *Escaping from crisis and pathology* The counselling paradigm tended to concentrate on the needs of people when they are in crisis. An important countervailing trend in recent pastoral care theory has been an emphasis on working holistically with people in the normal circumstances of their everyday lives and communities to maximize their well-being. In this connection, some recent theorists like James Fowler have explored the importance of the standard human life cycle and the specific tasks and challenges it throws up for faith and functioning.[12] Others have tried to create normative practical theologies for dealing with the ordinary situations of life such as the family or ageing.[13]

6. *Extending the scope and boundaries of pastoral care* Modern pastoral care theories were originally formulated in white-, male-, and clerically-dominated liberal Protestant denominations in North America. Gradually, the moorings to these origins are being slipped and pastoral care is becoming more inclusive. Pastoral care theorizing is now an inter-denominational activity. Since Vatican II with its emphasis on the humanizing role of the church and the importance of the lay apostolate, Roman Catholics in particular have begun to contribute more.[14] Feminist perspectives and pastoral care for and by women are gradually beginning to assume a more prominent role.[15] These are not only making

women visible as agents and recipients of pastoral care, but also expanding the scope of pastoral care into areas once considered 'taboo' or marginal, e.g., child abuse, domestic violence, divorce, long term disability and illness. The inter-cultural nature of appropriate pastoral care theory is being explored. The distinctive needs and contributions of, for example, black people in pastoral care are being recognized. The tensions and opportunities afforded by an international dimension in the pastoral care movement are becoming apparent. And finally, there is starting to be an inter-religious dimension to pastoral care, represented strongly in the United States by increasing interest in the subject amongst liberal Jewish rabbis. Interestingly, and disappointingly, the North American literature of pastoral care remains dominated by the professional perspective – it is written by and for professional or official pastoral carers. Perhaps the next challenge which it should tackle is that of helping to render lay people the subjects rather than the objects of care.

Many of the trends cited above, and others, are exemplified in the single most important book to be produced in the sphere of pastoral care anywhere in the last decade, the *Dictionary of Pastoral Care and Counseling*.[16] Now, for the first time, readers can gain access to a comprehensive and substantial work which will bring them up to date on most of the most recent theorizing about pastoral care in the USA and elsewhere.

There are about six hundred contributors to this volume, the majority being North Americans. It contains articles by most of the major pastoral theologians working on that continent, e.g., Capps, Browning, Clinebell, but there are contributions from other continents and countries from Israel to Japan. The authorship is thoroughly inter-denominational and inter-disciplinary with a majority of authors being academics or highly qualified practitioners within religion or psychology. Many of the contributors are women, a refreshing contrast to the British pastoral scene, and some represent non-Christian viewpoints such as those of native North American religion and Judaism. The topic coverage of their articles is comprehensive, ranging from theories (e.g., object relations theory, personality theory, Jungian psychology, spiritual direction), through techniques (e.g., behaviour therapies, Transactional Analysis), to short biographical studies of prominent pastoral theologians down the ages (e.g., Augustine of

Hippo, Richard Baxter, Friedrich Schleiermacher, Seward Hiltner).

The *Dictionary* emphasizes theology as well as psychology (there is an article on the doctrine of God and its pastoral significance by David Tracy, and there are useful articles on the pastoral significance of the work of theologians such as Barth, Tillich and the Niebuhrs). The captivity of pastoral care within the counsell-ing paradigm is challenged by articles on, for example, the sociology of pastoral care, social justice, and liberation theology. Under-represented aspects of pastoral care, such as black pastoral care and feminist challenges to pastoral care are included. Of particular interest are many articles on the history of pastoral care in various traditions and contributions on the pastoral care movement as an international phenomenon (Western Europe, East Asia and Africa are just some of the areas which receive attention).

It is almost impossible to over-emphasize the importance of this *Dictionary*. It is a bench mark and textbook of where pastoral care theory and practice have got to and are going, particularly in North America, but also in other parts of the world. One sobering aspect of its coverage is that very few British authors contributed to it and coverage of the British pastoral care scene is comparatively tiny. On the international stage, then, Britain appears to be still rather a backwater so far as significant pastoral care theory and practice is concerned, especially compared to the lively, vibrant and innova-tive situation in North America. This prompts me to turn to developments on this side of the Atlantic to assess their shape and significance.

I criticized the North American writers on pastoral care *inter alia* for a certain trendyness, superficiality and remoteness, related to the fact that much of the US pastoral care industry is dependent on academics who are often not pastoral practitioners and who produce books at a quite alarming rate (see pp. 30ff. above). I think I still stand by this criticism. British writers on pastoral care at their best embody a sturdy, deep and practical contribution to pastoral care which is continuing to develop. The problem is that it is not developing very far or very fast. Up until about 1990 the SPCK 'New Library of Pastoral Care' was producing a steady stream of useful titles, often arising from or closely related to actual pastoral practice.[17] A number of other significant books on pastoral care were also published at the end of the 1980s by authors such as David Deeks, Michael Wilson and Duncan Forrester and his colleagues.[18] However, more recently there has been a disappointing lack of major publications in this field. One can only speculate on the reasons for this. One contributory factor may be that certain major authors who helped to shape and dynamize the pastoral care theory field in the 1980s have now moved on to other work. This would appear to be true in the case of Michael Jacobs who contributed three titles to the SPCK series and in that of Alastair Campbell who edited the British *Dictionary of Pastoral Care* published in 1987 and whose other books had a seminal influence on the regeneration of British pastoral care theory.[19] A further feature may be that younger or more recently appointed academics in the field have not yet got into their stride with publication (not helped by being over-pressed in a market-style higher education system) and may find it difficult to get into print in a recession-smitten book trade. A third factor may be that practitioners who might have once had more time to write books are themselves hard pressed, either in caring agencies which are under strain or within the churches where person power is at a premium and time and money for study leave is hard to obtain.

Whatever the reasons for lack of systematic, extended discourses on pastoral care theory, it cannot be said to reflect a lack of pastoral practice or pastoral education within Britain. There are probably more students studying pastoral care, counselling and practical theology now than ever before and there is no reason to suppose that empirical pastoral need has grown markedly less. (There are new courses on applied theology, ministerial education and pastoral theology at the Universities of Newcastle, Kent and Oxford as well as at a number of other colleges; the larger theological colleges also offer pastoral education on a wider scale than ever before.) It is to be hoped, therefore, that what we are presently experiencing is a temporary doldrum in publication and the production of innovative pastoral theory, not a permanent feature. This hope must not, however, be allowed to obscure the fact that pastoral theology and pastoral care are still grossly intellectually under-capitalized. It is a perverse tribute to our native contempt both for the intellect and practice that practical theology is still a poor relation, taught mostly by people who have little specific training in the subject area and who are not expected to stay in it for very long.

Turning to the content of British pastoral practice and theory, there are many similarities in trends with the North American situation. Although many of the British books cited above deal with practical pastoral situations from a more empirical standpoint than that of many North American authors, it is possible to see many similarities and parallels. This, of course, is not surprising as we have to import much of our theory from the far side of the Atlantic and we share many cultural similarities.

Much British pastoral writing finds little use for the religious and theological tradition. However, the recovery of some elements of it is represented by the work of Wesley Carr.[20] Carr's *The Pastor as Theologian* is a complex and demanding text which draws on psychodynamic thought and some of the classic Christian doctrines (incarnation, atonement, and creation/resurrection) to help pastors develop usable roles in ministry which are faithful both to tradition and to the realities of the present situation.

Unlike the North Americans, British pastoral care theorists show little enthusiasm for engagement in dialogue with the Bible (perhaps the Bible has a more central legitimating function in North American society in general and in churches in particular, especially with the fundamentalist movement providing an articulate and critical horizon for pastors and theologians).[21] However, there is a great deal more interest in hermeneutic and interpretative methods, especially when it comes to theological reflection. Book length contributions in this area have come from the pens of John Foskett and David Lyall, David Deeks and Laurie Green.[22] The imperative to find ways of interpreting practical and pastoral experience theologically has also given rise to a series of interesting papers on theological reflection in the main pastoral studies journal.[23] The impetus for this interest has come from the needs of theological educators working with students in pastoral studies, from modern developments in textual hermeneutics, from the empirical reflective methods on practice of liberation theologians, and from developments in reflective education throughout the professions.[24] Altogether, this looks like one of the more promising and sophisticated areas in British pastoral care.

The same cannot be said with quite such confidence in relation to the theme of recognizing the corporate, communal and socio-political dimensions of pastoral care. Although there is a trickle of interest in the form of the odd paper or book in this area there is relatively little interest in politicizing pastoral care or exploring its corporate and communal dimensions.[25] This is somewhat ironic when it is considered that British society has continued to become much more politicized over the last ten years.

On the question of re-siting pastoral care within the horizon of values and ethics, interest in this is perhaps most evident when someone calls for a retreat from non-judgmental counselling techniques back into a more definite pastoral identity.[26] As often as not, this call provokes the response that we have not yet learned all that we need to from counselling and therapeutic techniques.[27] All this is evidence that the debate over values and purpose in pastoral care is very much alive and well. It is just unfortunate that the debate never seems to advance very much.

It should be apparent from the titles mentioned as comprising the SPCK 'New Library of Pastoral Care' that the focus of pastoral care theory in Britain is gradually turning from the focus on crisis and pathology initially engendered by the encounter with counselling to a more holistic and preventive approach. This nurturing positive approach is particularly apparent in the work of Michael Wilson who for years has advocated a turn away from individualized problem-centredness to corporate growth in community.[28] It is good to see an interest evolving in improving, e.g., marriages, the ordinary working lives of ministers, the lives of families. One can only hope for the sake of all involved that this is a tendency which will prove to be permanent within the British pastoral care movement.

Finally, there is some sign that the scope and boundaries of pastoral care theory and practice in Britain are growing, if all too painfully slowly. Elaine Graham and her colleagues are starting to develop an indigenous women's pastoral theology which is broadening the purview of pastoral care into previously 'taboo' areas such as domestic violence, child abuse, single parenthood and divorce.[29] Emmanuel Lartey, a Ghanaian theologian trained in Britain is doing much to raise inter-cultural and inter-racial issues in pastoral care and counselling.[30] Some interesting work is being done on pastoral care between faiths, paticularly between Jews and Christians.[31] The British pastoral care and counselling network remains in contact with the wider international scene, though no recent work seems to have had the international impact on that scene since the publication of Alastair Campbell's *Redis-*

covering Pastoral Care over ten years ago. In the light of the low priority given to pastoral care and the small number of teachers in this discipline in Britain, however, we should perhaps be surprised that so much *is* happening rather than regretting its rather circumscribed extent.

Once one turns from the literature of pastoral care to ask what is happening 'on the ground' an already fragmented picture disintegrates even further. It is clear that old-fashioned pastoral care – hints and tips given by older clergy to younger ones in an apprenticeship model – still continues. At the same time, pastoral counselling courses for clergy and lay people abound and flourish, reflecting a fundamental belief in the merit and efficacy of counselling on the part of many. The participation of lay people and women in the official pastoral care of the churches grows as the churches themselves decline in numbers, reflecting as much the person power needs of the churches as enlightenment about the equality and talents of all within the Christian community. By contrast with this move to involve more people in pastoral care, there are moves from the Association of Pastoral Care and Counselling and the College of Health Care Chaplains, amongst others, to professionalize pastoral care and set out competencies and training courses for it in a much more definite and vigorous way which would lead to professional accreditation. Meanwhile, organizations like the Westminster Pastoral Foundation which set out to provide pastoral counselling within some kind of religious horizon have severed their links with the churches to become entirely secular – the Foundation now rather coyly calls itself WPF. Evangelical churches have taken up rather contrary positions on pastoral care and counselling. Some are rather taken with the notion of Christian counselling; others prefer the unmediated and untutored gifts and guidance of the Holy Spirit to increase the well-being of their members. In the mainstream churches, there is much interest in spirituality and prayer which is paralleled by the growth of the New Age spiritualities outside the church.[32] This has largely failed to attract the attention and interest of pastoral care practitioners and theorists, though it is clearly enormously dynamic in practical terms for many people, both clerical and lay. Finally, it is depressing to note that pastoral care contributes very little originally and overtly to wider debates about care and well-being in a secular society, importing from other disciplines and theories rather than exporting to them on the whole.

What interim verdict, then, can be made on the theory and practice of British pastoral care based on the evidence cited here? The judgment that I make is that pastoral care is variegated incoherent and fragmented, both in practice and in theory. There is energy in it, and it can be fruitful in small ways. However, despite thirty years of pastoral studies teaching in universities and colleges we still await a substantial flourishing of interest and expertise in pastoral care. The main driving force behind such interest as there is in pastoral care seems to come even now from the skills and theories of therapy and counselling. It is counselling with its relative theoretical and practical coherence and usefulness to which people either adhere or react.[33] Unfortunately, pastoral care is still not regarded as important enough either by the churches or by educational institutions to merit much credibility or resource. This means that, for better or worse, incoherence, fragmentation and variegation are here to stay for the immediate future. The area is likely to remain in the doldrums of lack of significant academic enquiry and practical innovation for some time to come. However, this need not prevent me from continuing to develop new aspects of critique in my comments on the original chapters of the book which follow.

Ethics and Pastoral Care

Of all the chapters in this book, it is this one I would most like to completely re-write. In its own terms and on the premises given, the chapter stands up perfectly well. However, I have come to think that the basic assumptions made about the nature of ethics are not necessarily helpful. Indeed, some of the practical problems identified in relating ethics to pastoral care are a product of these unhelpful assumptions.

The original chapter explores a set of uncomfortable and *prima facie* irreconcilable polarities – between the love of God and the justice of God, between the need for care and the need for values in practical theology, and between the need for compassion and the need for confrontation on the part of pastors in actual practical situations. Some intellectual and practical techniques were suggested for resolving these tensions, but I remained dissatisfied with their implicit polarization. It was not until I explored feminist thinking in general, and feminist ethical thinking in particular, more that I was able to identify the source of my dissatisfaction.

Feminist ethical thinking starts with the experience of women.[34] In broad terms, this focusses on connectedness, relationship, closeness and making things work in ordinary, concrete, practical human situations. Patriarchal ethics, which had shaped my own thinking tends, on the other hand, to be largely abstract, remote, detached, generalized, rationalistic, cognitive and encapsulated. It is often based round extreme and rare situations, usually problematic ones which pose as moral dilemmas; it appears individualistic, atomized, and either over- or under-optimistic about human nature and human action. It does not cope very well with particular situations in real life and it is unwilling to recognize social construction and context. Frequently, it has the feeling of a linguistic game. It may be useful for clarification of thought and concepts and producing a certain kind of intellectual muscle. However, it is unable to describe or contribute to the everyday lives of most people I know, especially in a creative and practical rather than a merely analytic and abstract kind of way.

Feminist ethics has shown me why it is difficult to relate ethics to pastoral care. This is because the traditional patriarchal way of thinking about ethics and indeed about God is abstract and disconnected from real-life situations in a counter-factual way. Much of theology and ethics was formulated by upper class white men who created ideas of God and the good in their own image.[35] It seems that for reasons of psychology and social upbringing, men tend to be much more concerned with abstract rules and principles than women who are inclined to give priority to preseving relationships in concrete situations.[36] Traditional ethics, formulated by men, has ignored the more holistic experience and perceptions of women, even thinking of women as less moral because less concerned with the rational element in moral perception. This has meant that it has missed out on vast swathes of actual moral insight and experience.

The feminist critique of ethics based on abstract principles rather than whole persons and actual relationships has been amplified from other quarters. Mary Midgley, a moral philosopher herself, has demonstrated the absurdity of trying to abstract elements of intuition and emotion from ethical thinking and moral action. To take emotions and the totality of human beings more seriously is rational not irrational, she argues.[37] This plea is underlined from a psychoanalytic perspective by Tom Kitwood.[38]

He argues that Western moralism has been dominated by white rationalistic men who have used ethics often as a form of social control. It has been distorted by its concentration on the intellectual, the ideal and the power of thought. It is a weak force for change, failing to deal adequately with issues of motivation, and not dealing with the moral activity of non-intellectuals. We need to attend instead to habitual human action towards others, ordinary people's moral ideas, their attempts at resolving moral dilemmas in theory and practice, moral character and integrity, and the social context of moral psychology, hitherto individualistic and concentrated on the theoretical aspects of moral development abstracted from social context.

The dominance of the view of persons as rational cognitive actors who think first and then act on their rational conclusions is untenable. Depth psychology suggests that persons are divided, having unconscious and preconscious levels of existence which constantly affect moral belief and action, often preventing genuine concern for others. Skill in theoretical moral judgment is not the same as skill in moral performance (as the lives of many academic ethicists reveal all too clearly!) and the development of the latter requires far more attention. Kitwood points up the socio-political and institutional factors impinging on moral development and action and criticizes the 'top-down', ideological and intellect-biassed nature of moral discourse formulated largely by the rich and powerful.

It would be good to see an awareness of the complexity, contextuality, developmental, practical, emotional, personal and fragmentary nature of human moral development and action as well as feminist insights into ethics informing the relationship of ethics to pastoral care. This would do much to relativize the importance of having the 'right' rational principles so prized by Browning, of reconciling these principles in theory and practice when they conflict, and of having to wonder how and when to confront people with them. At the same time, it would encourage pastoral carers to take the ordinary moral experience of people seriously and suggest that pastors should not be afraid to help people to explore and understand their experience more deeply instead of trying to conform themselves to some cognitive ideal. My conclusion is that we need to pay less attention to verbalized theories, paradoxes and polarities on the abstract level and to give more to the people and values which we encounter in everyday relationships. This will not mean that issues of value and morality will disappear or become universally unproblematic, nor does it mean abandoning a wider search for justice and equality. But it does mean that they can become matters of concrete concern and action for all people rather than matters of intellectual perplexity and contradiction for professional pastors. This might enable us to embody more clearly concern for others, as well as living down some negative aspects of the past:

> Moral discourse in western culture has been corrupted by two pernicious ingredients. One is a kind of 'pure' intellectualism . . . suggesting that we can know the good in some timeless, separate and disembodied . . . way. The other is a conglomeration of deprecating and masochistic ideas about human nature derived mainly from the Augustinian form of Christianity . . .[39]

It would also enable us to deal more creatively with some of the difficult polarities and dualisms which so plagued my original chapter.

Discipline and Pastoral Care

I have little to add to my original critique and reconstruction of discipline in pastoral care. The main thing is to re-emphasize the fact that discipline can easily become a tool of social control. A number of studies illustrate the way in which, e.g., the Catholic church historically used the confessional to gain and maintain a kind of uncritical social conformity.[40] As we have seen, ethics can be used as an instrument or social control by the rich and powerful who devise and articulate moral discourse, against the poor and weak who are regarded as immoral and feckless:

> There has always been a tendency for those who have privilege in societies with deeply structured domination to advance the view that human nature is 'essentially' self-seeking and un-trustworthy, and therefore to be curbed.[41]

At a time when Government is once again raising the fantasy of total moral decay in society and calling upon the churches to become involved in the process of teaching people 'right and wrong' it will be important for pastoral carers and others to be clear that calls for discipline and self-control lead to growth and self-development, not just to a kind of mindless conformity which suits those in power both in church and state. The last time I heard the word 'discipline' being used in Anglican circles, two clergy were being arraigned by their bishop for adhering to the free-thinking views of Don Cupitt and for admitting to not believing in the physical resurrection of the body. This small vignette is a parable of just how negative and coercive discipline may become.

Politics and Pastoral Care

It is curious that after a decade of British society becoming increasingly more politicized, the break up of consensus about the Welfare State, and a number of acrimonious public exchanges between church and state that pastoral care appears to be less politically aware and involved than it was a decade ago. No major books have been published on the political dimensions and implications of pastoral care since Selby's *Liberating God* in 1983. The lack of theoretical perspectives seems to reflect quietism and individualism in practice. The decline of political awareness and interest is difficult to explain. It may stem from a re-assertion of the innate conservatism of the church in a time when that institution is declining and becoming poorer. Perhaps people no longer believe in the possibility of real political change after so long under one government and the loss of credibility of alternatives to individualistic capitalism with the collapse of communism. In the case of hospital chaplains, the example I considered in the original chapter above, they, like many other public service workers are very much more clearly under the control of managers and are more insecure in their jobs. This makes it difficult for them to act as critics of their institutions and of the social order generally. The fact that it is very difficult to contemplate action for change and greater social justice does not mean that the challenge of politics to pastoral care has gone away. In a society where the gap between rich and poor continues to widen with enormous adverse consequences for the poor in terms of their health and well-being the need for socio-politically aware and committed pastoral care has never been greater.[42]

The Bible and Pastoral Care

I noted above that there is still little evidence to show that British pastoral theorists other than fundamentalists are interested in exploring the relationship of the Bible to pastoral care.[43] That this is not the case in America is evidenced by Donald Capp's curious book, *Reframing*. Having outlined the techniques of reframing, a psychological technique which involves helping people to change their perspective on events so that in turn they can change their attitudes and actions, Capps resorts to the Bible to show that (*a*) Jesus was a skilled reframer in that he used parables, stories and riddles which changed people's view of themselves and their world, and that (*b*) Job's comforters can be seen as exemplars of modern counselling techniques. Thus Eliphaz is a supportive counsellor, Bildad a crisis counsellor and Zophar an ethical, value and meaning counsellor! All of their methods are inadequate and it is God who gets it right in helping Job by reframing his situation for second order change.[44] It is difficult to work out what Capps is up to in using a piece of biblical text in this way. Is he being ironically deconstructive, indulging in parody, or just practising good, old-fashioned eisegesis? While reframing may or may not be a good pastoral technique it is difficult to see that hermeneutic value or respect is affirmed by trying to exemplify modern counselling techniques out of an ancient document. There certainly seems to be no sense in which the biblical text is allowed autonomously to question present world-views; it is merely used to amplify and dignify the use of one very particular pastoral technique which is thereby endowed with a halo of biblical (indeed divine!) authority and veracity. If Capps is pointing the direction for the use of the Bible in pastoral care theory and practice, it might be better if it was allowed to revert to being a closed and silent book.

Interlude

The final part of *A Critique of Pastoral Care* represents something of a protest against an instrumental, ratio-technical world-view pervading pastoral care. I argued that while the instrumental, technique-focussed view on people and problems offered many advantages, it presented too narrow a view of the chaotic, tragic, mysterious reality of experience.

In the last few years, it is probably true to say that people have come to feel that the world is even more mysterious and chaotic than it has ever been. Amidst a long world economic recession there have been almost endless succession of major social changes (the collapse of communism in Eastern Europe, the radical re-shaping of the Welfare State in Britain being but two examples). Paradoxically, this seems to have actually increased the demand for techniques of ratio-technical control in both personal and institutional life.

On the individual level, there has been an explosion of counselling and the search for professional techniques of interven-tion. Reframing, which helps professionals intervene briefly (therefore economically) and directively in individuals' lives, is just one example of the search for quick and efficient 'fixes' to complex human problems.[45] Another set of techniques which profoundly affecting the shape and character of social institutions (including the churches) are those of general management.

Management techniques, to the greater use of which the Archbishop of Canterbury has committed the Church of England, embody powerful visions, metaphors and understandings of reality. Human beings can control the world and create a better future if they use the right techniques. Individuals must be subordinate to greater goals decided by their superiors. Rela-tionships are fundamentally hierarchical and require clear lines of upward accountability and downward responsibility. Everything worth doing can in some way be measured. Clear directions can be set for the future and they can then be attained. Goals should be limited and clearly expressible in a single mission statement which determines the work of all in the organization. Productivity and profitability determines the value of all individual and organiza-tional endeavour. The guiding metaphors of managerialism, based on undergirding concept of competing in a hostile market-place, can be characterized as narrow, over-optimistic, Pelagian and utopian (in a way which puts Marx to shame!). They are trivializing, and unrealistic about the nature and pluriformity of human beings (who have many goals not just one mission), as well as about the chaotic nature of the world in which we live.

The beautiful simplicity of vision offered by managerialism is seductive in a time of uncertainty. It is likely to influence pastoral care in two ways. First, managerial techniques are beginning directly to shape the way in which professional ministry and pastoral care is carried out.[46] Secondly, the implicit theologies and world-views of managerialism will affect the essential nature and character of the churches in which they are used, together with people's views of themselves and each other, possibly threatening the emergence of pluriformity, shared authority, leadership from the bottom and perspectives from the margins.[47] In the light of the continued growth of the quasi-scientific nostrums of management and counselling, I believe my chapters on failure and laughter have potentially more critical power and relevance than they did when I first penned them.

Failure in Pastoral Care

Having affirmed the value of acknowledging the 'surd' dimen-sions of failure and laughter in pastoral care as in human activity generally, I do have one reservation about the chapter on failure. In writing it, I was much under the influence of Maria Boulding's powerful and inspiring book, *Gateway to Hope*. It was she who described Jesus as 'history's greatest failure'. It was in the light of that description that I considered the Christian theological tradition. I have subsequently come to see this tradition as far more confused, paradoxical and ambiguous. Graham Shaw, for example, suggests that St Paul was essentially rather an over-weening triumphalist waiting for the day of Christ's triumph which would result in the exaltation of his faithful followers as well.[48] In this sense, all the New Testament writers can be seen to be writing with a sense of sure and complete triumph. One of my reviewers noted that if Jesus was in fact history's greatest failure no one would have heard of him. All this requires that I acknowledge that Jesus was less of a failure than I presented him as being. It also raises the question of to what extent those who feel or experience failure can really identify with Jesus or he with them. To do justice to this question and the complex, mixed messages about triumph and failure within the Christian tradition would take a book in itself. I hope to do some more work on this in relation to the themes of guilt and shame in the near future. In the meantime, I think the chapter still has practical value for those who face up to the sharp pain and reality of failure in pastoral care.

Laughter and Pastoral Care

A Critique of Pastoral Care was completed just as the academically fashionable intellectual movement of post-modernism was coming into the centre of British academic life. Post-modernism is notoriously difficult to define and understand – there is even debate about whether it really exists as a discrete set of ideas and assumptions. However, some of its main features may be taken to be (*a*) there is no reality outside language so language and signs *are* reality – this means, *inter alia*, that language cannot refer and there is no way to get at, e.g., the objective existence of God or even of physical phenomena; (*b*) there is no meta-language, meta-narrative, or meta-theory through which all things can be connected or represented – universal and eternal truths, if they exist at all, cannot be specified; (*c*) we must take seriously the reality of ephemerality, fragmentation, discontinuity and the chaotic.[49] All of which seems to resonate well with the judgment made by a reviewer that this book, and pastoral care in general, seem incomplete and without coherent underlying assumptions.[50] Perhaps pastoral care is a proto-post-modern activity!

Whatever the reality of that speculation, it is important to point up the potentially creative challenge presented to pastoral care by post-modern writers, specifically by Don Cupitt. The reason that the challenge is presented here in my comments on laughter is because irony – the possibility of standing apart from and relativizing one's own language and understanding – is one of the key notes of the post-modern world-view.[51] Cupitt, in his many books, accepts the tenets of post-modernism and believes that we live in a contingent world of signs.[52] There is no heaven above or hell beneath, no objective God who can be accessed by prayer, no hierarchical order of the universe which is more real than what we perceive. We skim along the surface of language and signs like flies on a pond and our real life is coterminous with our involvement with this surface – there is no depth which we can plumb, or life beyond this. In this apparently tragic situation we have the possibility of participating fully in the world of sign-making and language. We can be artists of meaning and understanding, committed to what we are doing because of its creative pleasure, but ironical because we recognize that our creations are contingent and must be placed alongside the creations of others – there is no final vocabulary or metaphor which is permanent, eternally valid or endlessly authoritative: 'Everything is secondary, and religion is a joyful – and also a self-mocking and ironical – acceptance and affirmation of transcience.'[53] In a Zen-like way, Cupitt suggests that we must take the world and our lives infinitely seriously while realizing that, like our classical view of God, we are creators, those who make words flesh, who can literally play with meanings, metaphors and symbols adding our own values to life. Cupitt sees this as the real meaning of incarnation – we now have the task of doing what only God could do, being creative through the use of our own words.

I would not want to claim that Cupitt's thought is uncontroversial or worthy of attention in every respect, but I do want to argue that his work is suggestive for pastoral care. In the first place in its unrelenting humanism, it forms a critique of historic, dogmatic, monolithic hierarchical Christian practice which has done so much to reduce human potential. Cupitt argues, for example, that Christian ethics has been little more than applied sexism and a way of exacting social conformity at the price of human joy and spontaneity.[54] In the second place, many of Cupitt's ideas are positively suggestive for, and consonant with, contemporary pastoral care. He places great value on human life in the present, analysing the contemporary human condition and looking for theoretical and practical ways to address this. He affirms the embodied human being, the importance of life valuing life, the place of desire, the equality of women, the importance of creation, the search for meaning, and the transforming possibilities of words, metaphors and stories. It is worth reading his work just to clear one's mind of half-truths and misconceptions about the world and theology. But more than this, the seriousness (and lightness) with which Cupitt explores contemporary reality deserves a considered response and dialogue from pastoral practitioners and theorists. If, living in a post-modern world, the fragmentation and incompleteness of pastoral care allows the possibility of trying to see what it might be to be a post-modern pastor relating better to other who also live in fragmented and incomplete worlds then a partial defect may be turned to very considerable relevance and advantage.

Conclusion

A week may be a long time in politics, but in the theory and practice of pastoral care five years is quite a short time. The trends I identified in the first edition of this book have in many ways continued during this period. This is a good thing in the sense that my critique remains broadly relevant. It is a bad thing, however, in so far as it means that not as much of fundamental significance has happened as one might hope. North American writers continue to be prolific, but often not profound; their tenure-tracing, professionalized approach to writing about pastoral care can be deeply unappealing. In Britain, on the other hand, development is blotchy and uneven. 'There is a lot of periphery but not much core', is how one of my colleagues describes it. She neatly characterizes our native pastoral care literature as 'still quite churchy, moderately clerical, reluctantly patriarchal and resolutely untheoretical.'[55]

It is my hope that in five years' time there may be many new developments in pastoral care for which a new critique can be offered and that a core to pastoral care theory and practice will have emerged in addition to the lively periphery which is presently there. However, given that one reviewer of this book noted five years ago that, 'The literature (of pastoral care) now being produced is unpredictable in quality and without a set of coherent underlying assumptions linking one work to another,' I have to admit that I travel in general hope rather than in specific expectation.[56]

Notes

Notes

Introduction

1. Alastair V. Campbell (ed.), *A Dictionary of Pastoral Care*, SPCK 1987, now goes some way towards remedying this situation, but the articles contained therein are necessarily rather brief.

2. The most important single contribution to pastoral care theory in the USA recently has been the publication of the 'Theology and Pastoral Care' series under the editorship of Don S. Browning.

Titles so far published are: Herbert Anderson, *The Family and Pastoral Care* (1984), Don S. Browning, *Religious Ethics and Pastoral Care* (1983), Alastair V. Campbell, *Professionalism and Pastoral Care* (1985, published in the UK as *Paid to Care?* (SPCK 1985)), Donald Capps, *Life Cycle Theory and Pastoral Care* (1983), *Pastoral Care and Hermeneutics* (1984), Regis A. Duffy, *A Roman Catholic Theology of Pastoral Care* (1985), Robert L. Katz, *Pastoral Care and the Jewish Tradition* (1985), K. Brynholf Lyon, *Toward a Practical Theology of Aging* (1985), Thomas C. Oden, *Care of Souls in the Classic Tradition* (1984), Elaine Ramshaw, *Ritual and Pastoral Care* (1987), Nelson S. T. Thayer, *Spirituality and Pastoral Care* (1985), Ralph L. Underwood, *Empathy and Confrontation in Pastoral Care* (1985). All are published in Philadelphia by Fortress Press. Many will be alluded to in the chapters which follow. The aim of the series, as outlined by Don Browning, is to '(1) retrieve the theological and ethical foundations of the Judaeo-Christian tradition for pastoral care, (2) develop lines of communication between pastoral theology and the other disciplines of theology, (3) create an ecumenical dialogue on pastoral care, and (4) do this in such a way as to affirm yet go beyond the recent preoccupation of pastoral care with secular psychotherapy and the other social sciences.' (Browning, op. cit., p. 9).

1. What is Pastoral Care Anyway?

1. William V. Arnold, *Introduction to Pastoral Care*, Philadelphia: Westminster 1982, p. 10.

2. Michael H. Taylor, *Learning to Care*, SPCK 1983, chs 2 and 3.

3. William A. Clebsch and Charles R. Jaekle, *Pastoral Care in Historical Perspective*, New York: Aronson 1975.

4. Ibid., p. 13.

5. Peter Brown, *Augustine of Hippo*, Faber 1969.

6. Anthony Russell, *The Clerical Profession*, SPCK 1980; Peter Davie, *Pastoral Care and the Parish*, Blackwell 1983. Further material on the history of pastoral care may be gained from John C. McNeill, *A History of the Cure of Souls*, New York: Harper & Row, 1977.

7. But see Peter Ribbins, 'Pastoral care in schools' in Alastair V. Campbell (ed.), *A Dictionary of Pastoral Care*, SPCK 1987.

8. See Taylor, op. cit., chs 2 and 3.

9. Martin Thornton, *Pastoral Theology: A Reorientation*, SPCK 1961. A more recent book which maintains the priority of spiritual direction in pastoral care but also engages in dialogue with the contemporary counselling movement is Kenneth Leech, *Soul Friend*, Sheldon Press 1977.

10. Frank Wright, *The Pastoral Nature of the Ministry*, SCM Press 1980, p. 9.

11. Eduard Thurneysen, *A Theology of Pastoral Care*, Richmond, Va.: John Knox Press 1962, p. 15.

12. Clebsch and Jaekle, op. cit., p. 4 (emphasis omitted). Clebsch and Jaekle draw heavily on the thinking of Seward Hiltner in arriving at this definition. See further e.g. Seward Hiltner, *Preface to Pastoral Theology*, Nashville: Abingdon 1958.

13. Cf. McNeill, op. cit., p. 330.

14. Colossians 1.28 (RSV). I owe the application of this passage to pastoral care to Dr Haddon Willmer of the University of Leeds.

15. Alastair V. Campbell, *Rediscovering Pastoral Care*, Darton, Longman & Todd 1981.

16. Wright, op. cit., ch. 1.

17. Roger Hooker and Christopher Lamb, *Love the Stranger*, SPCK 1986, contains a discussion of the importance of patience and waiting in pastoral care.

18. Alastair V. Campbell, *Paid to Care?*, SPCK 1985, p. 1.

19. This typology of the components of ministry is drawn from Henri J. M. Nouwen, *Creative Ministry*, New York: Doubleday 1978.

20. See further e.g. William H. Willimon, *Worship as Pastoral Care*, Nashville: Abingdon 1978; S. Pattison, 'Pastoral Care and Worship' in J. G. Davies (ed.), *A New Dictionary of Liturgy and Worship*, SCM Press 1986.

21. Howard Clinebell, *Basic Types of Pastoral Care and Counselling*, SCM Press 1984, p. 43.

2. *Stepping Westwards*

1. R. A. Lambourne, 'With love to the USA' in M. A. H. Melinsky, *Religion and Medicine*, London: SCM Press 1970, pp. 132–45.

2. Thomas C. Oden, *Care of Souls in the Classic Tradition*, Philadelphia: Fortress 1984, p. 32. For more on Clinical Pastoral Education see D. Lyall, 'Clinical Pastoral Education' in Alastair V. Campbell (ed.), *A Dictionary of Pastoral Care*, SPCK 1987.

3. Oden, op. cit., pp. 22–4.

4. See Howard J. Clinebell, *Basic Types of Pastoral Care and Counselling*, SCM Press 1984, pp. 46–9.

5. I have followed Fierro in my characterization of the features of the theology of Bultmann and Tillich here. See A. Fierro, *The Militant Gospel*, SCM Press 1977, ch. 1.

6. Howard J. Clinebell, *Basic Types of Pastoral Counseling*, Nashville: Abingdon 1966; Clinebell, *Basic Types of Pastoral Care and Counselling*. Clinebell's other books reveal the width and depth of his commitment to drawing on many types of counselling theory. See e.g. Howard J. Clinebell, *Growth Counseling*, Nashville: Abingdon 1979, *Contemporary Growth Therapies*, Nashville: Abingdon 1981.

7. William V. Arnold, *Introduction to Pastoral Care*, Philadelphia: Westminster 1982, p. 9.

8. Gerard Egan, *The Skilled Helper*, second edition, Monterey: Brooks-Cole 1982, Eugene Kennedy, *On Becoming a Counsellor*, Dublin: Gill & Macmillan 1977.

9. Robert L. Katz, *Pastoral Care and the Jewish Tradition*, Philadelphia: Fortress 1985.

10. R. A. Lambourne, 'Objections to a National Pastoral Organisation', *Contact 35*, 1971, 24–31. Lambourne's papers remain seminal in thinking about pastoral care and are collected together in Michael Wilson, (ed.), *Explorations in Health and Salvation*, Institute for the Study of Worship and Religious Architecture, University of Birmingham 1983 obtainable from Department of Theology, University of Birmingham, Birmingham B15 2TT. See also Clinebell's reply to Lambourne in *Contact 36*, 1971, 26–9. A good discussion and *resumé* of this debate is to be found in Alastair V. Campbell, *Paid to Care?*, SPCK 1985.

11. Frank Wright, *The Pastoral Nature of the Ministry*, SCM Press 1980, ch. 1.

12. Bernice Martin, *A Sociology of Contemporary Cultural Change*, Blackwell 1981, p. 193.

13. Ibid., p. 190.

14. See e.g. Thomas C. Oden, *Kerygma and Counseling*, San Francisco: Harper & Row, 1978 which explores analogies between the psychotherapeutic process and divine self-disclosure, and Thomas C. Oden, *Game Free*, New York: Harper & Row 1974, which looks at some of the relationships raised by Transactional Analysis.

15. Oden, *Care of Souls in the Classic Tradition*, p. 24.

16. Ibid., p. 24.

17. Thomas C. Oden, *Pastoral Theology*, San Francisco: Harper & Row 1983.

18. Clinebell, *Basic Types of Pastoral Care and Counselling*, p. 10.

19. Ibid., p. 10.

20. Ibid., pp. 31–45.

21. See ibid., pp. 62–4.

22. See above Introduction, n. 2.

23. Oden, *Care of Souls in the Classic Tradition*, p. 24.
24. See further, e.g., Wesley Carr, *Brief Encounters*, SPCK 1985, ch. 4.

3. Ethics and Pastoral Care

1. The foregoing points are contained in David Cook, *The Moral Maze*, SPCK 1983, introduction.
2. Thomas C. Oden, *Care of Souls in the Classic Tradition*, Philadelphia: Fortress 1984, p. 24.
3. Felix Biestek, *The Casework Relationship*, George Allen & Unwin 1961; Alastair V. Campbell and Roger Higgs, *In that Case*, Darton, Longman & Todd 1982; R. John Elford, 'Moral issues in Pastoral Care' in Alastair V. Campbell, (ed.), *A Dictionary of Pastoral Care* SPCK 1987.
4. Don S. Browning, *The Moral Context of Pastoral Care*, Philadelphia: Westminster 1976.
5. Op. cit., p. 98.
6. Ibid., p. 99.
7. Ibid., p. 106.
8. Ibid., p. 26.
9. See, e.g. Viktor E. Frankl, *The Doctor and the Soul*, Penguin Books 1972; William Glasser, *Reality Therapy*, New York: Harper & Row 1965.
10. See Alastair V. Campbell, *Paid to Care?*, SPCK 1985, p.1.
11. Don S. Browning, *Religious Ethics and Pastoral Care*, Philadelphia: Fortress 1983. Some of the articles in Don S. Browning (ed.), *Practical Theology*, San Francisco: Harper & Row 1983, amplify and give background to *Religious Ethics and Pastoral Care*.
12. Op. cit., pp. 51–2.
13. Ibid., pp. 50–2.
14. The five stages of practical moral reasoning are outlined in ibid., ch. 6.
15. 'We can ask, for example, concerning any particular individual, What are (1) her dominant metaphors of ultimacy; (2) her moral style and patterns; (3) the patterns, modalities, or themes of interaction she used to meet her ends; (4) the social and cultural forces that shape her context; and (5) the roles and practical rules by which she tries to live her life?' (Ibid., p. 101).
16. For a consideration of some of the problems associated with using 'secular' insights and social science disciplines see Stephen Pattison, 'The use of the behavioural sciences in pastoral studies' in Paul H. Ballard (ed.), *The Foundations of Pastoral Studies and Practical Theology*, Cardiff: Faculty of Theology 1986.
17. John C. Hoffman, *Ethical Confrontation in Counseling*, Chicago: University of Chicago Press 1979, p. 2.
18. See further Howard Clinebell, *Basic Types of Pastoral Care and Counselling*, SCM Press 1984, ch. 6; Geoffrey Peterson, *Conscience and Caring*, Philadelphia: Fortress 1982, ch. 2.
19. These characteristics are largely culled from Ian T. Ramsey, 'On not being judgmental', *Contact 30*, 1970, 2–15.

20. See Ramsey, op. cit.

21. See further Paul Halmos, *The Faith of the Counsellors*, Constable 1965.

22. Browning, *Religious Ethics and Pastoral Care*, p. 122.

23. Ralph L. Underwood, *Empathy and Confrontation in Pastoral Care*, Philadelphia: Fortress 1985.

24. Ibid., p. 90.

25. Ibid., pp. 92–4.

26. In Freudian terms, an appeal is made to the ego-ideal rather than the superego. The ego-ideal represents the area of positive aspiration in the psyche rather than that of negative parental prohibition. See further Hoffman, op. cit., ch. 4.

27. Browning characterizes the nature of this exploration as 'flexibility and playfulness' (*Religious Ethics and Pastoral Care*, p. 101).

4. *Discipline and Pastoral Care*

1. See p. 13 above.

2. Seward Hiltner, *Preface to Pastoral Theology*, Nashville: Abingdon 1958, p. 65.

3. Cf. II Cor. 2.5ff. C. K. Barrett regards the exercise of corporate discipline over offenders as one of the signs of the apostolicity of the church. See further C. K. Barrett, *The Signs of an Apostle*, Epworth 1970.

4. George Herbert, *The Country Parson*, SPCK 1981, p. 69.

5. Op. cit., p. 31.

6. Ibid., p. 55.

7. Ibid., p. 76.

8. Ibid., p. 79.

9. Don S. Browning, *The Moral Context of Pastoral Care*, Philadelphia: Westminster 1976, p. 20.

10. Op. cit., p. 21.

11. Ibid., p. 21.

12. See Jürgen Moltmann, *The Church in the Power of the Spirit*, SCM Press 1977; Wolfhart Pannenberg, *Christian Spirituality and Sacramental Community*, Darton, Longman & Todd 1984.

13. For this typology see Avery Dulles, *Models of the Church*, Dublin: Gill & Macmillan 1976, chs 2 and 6.

14. John Habgood, *Church and Nation in a Secular Age*, Darton, Longman & Todd 1983, ch. 5.

15. See further e.g., Stanley Hauerwas, *A Community of Character*, University of Notre Dame Press 1981; Craig Dykstra, *Vision and Character*, New York: Paulist Press 1981: James M. Gustafson, *Can Ethics be Christian?*, University of Chicago Press 1975. The search for distinctive Christian identity is also implicit in less directly ethical strains of theological thought in the USA. See e.g. George Stroup, *The Promise of Narrative Theology*, SCM Press 1984.

16. Browning, op. cit., p. 59.

17. See Thomas C. Oden, *Care of Souls in the Classic Tradition*, Philadelphia: Fortress 1984, p. 38.

18. See, e.g., Pannenberg, op. cit., David Clark, *Basic Communities*, SPCK 1977.

19. E. Mansell Pattison, *Pastor and Parish – A Systems Approach*, Philadelphia: Fortress 1977. For a fuller summary of this approach see Stephen Pattison, 'Pastoral Care of Systems' in Alastair V. Campbell (ed.), *A Dictionary of Pastoral Care*, SPCK 1987.

20. Regis Duffy, *A Roman Catholic Theology of Pastoral Care*, Philadelphia: Fortress 1983.

21. Op. cit., p. 11.

22. Ibid., p. 40.

23. Richard Foster, *Celebration of Discipline*, Hodder & Stoughton 1981. Cf. also Kenneth Leech, *Soul Friend*, Sheldon Press 1977.

24. Henri J. M. Nouwen, Donald P. McNeill, Douglas A. Morrison, *Compassion*, Darton, Longman & Todd 1984. p. 90.

25. Anthony C. Meisel and M. L. del Mastro, *The Rule of Saint Benedict*, New York: Doubleday 1975, p. 43.

26. Christopher Holdsworth, *Steps in a Large Room*, Quaker Home Service 1985, p. 19.

27. Behaviourist psychologists have shown that desired behaviour and attitudes are much more effectively reinforced by positive reward than by punishment. Rather than killing, then, it seems that kindness may in fact give life!

28. Cf. Alastair V. Campbell, *Paid to Care?*, SPCK 1985, p. 4. Friendship as the normal relationship between Christians is also advocated by Moltmann. See Moltmann, op. cit., p. 314ff. The use of this term is not without problems, however. See Gilbert C. Meilaender, *Friendship*, Notre Dame: University of Notre Dame Press 1985.

29. A very similar approach to that adopted by Herbert can be found as recently as the 1930s when the pastoral lectures of Bishop Edward King to students in Oxford were published, not as an antique curio, but as a real help to the newly-ordained and those preparing for ordination. See Eric Graham, *Pastoral Lectures of Bishop Edward King*, Mowbray 1932, ch. 3.

30. For more on discrepancies of understanding and perspective in helping encounters see John E. Meyer and Noel Timms, *The Client Speaks*, Routledge & Kegan Paul 1973; G. Stimpson and B. Webb, *Going to see the Doctor*, Routledge & Kegan Paul 1975.

31. Graham, op. cit., p. 51.

32. See, e.g., William D. Horton, 'Visiting', in Cyril Rodd (ed.), *The Pastor's Problems*, T. and T. Clark 1985.

33. William B. Oglesby, *Biblical Themes for Pastoral Care*, Nashville: Abingdon 1980, ch. 2.

34. Op. cit., p. 72.

35. Cf. Luke 4.30; 8.37.

36. Cf. Graham, op. cit., p. 53: 'THE VISITATION OF MIDDLE-CLASS

PEOPLE (e.g. farmers, tradesmen, etc.). This is a most difficult task; you can't talk religion with them. But consult with them on all the parish matters you can (e.g. about the allotment ground, etc.). Talk openly; such people do not understand hints or innuendos. Warn him of his responsibility for others, e.g. his servants; and speak when he is alone, and not when he is busy.'

5. *Politics and Pastoral Care*

1. This chapter is based on Stephen Pattison, 'Pastoral Care in Psychiatric Hospitals: An Approach Based on Some of the Insights and Methods of Liberation Theology' unpublished PhD dissertation, University of Edinburgh 1982. See also Stephen Pattison, 'Political Theology and Pastoral Care' in Alastair V. Campbell (ed.), *A Dictionary of Pastoral Care*, SPCK 1987. I would like to acknowledge the support of the Department of Education and Science in carrying out this research.

2. Frank Wright, *The Pastoral Nature of the Ministry*, SCM Press 1980, p. 73.

3. Dieter T. Hessell, *Social Ministry*, Philadelphia: Westminster 1982; Howard Clinebell, *Basic Kinds of Pastoral Care and Counselling*, SCM Press 1984, ch. 2. Cf. also Harvey Seifert and Howard J. Clinebell, *Personal Growth and Social Change*, Philadelphia: Westminster 1969. The only other American book closely related to this subject is Charles F. Kemp, *Pastoral Care with the Poor*, Nashville: Abingdon 1972. There are, however, several important papers which will be referred to below.

4. The book is Peter Selby, *Liberating God*, SPCK 1983. Cf. also Alastair V. Campbell, 'The politics of pastoral care', *Contact 62*, 1979, 2–15, A. O. Dyson, 'Pastoral theology: towards a new discipline', *Contact 78*, 1983, 1–8, Michael Wilson, 'Personal care and political action', *Contact 87*, 1985, 12–22.

5. Many of Lambourne's papers demonstrate a very direct concern for the socio-political dimension and they form a fine and stimulating resource. They are collected together in Michael Wilson, (ed.) *Explorations in Health and Salvation*, University of Birmingham Institute for the Study of Worship and Religious Architecture 1983, obtainable from the Secretary, Dept. of Theology, University of Birmingham, B15 2TT.

6. See David Jenkins, 'The God of freedom and the freedom of God', *The Listener* 18 April 1985; David Sheppard, *Bias to the Poor*, Hodder & Stoughton 1983.

7. Alastair V. Campbell, 'The state of the art', *Contact 88*, 1985, 2–8.

8. See above ch. 2 for a fuller discussion of the influence of pastoral counselling and the pastoral psychology movement.

9. Dorothee Sölle, *Choosing Life*, SCM Press 1981 p. 82.

10. See e.g. Paul Tillich, *The Courage to Be*, Collins 1962.

11. Jose Comblin, 'What sort of service might theology render?' in Rosino Gibellini (ed.), *Frontiers of Theology in Latin America*, SCM Press 1980, p. 74.

12. J. G. Davies, *Christians, Politics and Violent Revolution*, SCM Press 1976, p. 102.

13. David Jenkins, *The Contradiction of Christianity*, SCM Press 1976, p. 102.

14. For a much more detailed discussion of individualism see Steven Lukes, *Individualism*, Blackwell 1973.

15. A good discussion and *resumé* of secularization is to be found in John Habgood, *Church and Nation in a Secular Age*, Darton, Longman & Todd 1983, ch. 1.

16. Paul Halmos, *The Faith of the Counsellors*, Constable 1965, ch. 5.

17. See further Anthony Russell, *The Clerical Profession*, SPCK 1980, ch. 8.

18. Clinebell, op. cit., p. 26.

19. Ibid., pp. 31–2.

20. Selby, op. cit.

21. Ibid., p. 76.

22. Robert H. Bonthius, 'Pastoral care for structures – as well as persons', *Pastoral Psychology 18*, 1967, 10–19, p. 10.

23. Ibid., p. 19. Bonthius writes from the context of the US community mental health movement of the 1960s.

24. See ch. 3 above, also Don S. Browning, *The Moral Context of Pastoral Care*, Philadelphia: Westminster 1976.

25. Selby, op. cit., p. 50.

26. R. A. Lambourne, 'With love to the USA', in M. A. H. Melinsky (ed.), *Religion and Medicine*, SCM Press 1970, p. 135.

27. Selby, op. cit., ch. 1.

28. R. A. Lambourne, 'Personal reformation and political formation in pastoral care' *Journal of Pastoral Care 25*, 1971, 182–7.

29. James Mathers, 'The pastoral role: a psychiatrist's perspective' in M. A. H. Melinsky (ed.), *Religion and Medicine 2*, SCM Press 1973.

30. Ibid., pp. 83–4.

31. William E. Hulme, 'Concern for corporate structures of care of the individual?' *Journal of Pastoral Care 23*, 1969, 153–63. Cf. Seifert and Clinebell, op. cit.

32. Don Browning, 'Pastoral care and models of training in counselling' *Contact 57*, 1977, 12–19, pp. 17–18.

33. R. A. Lambourne, *Community, Church and Healing*, Darton, Longman & Todd 1963.

34. Bonthius, op. cit., p. 11.

35. See ch. 4 above.

36. See further W. H. C. Frend, *The Donatist Church*, Oxford University Press 1952, ch. 15; Peter Brown, *Augustine of Hippo*, Faber 1969, ch. 21.

37. John T. McNeill, *A History of the Cure of Souls*, New York: Harper & Row 1977, p. 201.

38. See Russell, op. cit., chs 8–15.

39. The enquiries are detailed and summarized in Virginia Beardshaw, *Conscientious Objectors at Work*, Social Audit 1981.

40. Philip J. Wogaman, *A Christian Method of Moral Judgment*, SCM Press 1976, ch. 5.

41. Paul Halmos, *The Personal and the Political*, Hutchinson 1978, ch. 6.

42. Hessell, op. cit., ch. 10.

43. Wogaman, op. cit., p. 114.

44. Davies, op. cit., p. 30.

45. Ibid., p. 184.

46. T. Greening, 'The "Gestalt prayer": final version?' *Journal of Humanistic Psychology 17*, 3, 1977, p. 78.

6. *The Bible and Pastoral Care*

1. There are some short articles by British writers. See e.g. Christopher Wigglesworth, 'Pastoral use of the Bible' in Alastair V. Campbell (ed.), *A Dictionary of Pastoral Care*, SPCK 1987; Henry McKeating, 'The pastor and his Bible' in Cyril Rodd (ed.), *The Pastor's Problems*, T. and T. Clark 1985.

2. See further Edward Farley, *Theologia*, Philadelphia: Fortress 1983; J. L. Houlden, *Connections*, SCM Press 1986, ch. 2.

3. I have drawn below upon the following works to varying degrees: James Barr, *The Bible in the Modern World*, SCM Press 1973, *Explorations in Theology 7*, SCM Press 1980, *Escaping from Fundamentalism*, SCM Press 1984; Edward Farley and Peter C. Hodgson, 'Scripture and tradition' in Peter Hodgson and Robert King (eds), *Christian Theology*, SPCK 1983; David Kelsey, *The Uses of Scripture in Recent Theology*, SCM Press 1975; Dennis Nineham, *The Use and Abuse of the Bible*, SPCK 1978; Robert M. Grant and David Tracey, *A Short History of the Interpretation of the Bible*, SCM Press 1984.

4. Farley and Hodgson, op. cit., p. 36.

5. Cf. Barr, *Explorations in Theology 7*, ch. 3.

6. Cf. Barr, *The Bible in the Modern World*, ch. 4 for a discussion of the Bible as literature. The most obvious protagonist of the viewpoint is Rudolph Bultmann.

7. See further Farley and Hodgson, op. cit.

8. See further e.g., Houlden, op. cit., ch. 5.

9. See further e.g., Nineham, op. cit.

10. See further e.g., Grant and Tracey, op. cit., Donald Capps, *Pastoral Care and Hermeneutics*, Philadelphia: Fortress 1984, ch. 1, Anthony C. Thiselton, *The Two Horizons*, Paternoster 1980.

11. See further Farley and King, op. cit., pp. 51ff., Barr, *Explorations in Theology 7*, ch. 4.

12. For a very reductionist liberal view of the Bible see Nineham, op. cit. For more on fundamentalism see Barr, *Escaping from Fundamentalism*.

13. Jay E. Adams, *Lectures on Counseling*, Grand Rapids: Baker 1978, p. 181.

14. Ibid., p. 183.

15. Cf. W. David Stacey, *The Pauline View of Man*, Macmillan 1956.

16. Cf. Adams, op. cit., pp. 204–9.

17. Cf. eg., William Glasser, *Reality Therapy*, New York: Harper & Row 1965.

18. See e.g., Lawrence J. Crabb, *Basic Principles of Biblical Counselling*, Marshall, Morgan & Scott 1975, p. 85.

19. Cf. Duncan Buchanan, *The Counselling of Jesus*, Hodder & Stoughton, 1985.

20. Thiselton, op. cit., p. 61.

21. Howard Clinebell, *Basic Types of Pastoral Care and Counselling*, SCM Press 1984, pp. 50–1.

22. Op. cit., pp. 52–3.

23. See Alastair V. Campbell, *Rediscovering Pastoral Care*, Darton, Longman & Todd 1981, especially chs 3, 4 and 5.

24. See further e.g., Donald Capps, *Pastoral Care and Preaching*, Philadelphia: Westminster 1980, *Pastoral Care and Hermeneutics* (1984).

25. Donald Capps, *Biblical Approaches to Pastoral Counseling*, Philadelphia: Westminster 1981.

26. Op. cit., p. 12.

27. Ibid., ch. 2.

28. See, e.g., Psalm 38.

29. Capps, op. cit., p. 73.

30. Ibid., p. 98. Emphasis added.

31. William B. Oglesby, *Biblical Themes for Pastoral Care*, Nashville: Abingdon 1980.

32. Oglesby, op. cit., p. 33. Emphasis added.

33. See ibid., ch. 2, also ch. 4 above for a fuller description of the themes of initiative and freedom related to visiting.

34. Oglesby, op. cit., pp. 224–5.

35. James Smart, *The Strange Silence of the Bible in the Church*, SCM Press 1970, p. 23.

36. Ibid., p. 24.

Interlude

1. I have drawn extensively on Peter L. Berger, Brigitte Berger and Hansfried Kellner, *The Homeless Mind*, Penguin 1974, ch. 1 for this description of technological consciousness.

2. See Brigitte and Peter Berger, *The War Over the Family*, Penguin 1984, ch. 1. Cf. D. H. J. Morgan, *The Family, Politics and Social Theory*, Routledge & Kegan Paul 1985, ch. 2.

3. Gerard Egan, *The Skilled Helper*, Monterey, California: Brooks Cole 1982. For systems theory cf. E. Mansell Pattison, *Pastor and Parish – A Systems Approach*, Philadelphia: Fortress 1977; Sue Walrond-Skinner, *Family Therapy*, Routledge & Kegan Paul 1976.

4. See. e.g. Jay Haley, *Problem-Solving Therapy*, New York: Harper & Row 1976.

5. Thomas C. Oden, *Care of Souls in the Classic Tradition*, Philadelphia: Fortress 1984, introduction and ch. 1.

6. Nelson S. T. Thayer, *Spirituality and Pastoral Care*, Philadelphia:

Fortress 1985, ch. 1.

7. Regis Duffy, *A Roman Catholic Theology of Pastoral Care*, Philadelphia: Fortress 1983.

8. Donald Capps, *Biblical Approaches to Pastoral Counseling*, Philadelphia: Westminster 1981.

9. Henri J. M. Nouwen, *The Wounded Healer*, New York: Doubleday 1979, *Creative Ministry*, New York: Doubleday 1978; Alastair V. Campbell, *Rediscovering Pastoral Care*, Darton, Longman & Todd 1981.

10. Donald Capps, *Life-Cycle Theory and Pastoral Care*, Philadelphia: Fortress 1983.

11. See further Ruth Wilkes, *Social Work with Underprivileged Groups*, Tavistock 1981, ch. 8.

12. See further Thayer, op. cit., ch. 1.

13. Craig Dykstra, *Vision and Character*, Paulist Press 1981, pp. 36ff.

14. John V. Taylor, 'On not solving the problem' (source and place of publication unknown).

15. Ibid.

16. Wilkes, op. cit., ch. 6.

17. Ibid., p. 59.

18. Dykstra, op. cit., p. 99.

19. Ibid., pp. 99ff.

20. Egan, op. cit., pp. 5f.

7. *Failure in Pastoral Care*

1. Jean Vanier, *Man and Woman He Made Them*, Darton, Longman & Todd 1985, p. 4.

2. Norman MacCaig, *Collected Poems*, Chatto & Windus 1985, p. 348.

3. See further Karl Menninger, *Whatever Became of Sin?*, Hodder & Stoughton 1975.

4. Dag Hammerskjold, *Markings*, Faber 1964, p. 76.

5. Henri J. M. Nouwen, *The Wounded Healer*, New York: Doubleday 1979.

6. Alastair V. Campbell, *Rediscovering Pastoral Care*, Darton, Longman & Todd 1981, ch. 4.

7. R. S. Thomas, *Selected Poems*, Granada 1979, p. 119.

8. Bill Jordan, *Helping in Social Work*, Routledge & Kegan Paul 1979, pp. 13–14.

9. See John de Wit, 'Success' in *The Bishopric* 7, 1985, 13–22.

10. Maria Boulding, *Gateway to Hope*, Fount 1985, p. 9.

11. Ibid., p. 9.

12. For more about risk see, e.g. C. Paul Brearley, *Risk in Social Work*, Routledge & Kegan Paul 1982. For creation as God's risk see Frances M. Young, *Can These Dry Bones Live?*, SCM Press 1982.

13. David Brandon, *Zen in the Art of Helping*, Routledge & Kegan Paul 1976, ch. 3.

14. Ibid., p. 6.

15. See further Jordan, op. cit., ch. 2.

16. Boulding, op. cit., p. 16.

17. Pierre Teilhard de Chardin, *Le Milieu Divin*, Fontana 1964, p. 68.

18. Boulding, op. cit., p. 17.

19. Ibid., p. 71.

20. Ibid., p. 9.

21. Rowan Williams, *Resurrection*, Darton, Longman & Todd 1982, p. 36.

22. Boulding, op. cit., p. 75.

23. Ibid., p. 72.

24. For more on shame see, e.g., Helen Merrell Lynd, *On Shame and the Search for Identity*, New York: Harcourt Brace 1958.

25. Boulding, op. cit., p. 118.

26. Nouwen, op. cit., p. 89.

27. Boulding, op. cit., p. 114.

28. Jordan, op. cit., pp. 15–16.

29. Ibid., p. 14.

30. Lionel Blue, *Bright Blue*, BBC 1985. For Blue's biographical background see Lionel Blue, *A Backdoor to Heaven*, Fount 1985.

31. Henri J. M. Nouwen, *Creative Ministry*, New York: Doubleday 1978, p. 65.

32. Boulding, op. cit., pp. 12, 74.

8. *Laughter and Pastoral Care*

1. The latter part of this title is drawn from Arthur Koestler, *The Act of Creation*, Hutchinson 1964, p. 62.

2. Frank Moore Colby, quoted in Anthony J. Chapman and Hugh C. Foot, 'Introduction' in Tony Chapman and Hugh Foot, (eds), *Humour and Laughter: Theory, Research and Applications*, Wiley 1976, p. 1.

3. Koestler, op. cit., p. 51.

4. Lionel Blue, *To Heaven with Scribes and Pharisees*, Darton, Longman & Todd 1975, p. 68.

5. In characterizing laughter as a sign of transcendence in everyday life I am using the words of Peter Berger but distorting the concept they denote in Peter Berger, *A Rumour of Angels*, Penguin 1969, ch. 3.

6. Howard Clinebell, *Basic Types of Pastoral Care and Counselling*, SCM Press 1984, p. 425.

7. Alastair V. Campbell, *Rediscovering Pastoral Care*, Darton, Longman & Todd 1981, ch. 5.

8. Cf. Heije Faber, *Pastoral Care in the Modern Hospital*, SCM Press 1971, pp. 81–92. The clown image receives its fullest exposition in a book about pastoral care in psychiatric hospitals, Roger Grainger, *Watching for Wings*, Darton, Longman & Todd 1979.

It is probably not an accident that this image has been formulated in the **highly secular,** technologically sophisticated and expert-dominated setting of the hospital where an individual pastor can feel marginalized and literally stupid or ignorant. The notion of being a prophetic fool, a sign of contradiction, allows pastors in this and other modern settings where they feel peripheral to maintain some self-respect and sense of functional usefulness. Cynics might say that it is an ideological device for justifying the place of pastors where there is no longer a place for them. Other criticisms could be made. First, perhaps the image of folly is anachronistically idealized and made to sound rather pleasant and desirable ('There is a fool in Shakespeare so it must be respectable to be one.') When people like St Paul were talking of fools they were talking of those who were treated as insane and outside society. This was, and is, a very painful position which seems incompatible with much of professional pastoral care today. Secondly, the vocation to be a fool in the Christian tradition involved the whole person. It was not simply a partial role that was assumed at the convenience of someone in a responsible position for a particular purpose. When people were thought to be fools and outcasts they were therefore wholly rejected, not just in one aspect, or from time to time. Thirdly, even if some pastors do have the courage to become outcasts in a particular situation, there is always the danger that far from changing the system prophetically, they may actually shore it up and help it to define its values more sharply and with a better conscience. The image of fool, like that of the prophet, is a very individualistic one. It is easy for social institutions to take a delight in having a resident critic who is a real asset in allowing the expression of negative feelings about bad aspects of situations while posing no potent threat to the *status quo* in practice. Thus fools become lovable rather than shocking, and a dynamic of collusion is set up. The Christian fools of old forsook human love and acceptance for the love of God. Most Christian pastors today need the love and approval of those amongst whom they work, at least to some extent. This is nothing to be ashamed of, but there is a real question mark against their being able to forsake acceptability to adopt in any real sense the hard way of the fool or prophet. Some pastors have a considerable talent for amusing people, making them laugh or even stopping them in their tracks and making them think. All these things are admirable in their own way and have their place in pastoral care. Whether they can legitimately claim the mantle of folly without romanticizing or debasing it is, however, very debatable.

9. At the beginning of a very short section on laughter as such, entitled 'Laughter in Heaven', Campbell himself remarks, 'Yet how serious the folly of pastoral care is now becoming it seems!' (Campbell, op. cit., p. 63). Despite this and another comment at the beginning of the chapter with which any writer on this subject must fully empathize – 'the feeling must remain that somewhere in the wings the fool is having the last laugh' – Campbell's account of folly does not explore humour and laughter very fully.

10. Cf. Blue, op. cit., ch. 4.

11. See his autobiography, Lionel Blue, *A Backdoor to Heaven*, Collins 1985.

12. Lionel Blue, *Bright Blue*, BBC 1985, pp. 52–4.

13. Blue, *To Heaven with Scribes and Pharisees*, p. 69.

14. Church of England, *Alternative Service Book*, Clowes, SPCK and Cambridge University Press 1980, p. 155. Cf. Blue, op. cit., p. 68.

15. Cf. Romans 11.16–24. It is important not to romanticize the Jewish tradition here. Robert L. Katz, *Pastoral Care and the Jewish Tradition*, Philadelphia: Fortress 1985 disappointingly contains not one reference to humour and no jokes or humorous anecdotes.

16. See Jürgen Moltmann, *Theology and Joy*, SCM Press 1973, p. 49.

17. Harvey Cox, *The Feast of Fools*, New York: Harper & Row 1970. p. 140.

18. See further John Saward, *Perfect Fools*, Oxford University Press 1980.

19. See ibid., ch. 6. Saward describes Francis' joy as 'rich, full-bodied, enthusiastic mirth in the Lord Jesus' (p. 86).

20. Cox, op. cit., p. 156, Julian of Norwich, *Enfolded in Love*, Darton, Longman & Todd 1980.

21. Quoted in Rowan Williams, *The Wound of Knowledge*, Darton, Longman & Todd 1979, p. 134.

22. Cox, op. cit., p. 157.

23. Moltmann, op. cit., p. 28.

24. Daniel W. Hardy and David F. Ford, *Jubilate*, Darton, Longman & Todd 1984, pp. 71ff.

25. 'Humour and Faith' in Reinhold Niebuhr, *Discerning the Signs of the Times*, SCM Press 1946.

26. Ibid., p. 115.

27. Moltmann, op. cit., p. 27.

28. Saward, op. cit., p. 101.

29. Koestler, op. cit., p. 29.

30. See further James B. Nelson, *Embodiment*, SPCK 1979, J. G. Davies, *Liturgical Dance*, SCM Press 1984, ch. 4 for more on Christian suspicion of the body.

31. See Koestler, op. cit., pp. 52–3. Alastair V. Campbell, *The Gospel of Anger*, SPCK 1986 considers how Christians deal with strong negative and destructive emotions.

32. This account is based on Koestler, op. cit., chs 1 and 2.

33. See ibid., ch. 3, also Sigmund Freud, *Jokes and their Relation to the Unconscious*, Penguin 1976.

34. Quoted in Koestler, op. cit., p. 53. Other writers like Bacon suggest, equally offensively to our ears, that deformed people and lunatics are prime and appropriate objects for the mirth of their fellows.

35. These three theories are lucidly laid out and summarized in D. I. Lloyd, 'What's in a laugh? Humour and its educational significance', *Journal of the Philosophy of Education 19*, 1985, 73–9.

36. Chapman and Foot, op. cit., p. 4.

37. Lloyd, op. cit., p. 77.

38. Helen Merrell Lynd, *On Shame and the Search for Identity*, New York: Harcourt Brace 1958, p. 147.

39. See Koestler, op. cit., pp. 29–30.

40. See Harvey Mindess, 'The use and abuse of humour in psychotherapy' in Tony Chapman and Hugh Foot (eds), *Humour and Laughter: Theory, Research and Applications*, Wiley 1976, p. 335.

41. Angela Wood, 'Telling it like it is: Teaching Judaism through story and humour', *British Journal of Religious Education 3*, 1981, 151–6, p. 151.

42. Donald Evans, *Struggle and Fulfilment*, Collins 1980, pp. 115–16.

43. Ibid.

44. Harry Williams, *Tensions*, Mitchell Beazley 1979, p. 111.

45. See Cox, op. cit., p. 154.

46. Bill Jordan, *Helping in Social Work*, Routledge & Kegan Paul 1979, p. 120.

47. Cf. Mindess, op. cit., p. 341.

48. Henri J. M. Nouwen, *Clowning in Rome*, New York: Doubleday 1979, p. 88.

49. Patrick Kavanagh, 'Lough Derg', quoted in Hardy and Ford, op. cit., p. 73.

Afterword

1. A promising methodological start to the process of hearing people speak for themselves and only then moving to a professional or theological standpoint in the pastoral care literature is James Woodward (ed.), *Embracing the Chaos*, London: SPCK 1990. Woodward's lead, also to be found in some feminist writings has yet to be followed up and fully developed.

2. Rodney J. Hunter (ed.), *Dictionary of Pastoral Care and Counseling*, Nashville: Abingdon 1990, p. xii.

3. An American reviewer noted that Pattison's 'grasp of North American pastoral care resources and trends is broad and his evaluative comments are universally fair.' (Brad A. Binau, 'Review of *A Critique of Pastoral Care*', *Journal of Pastoral Care 44*, 1990, pp. 82–4). This is reassuring, given that I never visited or studied in North America.

4. Thomas C. Oden, *Becoming a Minister* (1987); *Ministry Through Word and Sacrament* (1989); *Crisis Ministries* (1986); *Pastoral Counsel* (1989); New York: Crossroad Publishing.

5. Don Browning, *A Fundamental Practical Theology*, Minneapolis: Fortress 1991.

6. Donald Capps, *Pastoral Care and Hermeneutics*, Philadephia: Fortress 1984.

7. Charles V. Gerkin, *Prophetic Pastoral Practice*, Nashville: Abingdon 1991.

8. John Patton, *From Ministry to Theology*, Nashville: Abingdon 1990.

9. See David Duncombe, 'Prophetic dimensions of ministry in Clinical Pastoral Education', *Journal of Pastoral Care*, 44/4, 1990.

10. See Gerkin, op. cit.

11. Richard Bondi, *Leading God's People*, Nashville: Abingdon 1989; Gaylord Noyce, *The Minister as Moral Counselor*, Nashville: Abingdon 1989.

12. James Fowler, *Faith Development and Pastoral Care*, Philadelphia: Fortress 1987.

13. Donald Capps, *Lifecycle Theory and Pastoral Care*, Philadelphia: Fortress 1983; K Brynholf Lyon, *Towards a Practical Theology of Aging*, Philadelphia: Fortress 1985.

14. See, e.g., Bondi, op. cit.; Regis A. Duffy, *A Roman Catholic Theology of Pastoral Care*, Philadelphia: Fortress, 1985.

15. Maxine Glaz and Jeanne Stevenson Moessner, *Women in Travail and Transition*, Minneapolis: Fortress 1991; Carroll Saussy, *God Images and Self Esteem*, Louisville: Westiminster/John Knox Press 1991.

16. Hunter (ed.), op. cit.

17. Recent titles include Peter Speck, *Being There: Pastoral Care in Time of Illness* (1988); John Foskett and David Lyall, *Helping the Helpers: Supervision and Pastoral Care* (1988); Sue Walrond-Skinner, *Family Matters: The Pastoral Care of Personal Relationships* (1988); Peter Chambers, *Made in Heaven?: Ministry with Those Intending Marriage* (1988); Wesley Carr, *The Pastor as Theologian: The Integration of Pastoral Ministry, Theology and Discipleship* (1989); Michael Jacobs, *Holding in Trust: The Appraisal of Ministry* (1989); Nicholas Bradbury, *City of God?: Pastoral Care in the Inner City* (1989); Mary Anne Coate, *Clergy Stress: The Hidden Conflicts in Ministry* (1989); Christopher Perry, *Listen to the Voice Within: A Jungian Approach to Pastoral Care* (1991). All published in London by SPCK.

18. David Deeks, *Pastoral Theology: An Enquiry*, London: Epworth Press 1987; Michael Wilson, *A Coat of Many Colours*, London: Epworth Press 1988; Duncan B. Forrester (ed.), *Theology and Practice*, London: Epworth Press 1990.

19. Alastair V. Campbell, *Rediscovering Pastoral Care*, London: Darton, Longman and Todd, second ed. 1987; *Paid to Care?*, London: SPCK 1985; *The Gospel of Anger*, London: SPCK 1986.

20. Carr, op. cit.

21. See, however, Ian McDonald, 'The Bible and Christian Practice' in Forrester (ed.), op. cit.

22. See Foskett and Lyall, op. cit.; Deeks, op. cit.; Laurie Green, *Let's Do Theology*, London: Mowbray 1990.

23. See, e.g., Stephen Pattison, 'Some straw for the bricks: a basic introduction to theological reflection', *Contact 99*, 1989, pp. 2–9; Simon Robinson, 'Mechanisms in aiding theological reflection', *Contact 102*, 1990, pp. 23–9; Michael Northcott, 'The case study method', *Contact 103*, 1990, pp. 26–32.

24. For this latter see, e.g., Donald Schon, *The Reflective Practitioner*, Aldershot: Avebury 1991.

25. See further, however, Elizabeth Stuart, 'The prophet as an image of the pastor in the New Testament', *Contact 109*, 1992, pp. 24–30; Stephen Pattison, *Pastoral Care and Liberation Theology*, Cambridge: Cambridge University Press 1994.

26. See, e.g., Alan Billings, 'Pastors or counsellors?', *Contact 108*, 1992, pp. 3–9.

27. See, e.g., Nicholas Bradbury, 'Is the Church of England serious about training its pastors?' *Contact 108*, 1992, pp. 10–16; articles in *Contact 110*.

28. See Wilson, op. cit.

29. E.g., Elaine Graham and Margaret Halsey (eds), *Lifecycles: Women and Pastoral Care*, London: SPCK 1993.

30. Emmanuel Lartey, *Pastoral Counselling in Inter-Cultural Perspective*. Bern: Peter Lang 1987.

31. See Howard Cooper (ed.), *Soul Searching*, London: SCM Press 1988.

32. For the latter see Michael Northcott, 'The New Age and Pastoral Theology: Towards the resurgence of sacred', *Contact Pastoral Monograph*, 1992.

33. See Billings, op. cit. A recent conference for pastoral studies teachers attended by most of the fifty or so pastoral studies teachers in the country took as its title, 'From therapy to mission', illustrating, albeit negatively, the continuing power and interest of counselling as a paradigm for pastoral care.

34. For Christian feminist ethical thinking see, e.g., Beverly Wildung Harrison, *Making the Connections*, Boston: Beacon Press 1985; Sharon D. Welch, *A Feminist Ethic of Risk*, Minneapolis: Fortress 1990; articles in *Studies in Christian Ethics 5*: 1, 1992. For non-Christian feminist ethics and feminist approaches to morality in general see Nel Noddings, *Caring*, Berkeley: University of California Press 1984; *Women and Evil*, Berkeley: University of California Press 1989.

35. 'We have imaged the divine in masculine ways and then have found God distant.' (James Nelson, *The Intimate Connection*, London: SPCK 1992.)

36. For more on the possible psychological differences in morality between men and women see, e.g., Carol Gilligan, *In a Different Voice*, Cambridge, Mass.: Harvard University Press 1982.

37. Mary Midgley, *Heart and Mind*, London: Methuen 1983.

38. Tom Kitwood, *Concern for Others*, London: Routledge 1990.

39. Kitwood, op. cit., pp. 4–5.

40. See, e.g., Mike Hepworth and Bryan S. Turner, *Confession*, London: Routledge and Kegan Paul 1982.

41. Kitwood, op. cit., p. 216.

42. I extend this analysis and argument in my forthcoming book, *Pastoral Care and Liberation Theology*.

43. See however, McDonald, op. cit.

44. See Capps, *Reframing*, ch. 6.

45. Reframing means changing the conceptual and/or emotional setting or viewpoint in relation to which a situation is experienced and putting it in a different meaning frame so that its meaning, and therefore attitudes and behaviours towards it are completely changed. See further, Capps, *Reframing*, p. 17.

46. See Michael Jacobs, op. cit.

47. See further Stephen Pattison, 'A decade of managerialism?', *Crucible* July–September 1991, pp. 143–6.

48. Graham Shaw, *The Cost of Authority*, London: SCM Press 1983. This judgment is confirmed for me to some extent in Frances Young and David Ford, *Meaning and Truth in 2 Corinthians*, London: SPCK 1987; E. P. Sanders, *Paul*, Oxford: Oxford University Press 1991.

49. For more on post-modernism generally see, e.g., David Harvey, *The Condition of Postmodernity*, Oxford: Blackwell 1989.

50. Alastair Campbell, 'Review of *A Critique of Pastoral Care*', *Theology* 92, 1989, pp. 229–30.

51. See further, e.g., Richard Forty, *Contingency, Irony and Solidarity*, Cambridge: Cambridge University Press 1989.

52. Don Cupitt, *The Long-Legged Fly* (1987); *The New Christian Ethics* (1988); *Radicals and the Future of the Church* (1989); *Creation out of Nothing* (1990); *What is a Story?* (1991); *The Time Being* (1992). All published in London by SCM Press.

53. Cupitt, *The Long-Legged Fly*, p. 109.

54. See, e.g., Cupitt, *The New Christian Ethics*.

55. Elaine Graham, personal communication, 17 March 1993.

56. Campbell, 'Review'.

Index of Authors

Adams, Jay E., 115–18
Arnold, William V., 5, 22, 28

Barr, James, 108
Benedict, St, 57f., 70f.
Blue, Lionel, 167f., 170–4
Bondi, Richard, 199
Bonthius, Robert H., 90f.
Boulding, Maria, 158, 161f., 166, 168, 213
Brandon, David, 156
Browning, Don S., 28, 34, 36–46, 48, 63, 65, 67, 91, 196ff., 200, 209
Buchanan, Duncan, 118f.

Campbell, Alastair V., 5, 13f., 16, 22, 114, 122f., 137, 141, 151, 157, 163, 170f., 202, 204
Capps, Donald, 31, 123–6, 136, 138, 196ff., 200, 211
Carr, Wesley, 203
Clebsch, William A., 7, 11f., 15, 17
Clinebell, Howard J., 12, 17, 21ff., 28ff., 83, 89, 120f., 170, 198, 200
Comblin, Jose, 85
Cox, Harvey, 175
Crabb, Lawrence J., 118
Cupitt, Don, 210, 214f.

Davie, Peter, 8
Davies, J. G., 85
Deeks, David, 202, 203
Dykstra, Craig, 140
Duffy, Regis, 63, 66f., 71, 136

Eckhart, Meister, 175

Egan, Gerard, 23, 135
Evans, Donald, 186

Farley, Edward, 201
Ford, David F., 175f.
Forrester, Duncan, 202
Foskett, John, 25, 99, 203
Foster, Richard, 68f.
Fowler, James, 199

Gerkin, Charles, 198
Graham, Elaine, 204
Green, Laurie, 203

Habgood, John, 64
Halmos, Paul, 86
Hammarskjold, Dag, 149
Hardy, Daniel W., 175f.
Herbert, George, 59–62, 70, 72ff., 80
Hessell, Dieter T., 83, 102
Hiltner, Seward, 59
Hobbes, Thomas, 180
Hodgson, Peter C., 108
Holdsworth, Christopher, 72
Hulme, William E., 28, 93

Jaekle, Charles R., 7, 11f., 15, 17
Jacobs, Michael, 25, 202
Jenkins, David, 85
Jordan, Bill, 153, 166, 190

Katz, Robert L., 23
Kennedy, Eugene, 23
King, Edward, 76
Kitwood, Tom, 207f.